"More than just a workbook, Hyman and Pedrick define and demystify Obsessive-Compulsive Disorder. In addition they offer therapists and patients a highly specific and useful treatment program. *The OCD Workbook* should be an important addition to your collection of OCD treatment literature."

—Robert H. Ackerman, MSW, Clinical Assistant Professor, Department of Psychiatry, State University of New York, Health Science Center at Brooklyn

"What a delight to read *The OCD Workbook*! In my twenty years of clinical practice and research involving people suffering from obsessive-compulsive disorder, this is the best self-help resource I have come across. Dr. Bruce Hyman, a clinical social worker, and Cherry Pedrick, a registered nurse, have written a terrific resource for persons with OCD and their families. Plus, this book should be on every therapist's bookshelf. Thoroughly grounded in the principles of evidence-based practice, *The OCD Workbook* is a very readable, interesting, and easy-to-understand manual. I highly recommend it!"

—Bruce A. Thyer, Ph.D., research professor of social work, School of Social Work, University of Georgia, Athens

"*The OCD Workbook* is extremely helpful to patients with OCD and their families. It is full of useful information on symptoms and causes of OCD and it provides an easy to follow step-by-step guide to combating this debilitating disorder. The authors have managed to make complex ideas, theories and treatment delightfully engaging, humorous and simple. For those who want to learn whether some of their behaviors or thoughts are obsessive or compulsive, a checklist of symptoms and assessment tools are provided. I would highly recommend this workbook to my patients and their families."

—Fugen Neziroglu, Ph.D., ABBP, Bio-Behavioral Institute, Great Neck, NY, Board Certified in Behavioral Psychology

"*The OCD Workbook* is a practical and comprehensive therapeutic guide. It will assist millions of people with OCD and their support persons in recovery from this serious disorder."

—Barbara Van Noppen, M.S.W., research associate, Department of Psychiatry in Human Behavior, Brown University

"*The OCD Workbook* is readable and informative. I would encourage my patients to read it to learn more about OCD, its symptoms, and how we can be partners in its treatment."

—Roberto A. Dominguez, M.D., professor, Department of Psychiatry, University of Miami School of Medicine

"The authors of this wonderful manual are to be congratulated for creating a comprehensive, balanced, and highly readable book. It should be a boon to patients and their family members, and anyone else who wants to know about OCD and related disorders. The book provides detailed instructions for self-treatment that are about the best I have seen. I urge therapists to get a hold of this book and study it. Not only will they learn to be better therapists, but they will also understand their patients better.

—Donald W. Black, M.D., Professor of Psychiatry, University of Iowa College of Medicine

THE OCD WORKBOOK

Your Guide to Breaking Free from
Obsessive-Compulsive Disorder

BRUCE M. HYMAN PH.D.
CHERRY PEDRICK, R.N.

New Harbinger Publications, Inc.

Distributed in Canada by Raincoast Books.

Copyright © 1999 by Bruce Hyman, Ph.D. and Cherry Pedrick, R.N.
New Harbinger Publications, Inc.
5674 Shattuck Avenue
Oakland, CA 94609

Cover design by SHELBY DESIGNS AND ILLUSTRATES
Edited by Kayla Sussell
Text design by Michele Waters

ISBN 157224-169-1 Paperback

Printed in the United States of America

New Harbinger Publications' Web site address: www.newharbinger.com

05   04   03

15   14   13   12   11   10   9   8

The OCD Workbook *is dedicated to the memory of Arnold Dresner, and to the millions of people who struggle with OCD, to their families who offer their support and understanding, and to the researchers and clinicians who have brought us this far in the treatment of OCD.*

Contents

Acknowledgments

This book has been made possible with the help of many people: Blanche Freund, Ph.D., who served as an advisor and mentor through the years of learning about behavioral treatment and OCD; my mother, Mildred Hyman, who has been a perpetual joy in my life; Cherry Pedrick, who helped make the collaboration of this book the pleasure it turned out to be; my wife, Robin, for whom my love grows more and more "obsessive" and "compulsive" every day; and to my patients, who teach me every day about gratitude, courage, and hope.

Bruce M. Hyman, Ph.D.

Bruce Hyman made co-authoring *The OCD Workbook* a wonderful experience. I am grateful to my husband, Jim, and my son, James, for their support and encouragement throughout the process of writing this book. I thank Michael Jenike, M.D., for his insight and vast knowledge about the brain. Thank you to my cats, Melody, Spunky, and Little Kitty, for the entertainment and cuddles during the lonely days of writing. Most of all, I thank my God for making it all possible.

Cherry Pedrick, R.N.

We would both like to thank Kayla Sussell who helped us put our ideas on paper with clarity and conciseness, Kristin Beck for believing in this project from the beginning, Kirk Johnson for the elegant cover design, Lauren Dockett for her prompt help with publicity, and all the others at New Harbinger Publications who made this book a reality.

Introduction

The great thing in this world is not so much where we are, but in what direction we are moving.

—Oliver Wendell Holmes

Who We Are

"I have to go back, I have to go back and see if I locked the door." I stared at the door of our house. I had to check it again. Turning off the ignition, I jumped out of the car.

"I saw you lock it, Mom," my son James called after me, obviously annoyed. He didn't want to be late for school again. "You checked it twice."

I knew I had locked the door. I always locked it, so why did I need to check it again? I couldn't explain. I just had to check again. This happened more and more often until I was regularly returning home just to see if the doors were locked. In the middle of the day, without warning, my fears would hit me. Did I lock the door? Did I turn off the coffeepot, the lights? Soon I was checking and rechecking appliances, locks, car brakes, and paperwork. When the constant checking began to interfere with my job as a home health nurse, I sought treatment.

I was diagnosed with obsessive-compulsive disorder, a neurobiological disorder that affects 2.5 percent of the population. As a nurse, I was somewhat familiar with obsessive-compulsive disorder (OCD), but I was not prepared for the struggle ahead. My need to recover motivated me to read every book and article about OCD I could find. This led to writing several magazine articles and a continuing education home study course for nurses. The research and writing helped me apply cognitive-behavior therapy principles to my own illness.

As my OCD improved, I reached out to others who were struggling with the same disorder. I met many people who were suffering from a lack of knowledge and support. I discovered support systems on the Internet and through the Obsessive-Compulsive Foundation. Help is available for people struggling with OCD, but there is a great need to get information to the people who need it.

My brilliant computer nerd son offered to make a website for me. A website! What would I do with a website? I soon found out. He made a beautiful home page dedicated to educating others about OCD. Thousands of people have stopped by "Cherry's Website" at http://members.aol.com/Cherlene on their educational journey. From there, links take them to the best OCD sites on the Internet.

I met Dr. Bruce Hyman at the 1997 Obsessive-Compulsive Foundation conference. He was writing a book—a workbook designed to give people with OCD the tools to work on their problem. For the past two years, he had been seeking a medical professional with OCD who could write about the experience of having OCD from the patient's point of view. We discovered we could each fill a need in writing a book about OCD. Together, the two of us bring important expertise to this project. My nursing background helps me to understand the medical aspects of OCD and its treatment. Having the disorder myself helps me relate the information with compassion and understanding. It's my hope that our combined expertise in helping people with OCD will make a difference to the people who will read this book.

—Cherlene (Cherry) Pedrick, R.N.

No, I don't have OCD . . . but in 1987, after seven years of conducting a general clinical psychotherapy practice, a middle-aged male was referred to me for treatment of severe washing and checking rituals. He took two-hour showers, obsessively avoided touching unfamiliar objects, feared dirt and germs, and washed his hands seventy-five times a day.

Having never been consulted previously by a person with OCD, I was baffled by his strange behavior and moved by his profound suffering. When I realized that my traditional training was ill-suited to truly helping him, I embarked upon a mission to learn everything I could about OCD and to seek guidance from whoever in the country might have specialized knowledge of it. This led me in 1988 to the Anxiety Disorders Unit at the former Medical College of Pennsylvania (now called Allegheny College of Health Sciences), directed by Dr. Edna Foa. There I observed the successful use of intensive behavioral treatment methods with OCD patients. Having a previous foundation in cognitive-behavioral treatment methods, in time I was able to adopt the methods for use with my own OCD patients.

Subsequently, I received several years of ongoing clinical case consultation from Dr. Blanche Freund. In 1992 I established the Obsessive-Compulsive Resource Center of South Florida with offices in Hollywood and Boca Raton, Florida. Presently, approximately 80 percent of my busy practice is devoted to the treatment of adults and children with OCD and related disorders.

The idea of writing a book on OCD grew out of my awareness that very few people with OCD are receiving the proper help. Although our culture has come a long way toward greater understanding and destigmatization of psychiatric disorders, including OCD, much fear and ignorance persists. Far too many people struggling with OCD fear the embarrassment and discomfort of seeking help and confronting the disorder. Those who do seek help for OCD are often disappointed by the results. Many of my patients report having sought help from several well-intentioned, but misinformed, health care professionals before they found someone truly knowledgeable about OCD. Due to the often desperate nature of the disease, people will seek help from almost any source that offers the remotest hope for relief. Frequently, these disappointing encounters with the health care system result in further emotional pain, guilt, discouragement, and mistrust. Many give up hope and lose confidence in their ability to break free from the power OCD has over their lives.

There is still no medical cure. You will probably still have OCD after reading this book but you also will have the weapons you need to fight against the disorder. My goal in writing this book is to help people with OCD get "on track" in their battle with OCD by guiding them step-by-step through the process of change.

Most of the treatment techniques in this book are not new. They have been presented in other self-help books, as well as in clinical texts for professional psychologists. *The OCD Workbook* presents current theories about behavioral change processes in clear and understandable language. It is the product of more than ten years of experience treating many hundreds of people with every conceivable type of OCD.

—Bruce M. Hyman, Ph.D., LCSW

How This Book Can Help You

The OCD Workbook is not intended as a substitute for psychiatric or psychological treatment by a qualified mental health professional. Rather, it should be used in the following ways:

1. In conjunction with ongoing psychiatric or psychological treatment. For example, you may be seeing a highly qualified professional who does not specialize in treating OCD. This book can be used to assist your therapist in the role of coach, guide, or advisor as you work through the steps toward getting control of your OCD.

2. By people reluctant to seek professional help for one reason or another. You may have a desire to learn as much about OCD as possible, using this book as a guide for self-directed intervention. If you think you have OCD, we urge you to see a mental health professional who is experienced in the diagnosis and treatment of OCD. A psychiatrist or psychologist can confirm an OCD diagnosis and help you decide if self-directed cognitive-behavior therapy is appropriate for you.

3. By family members seeking a greater understanding of OCD. Just as it is not recommended that a doctor treat his/her own family for other diseases, we do not recommend that family members take on the role of psychotherapist using this book, even if trained as therapists. However, family members can provide valuable support as the person with OCD works through the self-help process outlined in this book. Part II describes how a trusted friend or family member can play the role of behavioral assistant.

About This Book

The OCD Workbook is divided into four parts. After reading Part I (chapters 1 through 3), you will understand what OCD is, how it is diagnosed, what the symptoms are, and how the disorder is currently treated. Included in these chapters are the most commonly accepted theories about the cause of OCD and the biological changes in the brains of people with OCD. Chapter 3 contains a review of the most effective treatments for OCD—medication and cognitive-behavior therapy.

Part II (chapters 4 through 8) is the heart of this book. There are step-by-step instructions to guide you through the Self-Directed Program for combating OCD. Attitudes that both help and hinder recovery are discussed. Establishing proper expectations of progress is addressed, especially the need for self-tolerance and patience. When you commit yourself to the Self-Directed Program, you will be asked to set aside a period of three to six weeks during which the program will be a top priority in your life. The reward of freedom from the distress of OCD will make this sacrifice worthwhile. Note that we don't say freedom from OCD, but freedom from the distress. You will find that you can live with a little bit of OCD in your life much more easily than you can with a lot of OCD.

Part II includes instructions for using *The OCD Workbook* alone or with a therapist functioning as a coach. Whether there is a need for professional counseling is discussed. If you don't have a therapist available for support, a trusted friend or family member may take on the role of behavioral assistant.

Part III (chapters 9 through 15) is an introduction to the specific symptoms and disorders in the OCD spectrum. You will learn powerful strategies for coping with less common, but debilitating disorders related to OCD. These include pure obsessions, scrupulosity, "Hit 'n Run" OCD, hoarding, trichotillomania, and body dysmorphic disorder.

Part III also includes valuable information on other disorders that often accompany and complicate OCD, including depression, ADHD, and Tourette's syndrome. You will be introduced to cognitive-behavior therapy techniques used to treat these disorders.

It happens to children too. OCD begins in childhood in 30–40 percent of reported cases. Months or years may pass before parents and teachers realize the child has a problem. You will learn how to apply the principles in this book to OCD in children.

Part IV (chapters 16 and 17) gives detailed information about reaching out to others for help with your struggle. Your family can play an important role in your recovery. Professional help also may be needed. We will offer you guidance in selecting a qualified mental health professional. Support groups also can be quite helpful in overcoming the shame and isolation that are often experienced with OCD. You will be referred to resources that can assist you in locating OCD support groups.

The appendix is a valuable collection of resources. You may have certain people in your life who are clueless when it comes to OCD. They probably wonder why you act strangely. Or maybe you have kept it secret and "coming out" will be a surprise to the people in your life. We have included a concise description of the disorder "A Brief Introduction to Obsessive-Compulsive Disorder for Family and Friends." You may copy this to give to teachers and school counselors, family members, and spiritual advisors.

PART I

CHAPTER 1

What Is OCD?

There is perhaps nothing so bad and so dangerous in life as fear.

—Jawaharlal Nehru

The people you will meet in this chapter are representative of the millions of people who have obsessive-compulsive disorder, or OCD. They struggle with a neurobiological disorder that fills their minds with unwanted thoughts and threatens them with doom if they do not perform repetitive, senseless rituals. They are not a rare group. About one out of forty people has OCD.

Obsessive-compulsive disorder is characterized by obsessions and/or compulsions that are time-consuming, distressing, and/or interfere with normal routines, relationships with others, or daily functioning. *Obsessions* are persistent impulses, ideas, images, or thoughts that intrude into a person's thinking and cause excessive worry and anxiety. *Compulsions* are mental acts or repetitive behaviors performed in response to obsessions to relieve or prevent worry and/or anxiety. They often have the intent of magically preventing or avoiding some dreaded event such as death, illness, or some perceived misfortune.

OCD has many faces, but the style and manner of the thoughts and behaviors presented by people with the disorder are remarkably and unmistakably consistent.

Basic Types of OCD

Checkers live with an excessive, irrational sense of being held responsible for possible dangers and catastrophes that may befall others as a result of the checkers' "imperfect" actions. They feel compelled to repeatedly check objects such as doors, locks, and the Off settings on household appliances to feel assured they've averted potential disasters they might have caused had they not checked.

Washers and cleaners have obsessions about the possibility of contamination by dirt, germs, viruses, or foreign substances. They live with the constant dread of either being harmed or causing harm to others by the actions of those agents of contamination.

Orderers feel they must arrange certain items in a particular, exact, or "perfect" way. They become extremely distressed if their things are moved, touched, or rearranged.

Pure obsessionals experience unwanted, intrusive, horrific thoughts and images of causing danger or harm to others. Instead of behavioral rituals, many engage in repetitive thoughts, such as counting, praying, or repeating certain words, to counteract their anxious thoughts. They may also mentally review situations obsessively to ward off doubt and relieve anxiety.

Hoarders collect insignificant items and have difficulty throwing away things that most people would consider "junk."

People with scrupulosity obsess about religious or moral issues. Their compulsions may involve prayer and seeking reassurance from others regarding their moral "purity."

Many people can identify with all these forms of OCD to some extent. Who hasn't checked to see whether the door is locked a second time? One person's prized, dusty old newspaper collection may be a pile of worthless junk to another. However, when behavior significantly interferes with daily living, OCD could be the problem.

Maybe you have a few of the symptoms described above but they do not interfere significantly with your life. Read on—you may realize that your habits do indeed interfere with your life. Even if your symptoms are not severe enough to warrant a diagnosis of OCD, you may benefit from the same cognitive-behavior therapy principles used to help people with full-blown OCD.

It is common for people with OCD to suffer from a variety of OCD symptoms. For example, Cherry Pedrick has problems with checking, mental rituals, and hand washing. Many people with OCD may have one predominant symptom for years, only to have it go away, and another one begin. For example, someone who has been a washer for many years may lose the fear of contamination and becomes a checker. Or vice versa. There is no typical pattern.

Now we'd like to introduce you to people with OCD. Except for Cherry Pedrick, these people are composites of many people with OCD. You may observe similarities between yourself and one or more of the people described—but this is only coincidental.

Cherry's Story: "What If?"—An Unwanted Companion

My struggle with OCD began with the fear that I had not locked the door when I left the house. After some time passed, my need to check and worry increased until it invaded my entire life. I was returning to the house to check the door, coffeepot, or stove. Away from home, I often stopped what I was doing and returned to my car to make certain the emergency brake was set and the door was locked. "What if?" scenarios became my constant companions. "What if I left the car door unlocked, and a child got inside it and then got hurt? What if I didn't set the brake, and the car was bumped from behind and rolled forward and hurt someone?"

Obsessions revolved around the fear that I had done something—or did not do something—that could be harmful to others. I also had a problem with hand washing when I prepared meals, fearing that I might contaminate the food.

Mary's Story

Obsessive fears of becoming very sick from a disease took over Mary's life when her oldest son contracted a life-threatening virus. She began to avoid blood, dirt, germs, and red spots for fear of the possibility—no matter how remote—of getting sick and therefore not being able to take care of her son. Her fears continued and worsened for five years before she sought treatment. By that time, Mary was washing her hands about one hundred times a day, and her daily showering ritual took about one full hour.

She avoided going near hospitals, clinics, and doctor's offices because she considered them "contaminated." Certain streets were off limits too—streets where homeless people were likely to hang out because she felt that homeless people were more likely to have open sores than people with homes. She avoided anything that might have a red spot on it because there was a chance the spot could be camouflaging a bloodstain.

Mary felt really comfortable only in certain sections of her own home that she considered "safe and clean." These areas were off-limits to other family members, especially her husband. Because he worked for a parcel delivery company and made daily deliveries to local hospitals, Mary considered her husband was "contaminated." When he came home from work, he had to shower immediately and put his clothing in the washing machine so Mary wouldn't have to touch them.

Melody's Story

Although she couldn't remember a time when she didn't check excessively, Melody didn't consider her checking behavior a problem until she went to college. She moved out of her parents' home into a small apartment with a roommate. At first her roommate was thankful for Melody's concern. It made her feel safe to see Melody check the door, stove, and appliances every night. However, Melody's nightly rituals grew longer as more and more items were added that had to be checked every night.

Her roommate grew alarmed when she saw that Melody was checking the windows that were always locked and looking in the backs of closets and under the beds. Also, everything had to be checked in a certain order. If Melody was interrupted or her concentration was broken, she started over. Sometimes she started over just because "it didn't feel right."

Melody also made copies of her schoolwork and kept them in a box. In the evenings, she checked these copies over and over, afraid she had missed a crucial point or had written something offensive. She called home three or four times a day to check on her parents and her little brother. She also checked on her friends and others she had associated with during the day. Had she said the wrong thing? Had she harmed someone by coughing with her mouth uncovered? Entire evenings were often spent reviewing the day's events, looking for mistakes she might have made and ways she might have harmed someone.

Robert's Story

Checking was a problem for Robert, too, but most of his checking compulsions dealt with driving. One night he saw a man standing in the median between the lanes. He glanced in the rearview mirror and saw the man dart across the road behind his car. Had he hit him? He looked back and didn't see him on the other side of the street.

Robert made a U-turn at the next intersection and went back. He drove slowly by the spot where he had seen the man. No dead body. His eyes could see that, but he still wasn't sure. He turned around and drove by again. An hour later, he was late for his appointment and still unsure. He went home and waited anxiously for the news to come on TV. Surely they would report an accident if someone had been injured.

A week later, Robert drove by a woman riding a bicycle in the bike lane. Again, he felt the fear. Maybe he hit her! He looked in the rearview mirror. She was still there, riding calmly, oblivious to his fears. Soon, he was looking back and checking his mirror whenever he passed pedestrians and bicyclists. He got into the habit of watching the news each night at 11:00 P.M. to check for accidents in areas where he had driven.

Ben's Story

As a child, Ben had organized the toys in his room very carefully. Toy soldiers went in a box. Puzzles had their own place on the bookshelf. His books were sorted on the shelves according to their size. Short ones on the right, taller ones on the left. At school, the other children had whispered about Ben's rituals. He had placed his books under his chair in the same spot every day. His pencil always had a sharp point and was positioned at the top of his desk, exactly in the middle. An eraser was kept on the right-upper corner, not too close to the edge. His papers always were arranged carefully in the middle of his desk.

As an adult, Ben rarely had visitors in his home. It was too much effort to put things back in order after they left. He couldn't enjoy the few visits family members made because of the anxiety he experienced when something was moved out of its place.

Jack's Story

Going through the thresholds of doors was Jack's difficulty. If he had a "bad" thought or "something just didn't feel right," he had to go back and walk through the door again. When he passed through a doorway, he had to touch the right side, then the left, then the top of the doorway. If he felt okay, he walked through the door. If it didn't feel right, he took a step back, then a step forward, and then he repeated his touching ritual.

Sitting in a chair or standing up from a chair also involved a ritual. First, Jack touched the floor, then both sides of the chair, then he stood. Writing took a lot of effort and time. He had to retrace each letter twice. Consequently, everything took Jack much longer than most people. He set his alarm for 3:00 A.M. so he could leave the house by 7:00 A.M. Every minute task involved in getting dressed and groomed had to be done "just right."

Mark's Story

Guilt plagued Mark constantly. When "bad" thoughts—usually of a blasphemous or sexual nature—came to his mind, he prayed. But the prayer had to be right, or it wouldn't work. So the prayers had to be repeated over and over until they felt "just right." It was particularly painful to Mark that his bad thoughts invaded his mind most often while he was in church. As a result, he was tempted to stay away from church and to give up on his belief in God completely. But he also feared that if he left the church, that would make him feel even guiltier.

Liz's Story

"One person's trash is another person's treasure." For years, Liz justified her collection of stuff by repeating this phrase. But most of the items stashed in the boxes that lined her apartment were no one's treasures. Over time, the boxes became a burden. Liz tried to solve the problem by moving. She put the boxes in storage and started over but her new apartment quickly filled with boxes too.

Liz saved newspapers, magazines, receipts, and mail—even the advertisements and catalogs that filled her mailbox. She wasn't sure why she saved things. But the thought of throwing anything away made her feel extremely anxious.

Ann's Story

While preparing lunch for her two-year-old child, Ann picked up a knife to cut a tomato. Suddenly, out of the blue, the thought of plunging the knife into her daughter popped into her mind. Horrified by such a thought, she was overwhelmed by intense feelings of guilt. The thought returned the next day, again while she was in the kitchen. That evening, while bathing her daughter, the thought, *What if I drown my baby?* popped into her head. Again, the thought deeply disturbed her.

For the next several days she thought over and over again, *I must be a horrible mother to think such terrible thoughts! I'd better do whatever I can to stop these thoughts!* To keep herself from thinking such disturbing thoughts, she distracted herself by repeating, *I'm a good mother and I'd never do that,* over and over in her mind. But still the thoughts recurred, stronger and stronger. Whenever she was alone with her daughter, she felt anxious. She began to avoid touching knives or anything sharp in the presence of her little girl. She made sure that her mother (who knew nothing about the distressing thoughts) was present when she bathed her daughter.

Ron's Story

Unwanted thoughts plagued Ron also. In his mind, certain scenes played over and over like a continuous movie. They scared him because he feared they would come true. He was harming someone, usually his wife. He knew that he wouldn't harm his wife, so why did thoughts of harming her so overwhelm his mind? He could be enjoying a movie or a meal, and the thoughts would burst into his mind. When the thoughts weren't torturing his mind, the music played. The same tune played over and over for days. Just as unexpectedly, the tune changed; another tune replaced it and began to torment him.

You have just read some typical stories of people with OCD. Now briefly describe the story of *your* struggle with OCD.

_____

_____

_____

Now describe some of your worst OCD symptoms:

_____

_____

_____

Describe the progression of these symptoms from the beginning to the present. How have they changed during the months or years?

_____

_____

_____

OCD Through the Ages

In this century, OCD has been known by such names as "compulsion neurosis" and "obsessional neurosis." Obsessive-compulsive disorder was once thought to be a rare disease. In 1964, researchers estimated OCD affected only 0.05 percent of the population (one out of 2,000 people). In 1977, the estimate was 0.32 percent (three out of 1,000 people). Major studies now estimate a lifetime prevalence rate of 2.5 percent (Yaryura-Tobias and Neziroglu 1997b). Much of the reason for the mistaken rarity of OCD is the secrecy of people who have the disorder.

Sigmund Freud, the founder of psychoanalysis, believed OCD was a psychological disorder caused by internal conflict and used the psychoanalytic technique of "the talking cure" to treat it. Over the decades, the results of this treatment generally were not good, and OCD became known as a difficult disorder to treat. Freud admitted being puzzled by OCD. He promulgated his psychological theories, but he looked toward a future when a more thorough understanding of the brain's chemistry and anatomy would play an important role in understanding psychiatric illnesses.

That future is here. Psychology has moved from theories of the "mind" to research on the brain. Today technological advances include techniques like positron emission tomography (PET), single-photon emission computed tomography (SPECT), and magnetic resonance imaging (MRI). With these techniques, scientists can look at the deep structures and chemical reactions within the brain. We now know that OCD is not caused by unconscious conflicts, but by abnormalities in specific parts of the brain.

Recent discoveries in neurochemistry and pharmacology have helped scientists to link OCD with problems in the regulation of the brain chemical, *serotonin*, which plays a vital role in the control of our moods and behavior. Today, we have five medications that help to correct such a chemical imbalance—Anafranil, Prozac, Luvox, Paxil, and Zoloft. Some people with OCD will see a reduction of their symptoms with any one of these medications. Others will receive only minimal relief from them and such patients require still other medications as supplements. This tells us that serotonin imbalance is not the only cause. Clearly, there is still a lot more to be learned about brain chemistry and pharmacology.

Psychoanalysis was routinely used to treat OCD until the 1960s. While medication was beginning to be used successfully to treat OCD, therapy was changing too. In 1966, British psychologist Victor Meyer began using behavior therapy to treat hospitalized OCD patients with severe contamination fears.

Meyer and his colleagues combined intensive exposure to feared objects such as bathroom doorknobs and faucets with strict restrictions on showering and washing. In fact, he had the water shut off entirely for the hospital unit except to areas used exclusively for toileting. After several days of intensive treatment, the new, innovative therapy worked! Fourteen of his fifteen patients demonstrated rapid reduction of their OCD symptoms. Ten were much improved or symptom-free, four showed moderate improvement. Since Dr. Meyer's groundbreaking work, numerous studies around the world have demonstrated improvement of OCD symptoms using the behavior therapy techniques of exposure and ritual prevention (Steketee 1993).

Unlike psychoanalytic therapy, which emphasizes the role of hidden, unconscious forces directing our behavior that are out of our control, behavior therapy emphasizes the role of learning in human behavior and the capacity to change behavior through unlearning faulty behaviors and attitudes.

In the 1980s, researchers such as Paul Salkovskis and Paul Emmelkamp began to recognize the role of faulty beliefs and attitudes in maintaining OCD symptoms. They applied the ideas of cognitive therapy, originally developed in the 1960s and 70s by Ellis (1962) and Beck, Emery, and Greenberg (1985), to understanding OCD. Cognitive therapy involves recognizing and disputing the irrational beliefs and faulty thought patterns that result in abnormal behavior. Cognitive therapy was then applied as an adjunct to behavior therapy in the treatment of OCD (Yaryura-Tobias and Neziroglu 1997b). Together, this is called cognitive-behavior therapy, or CBT. It is the cornerstone of this book and it's a powerful tool in the struggle with OCD.

CHAPTER 2

So You Have a Problem:
What Is It?

Although the world is full of suffering, it is full also of the overcoming of it.

—Helen Keller

A Closer Look at OCD

In the United States, obsessive-compulsive disorder is the fourth most common psychiatric diagnosis with a lifetime prevalence rate of 2.5 percent. This means one out of every forty persons—over 6.6 million men, women, and children in this country suffer from OCD. Previous estimates were much lower—.05–.32 percent (one out of every 1,000-2,000 people). Estimates today are twenty-five to sixty times greater than those of 1964 and 1967 (Yaryura-Tobias and Neziroglu 1997a). Sixty-five percent of people with OCD develop the disorder before the age of twenty-five and only 15 percent develop it after the age of thirty-five. There is a slightly higher incidence of OCD in women. However, among children, boys with OCD outnumber girls by about two to one (Niehous and Stein 1997).

What do these statistics mean to the average person with OCD? It is confirmation that you are not alone. People with OCD tend to keep the illness a secret. As a result, you don't realize how many others share the same problems. Look around you next time you encounter a large number of people—at a baseball game, concert, mall, even waiting in line at the department of motor vehicles. An average of one out of forty people surrounding you has OCD.

Obsessive-compulsive disorder exists in every culture and on every continent. Studies in five other countries—Canada, Puerto Rico, Germany, Korea, and New Zealand—have revealed the same percentage of people with OCD (Niehous and Stein 1997).

The onset of OCD symptoms is usually gradual, although some people have reported a sudden onset. It is not uncommon for OCD symptoms to flare up during times of emotional stress at work or at home. Major life transitions such as leaving home for the first time, pregnancy, the birth of a child, the termination of a pregnancy, increased levels of responsibility, health problems, and bereavement may be linked to the onset or worsening of OCD symptoms.

The *DSM-IV-R* (*Diagnostic and Statistical Manual of Mental Disorders*, Fourth Edition) is the diagnostic "bible" for mental health professionals (American Psychiatric Association 1994). It states that:

> The essential features of Obsessive-Compulsive Disorder are recurrent obsessions or compulsions that are severe enough to be time-consuming (i.e., they take more than one hour a day) or cause marked distress or significant impairment. At some point during the course of the disorder, the person has recognized that the obsessions or compulsions are excessive or unreasonable. (DSM-IV-R, p. 417)

Obsessions are persistent ideas, impulses, images, or thoughts experienced as inappropriate and intrusive, and causing marked anxiety. The person has the sense that the thought is not within his or her control and that it is not the kind of thought that he or she would expect to have. However, the person can come to understand that the obsessions are the product of his or her own mind and are not imposed from without (Pedrick 1997).

The discomfort of an obsessive thought or impulse results in attempts to contain or neutralize the discomfort. Hence, people develop compulsions. Compulsions are mental acts, such as repeating words silently, praying, and counting, or repetitive behaviors, such as ordering, checking, and hand washing. The function of a compulsive ritual or behavior is to reduce the distress that accompanies an obsessive worry or fear. It has the effect of containing, controlling, or neutralizing anxiety. People with OCD do not derive gratification or pleasure from performing their compulsions. They often feel driven to do them to prevent some dreaded situation—usually harm to others, often to themselves. Compulsions are either not connected in a realistic way with what they are designed to neutralize or prevent, or are clearly excessive (Pedrick 1997).

What OCD Is Not

Important to understanding of OCD is knowing what OCD is not. Many forms of repetitive behavior may be mistakenly labeled as OCD.

Superstition, Rituals, and Prayer

The *DSM-IV-R* states:

> Culturally prescribed ritual behavior is not in itself indicative of Obsessive-Compulsive Disorder unless it exceeds cultural norms, occurs at times and places judged inappropriate by others of the same culture, and interferes with social role functioning. Important life transitions and mourning may lead to an intensification of ritual behavior that may appear to be an obsession to a clinician who is not familiar with the cultural context . . . Superstitions and repetitive checking behaviors are commonly encountered in everyday life. A diagnosis of Obsessive-Compulsive Disorder should be considered only if they are particularly time consuming or result in clinically significant impairment or distress (p. 420)

It is important to recognize that certain repetitive or ritualistic behaviors may be due to cultural or religious influences, not to OCD. Rituals and repetitive behaviors are part of the normal repertoire of behaviors we all possess. Prayer, for example, can be an important part of our daily lives. Most people perform some ritualistic and repetitive behavior in the normal course of daily life, and many people are superstitious. But when these behaviors take over, resulting in significant impairment, distress or anxiety, or are excessively time-consuming, OCD is suspected. One OCD expert, Robert Ackerman, aptly describes OCD as a "cult of one."

Almost everyone worries, at times excessively. The worries resulting from OCD are usually senseless and irrational. Ignoring them makes one feel anxious and nervous. Excessive worrying that is rational, but excessive, may be a symptom of depression. Many people are compulsive, but do not have OCD. They give careful attention to details and procedure and are overly concerned with rules, regulations, and doing things the "right" way.

On the other hand, the compulsions of the OCD patient are useless, repetitive behaviors and are performed to dispel anxiety. Most often, people with OCD consider their compulsions silly, useless, and troublesome, even embarrassing and shameful (Pedrick 1997).

Substance Abuse and Compulsive Gambling

Although many problem behaviors are considered "compulsive," they do not necessarily comply with the clinical definition of OCD, and therefore are not considered OCD. These include pathological gambling and the substance addictions, including drugs and alcohol. The main difference between OCD and these addictive, or impulse, disorders is that the obsessive thoughts and compulsive behaviors of OCD are, for the most part, unwanted and unpleasant. Unlike the addictions, OCD brings no anticipation of pleasure or satiation. OCD behaviors are done to reduce discomfort and worry, not for the instantaneous pleasure they bring.

Eating Disorders

The compulsive overpreoccupation with food and thinness found in such disorders as obesity, anorexia nervosa, and bulimia have features in common with OCD. Because many people with anorexia also have clear OCD symptoms, a strong relationship between these two disorders is suspected (Hecht, Fichter, and Postpischil 1983).

Obsessive-Compulsive Personality Disorder (OCPD)

When we think of a *personality*, we generally think of phrases describing people's overall behavior: "He has a nice, caring personality," or "She has a strong, tenacious, or domineering personality," etc. A *personality* is a consistent, enduring, "cradle to grave" set of learned and inherited responses to a multitude of situations and challenges in life. They are characteristics that don't change much throughout the life span.

When a personality "style" or a set of features of a personality causes an excess of stress or difficulty in life, a person is said to have a "personality disorder." According to the *DSM-IV-R*, people with obsessive-compulsive personality disorder (OCPD) are characterized by a preoccupation with details, rules, lists, orderliness, perfectionism, and mental and interpersonal control at the expense of flexibility, openness, and efficiency. They view the world in black-and-white, all-or-nothing terms. There are no gray areas. Anything short of perfection is unacceptable.

This pattern begins by early adulthood and is present in a variety of contexts in the person's life. In the area of work, people with this disorder tend to be highly efficient, reliable, and organized—but often excessively so. They may get overinvolved with the details of a task, often "losing the forest for the trees." In their personal lives, they spurn change and spontaneity, instead preferring predictability, repetition, and a highly routinized way of life. They tend to keep their emotions and behavior highly controlled, and appear rather cold and aloof to others.

Differences Between OCD and OCPD

Although people with OCD often have features of OCPD, only a small percentage of people with OCD (6–25 percent) actually have full-blown OCPD (Baer and Jenike 1998). The main difference between OCD and OCPD lies in the degree of life impairment. People with OCD suffer substantially from their problem, and they wish to be rid of it. People with OCPD, on the other hand, are rarely uncomfortable about it and rarely feel the need for help for their problems. They are often unaware of the problems that may be caused by their behavior until such problems are brought to their attention by co-workers or family members who have been adversely affected by their behavior.

When a person with OCD also has OCPD, certain characteristics such as rigidity, perfectionism, and the need for control make the OCD behaviors more difficult to change. This is mostly due to the OCPD person's reluctance to accept guidance and intervention from outside themselves—implying they are less than "perfect." Unfortunately, when they reach the point at which they are ready to wholeheartedly face their problems, all may seem lost. However, along with hitting "rock bottom" comes the opportunity for change.

The Symptoms of OCD

Although OCD can manifest in a very large variety of ways, the most common symptoms of OCD are checking compulsions and washing or cleaning compulsions. Other symptoms include the need for symmetry, unwanted sexual and/or aggressive thoughts, compulsive counting, the need to ask constantly for reassurance, ordering rituals, and hoarding.

Some people are "purely obsessional." This means that they have obsessions, but no compulsions. Such people are likely to have repetitious thoughts of an aggressive or sexual act that are reprehensible to them. Others exhibit "primary obsessional slowness." In these people, slowness is the primary symptom. They may spend hours every day getting washed, dressed, and eating.

The pattern of the occurrence of symptoms in OCD is extremely varied. While many people with OCD have one symptom throughout their lives, others often have multiple obsessions and compulsions. For example, a "checker" may also be a "washer." In addition, the symptoms may alternate and transform throughout the life span. For example, a person with intrusive thoughts in adolescence may get over that problem only to become a washer in early adulthood, and then become a checker in later life.

A list of OCD symptoms appears on the following pages. Recognizing these signs can help the person with OCD come out of a self-imposed closet and seek treatment. Make checkmarks next to the symptoms that apply to you. You will use this list in later chapters as you work your way through the Self-Directed Program. One (or more) of these symptoms is not sufficient to diagnose a person with OCD. Remember that OCD is diagnosed only when these behaviors result in significant impairment, distress or anxiety, or are too time-consuming.

Obsessions

Contamination Obsessions

Excessive fear or disgust, and preoccupation with avoiding:

- ❏ bodily waste or secretions—urine, feces, saliva, blood

- ☐ dirt or germs
- ☐ sticky substances or residues
- ☐ household cleansing agents or chemicals
- ☐ environmental contaminants—radon, asbestos, radiation, toxic waste
- ☐ touching animals
- ☐ insects
- ☐ becoming ill from contamination
- ☐ making others ill by contaminating them
- ☐ diseases—AIDS, hepatitis, sexually transmitted diseases

Hoarding, Saving, and Collecting Obsessions

- ☐ Worry about throwing things away, even seemingly useless items
- ☐ Urge to collect useless things
- ☐ Urge to pick up items from the ground
- ☐ Uncomfortable with empty space—feel need to fill it

Ordering Obsessions

- ☐ Preoccupation with symmetry, exactness, or order
- ☐ Excessive concern that handwriting be perfect or "just so"
- ☐ Concern with aligning papers, books, and other items a certain "perfect" way

Religious Obsessions, Scrupulosity

Excessive fear, worry, and preoccupation with:

- ☐ having blasphemous thoughts or saying bad things
- ☐ being punished for blasphemous thoughts
- ☐ concern with religious beliefs
- ☐ issues of right and wrong, morality
- ☐ dwelling on religious images or thoughts

Somatic Obsessions

Excessive fear, worry, and preoccupation with:

- ☐ having an illness or negative reactions of others to one's appearance

Aggressive Obsessions

Preoccupation and excessive, illogical fear of:

☐ harming yourself

☐ harming others

☐ acting on unwanted impulses—e.g., run someone over, stab someone

☐ harming others through your own carelessness

☐ responsibility for some terrible accident—or fire, burglary—especially if resulting from personal carelessness

☐ blurting out insults or obscenities

☐ doing something embarrassing or looking foolish

☐ violent or horrific images in your mind causing you to do harm to others

Sexual Obsessions

Unwanted, worrisome, and intrusive

☐ sexual thoughts, images, or impulses

☐ thoughts about molesting your own or other children

☐ thoughts about being or becoming a homosexual

☐ thoughts or images of violent sexual behavior toward others

Miscellaneous Obsessions

☐ Urge to know or remember certain things—slogans, license plate numbers, names, words, events of the past

☐ Fear of saying something wrong, not saying something just right, or leaving out details

☐ Worry about losing things

☐ Worry about making mistakes

☐ Easily bothered by certain sounds and noises—clocks ticking, loud noises, buzzing

☐ Easily bothered by the feel of clothing, textures on the skin

☐ Intrusive nonsense sounds, music, words

☐ Fear of saying certain words because of superstitious beliefs about particular words

☐ Fear of using certain colors for superstitious reasons

☐ Excessive superstitious fears with rigid adherence to them

☐ Excessive concern with lucky and unlucky numbers with rigid adherence to them

Compulsions

Cleaning and Washing Compulsions

Excessive, illogical, and uncontrollable

- ☐ hand washing, often performed in a ritualistic way
- ☐ showering or bathing, often performed in a ritualistic way
- ☐ ritualistic tooth brushing, grooming, shaving
- ☐ cleaning of the house, certain rooms, yard, sidewalk, car
- ☐ cleaning of objects, household items
- ☐ use of special cleansers or cleaning techniques
- ☐ avoidance of objects considered "contaminated"
- ☐ avoidance of specific places—cities, towns, buildings—considered "contaminated"
- ☐ concern with wearing gloves or other protection to avoid "contamination"

Checking Compulsions

Checking over and over (despite repeated confirmation):

- ☐ that you did not harm others without knowing it
- ☐ that you did not harm yourself
- ☐ that others did not harm you
- ☐ that you did not make a mistake
- ☐ that nothing terrible happened
- ☐ that you did not do something that could cause future harm
- ☐ some aspect of physical condition, health—pulse, blood pressure, appearance
- ☐ physical surroundings—locks, windows, appliances, stoves
- ☐ that jars are closed by excessive tightening
- ☐ that doors are closed by excessive, repeated shutting, closing

Hoarding, Saving, and Collecting Compulsions

- ☐ Saving, collecting seemingly useless items
- ☐ Pick up useless items from the ground
- ☐ Difficulty throwing seemingly useless items away: "Someday I may make use of this . . ."

Repeating, Counting, Ordering

☐ Reading and rereading things, sometimes for hours

☐ Excessive worrying that you didn't understand something you read

☐ Excessive writing and rewriting things

☐ Repeating routine activities—going in and out of doorways, repeated crossing of thresholds, getting up and down from a chair, combing hair, tying shoes, dressing and undressing over and over

☐ Doing certain activities a particular number of times

☐ Counting items—books on a shelf, ceiling tiles, cars going by

☐ Counting during compulsive activities, such as checking and washing

☐ Arranging items in a certain order—books, pencils, cupboards

Miscellaneous Compulsions

☐ Mental rituals—prayers, repeating "good" thoughts to counteract "bad" thoughts

Note: Unlike obsessions, these mental rituals are performed with the intention of reducing or neutralizing anxiety.

☐ Excessive need to repetitively ask others for reassurance when ample assurance is evident to others, and has already been provided by those around you

☐ Need to confess wrong behavior, even the slightest insignificant infractions of behavior toward others

☐ Superstitious behavior that takes excessive amounts of time

☐ Need to touch, tap, or rub certain items or people

☐ Measures, other than checking, to prevent harm to self or others—for example, avoidance of certain objects or extreme precautions to prevent highly unlikely harm or danger

☐ Eating ritualistically according to specific "rules"—arranging food or utensils, eating at certain times, eating foods in a particular order

Related Symptoms

☐ Pulling own hair—from scalp, eyebrows, eyelashes, pubic area

☐ Acts of self-damage or self-mutilation—picking skin

☐ Compulsive shopping

Note: compulsive shopping is often related to hoarding—buying a number of things for fear of running out, for example.

How Is OCD Diagnosed?

A diagnosis of OCD is made on the basis of the psychiatric examination, a history of the patient's symptoms and complaints, and the degree to which the symptoms interfere with daily functioning. Based on the nature, length, and frequency of the symptoms presented, the doctor will differentiate OCD from other medical diseases with similar symptoms. These include schizophrenia, phobias, panic disorder, and generalized anxiety disorder. A physical exam may be ordered to rule out other causes of the symptoms presented. As of yet, there is no blood test available to reliably diagnose OCD. So, how do mental health professionals distinguish between OCD and those people who just worry a great deal?

Studies have shown that 80–99 percent of people experience unwanted thoughts (Niehous and Stein 1997). But most people can hold unpleasant thoughts in their mind without too much discomfort—or they can easily dismiss the thoughts entirely. Their thoughts are shorter in duration, less intense, and less frequent. On the other hand, the obsessions of OCD usually have a specific onset, produce significant discomfort, and result in a powerful, overwhelming urge to neutralize or lessen them. The obsessions and compulsions of OCD significantly interfere with life. People with OCD recognize that they are excessive or unreasonable—most of the time. There are several tools that mental health professionals use to aid in the diagnosis of OCD.

The Yale-Brown Obsessive-Compulsive Scale (YBOCS) is a questionnaire used to help target obsessive-compulsive symptoms and assess their severity. It is also used to monitor and assess clinical response to treatment. There is also a children's version of the scale. Other assessment tools include the Compulsive Activity Checklist (CAC), the Leyton Obsessional Inventory (LOI), the Maudsley Obsessive Compulsive Inventory (MOCI), the Padua Inventory (PI), and the NIMH Global Obsessive-Compulsive Scale (NIMH Global OC).

OCD and Shame

People with OCD are typically secretive and shameful about their obsessive thoughts and compulsive behaviors. Many are successful in hiding their illness for years. Unlike many mental illnesses, people with OCD are aware, at least at times, of their inappropriate behaviors and thoughts. However, they are often unaware that their symptoms are part of a recognizable clinical condition that can be treated. Or they may fear that they'd be scorned, perhaps even "locked up" should they reveal their obsessions and compulsions to others.

Because of the secretiveness, many people wait years, even decades, to seek help. Meanwhile, the obsessive thoughts and compulsive behaviors become further ingrained in their total lifestyle. The average time between the onset of symptoms and seeking treatment is 7.5 years (Yaryura-Tobias and Neziroglu 1997b). Hopefully, further education about OCD will narrow this time period.

Due to the shame people with OCD feel, many won't consult a mental health professional. They may prefer instead to seek help for their symptoms from some other health professional. Alert nonpsychiatric physicians can detect symptoms of OCD in patients who come to see them for seemingly unrelated problems. The family doctor may be the first one to see signs of OCD in patients. Parents and family members may mention their concern about the person's frequent washing, counting, or checking. Excessive worry about having acquired immune deficiency syndrome (AIDS) and other illnesses, resulting in repeated needless consultations, should alert the physician.

Other doctors likely to detect signs of OCD include dermatologists, oncologists, infectious disease internists, neurologists, neurosurgeons, obstetricians, pediatricians, plastic surgeons, and dentists. Chapped hands and eczema-type conditions—from excessive hand washing—may be seen by dermatologists. People may present themselves to plastic surgeons for repeated consultations for what they feel are noticeable deformities. Gum lesions from excessive teeth cleaning can alert the dentist. Signs of OCD may be seen postpartum and during pregnancy. Neurologists and neurosurgeons see signs of OCD associated with Tourette's syndrome, head injury, epilepsy, choreas, and basal ganglia lesions or disorders. The informed physician with a keen eye will detect OCD and make the appropriate referral to a psychiatrist or other mental health professional, rather than dismissing the person as "odd" or "crazy."

People with OCD frequently suffer from depression. Approximately one-third have depression at the time they seek treatment. About two-thirds of people with OCD have had at least one episode of major depression in their lifetime (Jenike 1996). Many others suffer from lesser forms of depression. It is important for doctors and family members to watch for warning signs of depression.

Signs of Clinical Depression

- Weight loss ____

- Sleep changes ____

- Loss of appetite ____

- Lack of energy ____

- Feelings of sadness ____

- Crying or frequent tearfulness ____

- Suicidal thoughts, with or without a plan to carry it out ____

- Feelings of hopelessness or helplessness ____

- Lack of interest in things that were of interest before, or lack of enjoyment of life, especially without knowing why ____

Check off the signs that apply to you and show this list to your doctor. If you have suicidal thoughts, even occasionally, we urge you to seek help from a qualified mental health professional now. Most cities and towns have a suicide hotline that can help you find and obtain the help you need. If you are a friend or family member of someone who is talking about suicide, don't hesitate. *Get help immediately.*

Does OCD Run in Families?

Studies done since 1930 have demonstrated the presence of OCD traits in blood relatives of 20–40 percent of studied cases (Yaryura-Tobias and Neziroglu 1997b). There may be a higher rate of OCD, subclinical OCD, tics, and Tourette's syndrome among relatives of people with OCD (Alsobrook and Pauls 1998). Those with childhood-onset OCD may be more likely to have blood relative with OCD (Geller 1998).

What Causes OCD?

No one knows exactly what causes OCD but researchers are piecing together the puzzle. There is growing evidence that it is caused by subtle variations in brain structure and circuitry. The most widely held theory is that the cause is related to abnormal levels of one of the brain's vital chemical messengers—*serotonin*. Serotonin plays a role in many biological processes, including mood, aggression, impulse control, sleep, appetite, body temperature, and pain. Serotonin dysregulation has also been implicated in depression, eating disorders, self-mutilation, and schizophrenia. (Yaryura-Tobias and Neziroglu 1997b).

Serotonin is one of the chemicals, called *neurotransmitters*, that nerve cells use to transmit energy impulses and to communicate with one another. Neurotransmitters do their work in the small space between two nerve cells, called the *synaptic cleft*. The transmission ends when the neurotransmitters are absorbed back up into the transmitting cell—a process that is called *reuptake*. Increasing the available serotonin through medication appears to produce changes in the *receptors* in some of the membranes of the nerves. It is believed that these receptors may be abnormal in people with OCD (Jenike 1996).

Brain-imaging studies have demonstrated abnormalities in several parts of the brains of people with OCD. These include the thalamus, caudate nucleus, orbital cortex, and cingulate gyrus. A study by Jenike and associates compared the brains of people with OCD with those of control subjects—people without OCD. Magnetic resonance imaging (MRI) showed a larger cortex (Jenike, Breiter, Baer, et al. 1996).

The *thalamus* processes sensory messages coming to the brain from the rest of the body. The *caudate nucleus* is part of the *basal ganglia*, deep in the center of the brain. The caudate nucleus controls the filtering of thoughts. Sensory information is sorted here. Normally, unnecessary information is disregarded. People with OCD become overwhelmed with intrusive thoughts and urges the caudate nucleus does not filter out. The caudate of someone with OCD behaves like a doorman of an apartment building who does a poor job keeping out the undesirables.

The *orbital cortex* is in the front part of the brain, above the eyes. This is where thoughts and emotions combine. The caudate that is letting unnecessary thoughts and impulses through makes the job of the cortex much more difficult. The orbital cortex tells us when something is wrong and when we should avoid something. It's like an early warning system in the brain. It seems to work overtime in people with OCD.

The *cingulate gyrus* is in the center of the brain. It helps you shift attention from one thought or behavior to another. When it's overactive, we get stuck in certain behaviors, thoughts, or ideas. The cingulate is also the part of the brain that signals danger—that something horrible will happen if you don't carry out your compulsions.

Imagine all these parts of your brain screaming at you when your OCD symptoms are at their worst:

- The *thalamus* sends messages from other parts of the body, making you hyperaware of everything going on around you.

- The *caudate nucleus* opens the gate and lets in unwanted intrusive thoughts.

- The *orbital cortex* mixes thoughts with emotions, then tells you, "Something is wrong here! Take cover!"

- The *cingulate gyrus* tells you to perform compulsions to relieve the anxiety the rest of your brain has heaped on you.

- Meanwhile, your *synaptic clefts* are screaming, "Send in some more serotonin! We're running short here!"

By now you must be thinking, "No wonder I have problems!" Hopefully, you are also realizing OCD is not your fault. It's your brain! Of course we have simplified this greatly. Experts aren't even sure exactly what different parts of the brain do. As we said, the puzzle is still being pieced together.

Research has found that certain autoimmune diseases, such as Sydenham's chorea, rheumatic fever, pediatric streptococcal infections, and lupus, also may cause some cases of OCD. In some studies, an association of OCD with von Economo's encephalitis, hypothalamic lesions, head trauma, brain tumors, and epilepsy has been demonstrated. However, most cases of OCD occur without such causative explanations (Jenike 1998; Yaryura-Tobias and Neziroglu 1997b).

Studies have found that behavior therapy can bring about positive changes in brain function. Medication helps to correct the serotonin imbalance (Yaryura-Tobias and Neziroglu, 1997a). Together, these powerful treatment strategies can help you break free from the grip of OCD. What does all this mean for people struggling with OCD?

Although many processes remain unclear, there is increasing evidence that the real cause of OCD lies in problems with the circuitry, structure, and neurochemistry of the brain. Parents, spouses, and other family members are not to blame for OCD. People with OCD can help their brains function better with cognitive-behavior therapy and medication.

There is hope.

Portions of this chapter were adapted from a continuing education course for nurses, *Obsessive-Compulsive Disorder*, by Cherlene Pedrick, RN. It was published in 1997 by the National Center of Continuing Education, Inc., and is used here with permission.

CHAPTER 3

What Can Be Done?

Do the thing we fear, and the death of fear is certain.

—Ralph Waldo Emerson

OCD was once considered a hopeless, untreatable psychiatric illness. Within the past fifteen years, however, there has been huge progress in the effective treatment of OCD. Considerable clinical and scientific evidence has demonstrated that *cognitive-behavior therapy* (CBT) combined with medications is an effective treatment. Thanks to these developments, many persons with OCD now live happier, better lives.

The "cognitive" in cognitive-behavior therapy (CBT) refers to specific methods and techniques that help change the faulty *beliefs* prevalent in OCD. "Behavior" in cognitive-behavior therapy refers to specific methods for changing behavior—the actions—such as the compulsive rituals of OCD. The cognitive-behavior therapy technique considered most effective in the treatment of OCD is called *exposure and ritual prevention* (ERP). It is also referred to as *exposure and response prevention*. The Self-Directed Program presented in this book employs techniques of cognitive-behavior therapy, including exposure and ritual prevention.

This chapter will further define cognitive-behavior therapy. We will also summarize the current use of medication in OCD treatment. It is vitally important, however, that you refer to your prescribing physician or pharmacist for information about the specific OCD medication that is right for you.

We also will address the issue of so-called alternative treatments. Interest in alternative treatments is at an all-time high throughout the world, and includes homeopathic methods, acupuncture, biofeedback, and vitamin supplements, to name just a few. While these methods may be useful in the treatment of many conditions, their usefulness with OCD has yet to be demonstrated or proven. People with OCD are often suspicious of traditional medical approaches. Regardless, it is important to make certain that any treatment you consider is backed up by legitimate research studies and proof that it works better than a placebo. The wrong treatment can be harmful!

Medication Therapy

The most effective medications to treat OCD belong to the family of drugs known as antidepressants. The five most useful medications are fluvoxamine (Luvox), fluoxetine (Prozac), sertraline (Zoloft), paroxetine (Paxil), and clomipramine (Anafranil). Citalopram (Celexa), venlafaxine (Effexor), nafazodone (Serzone), and other antidepressants also may be useful, but more study is needed.

Anafranil is the oldest medication for OCD and belongs to an older family of drugs known as tricyclic antidepressants. It has been used all over the world since the 1970s and was approved for use in the United States in 1990. It was considered the very first breakthrough drug in the treatment of OCD. It has a powerful effect upon serotonin but also has effects upon dopamine and other chemical messengers in the brain. Now newer drugs that specifically target serotonin have been developed.

These newer drugs are called *selective serotonin reuptake inhibitors* (SSRIs)—drugs that are "selective" in their action on the brain chemical serotonin. They include Luvox, Prozac, Zoloft, and Paxil. Here is a brief overview of how these medications help OCD patients.

Anafranil and the SSRIs are not chemically related, but they all seem to work by making more serotonin available in the brain. Let's review the information from chapter 2 about the role of serotonin. Serotonin is one of the *neurotransmitters* (chemical messengers) that nerve cells in the brain use to communicate with each other. These neurotransmitters are active when they are present in the small space between two nerve cells called the *synaptic cleft*. For one nerve cell to communicate with another, these brain chemicals—or neurotransmitters—must be released into the synaptic cleft. When this communication or transmission between cells is completed, the chemicals are taken back up into the transmitting cell in a process that is called *reuptake*. Anafranil and the SSRIs slow the reuptake of serotonin, therefore making more of it available to the receiving cell, and thus prolonging its effect on the brain.

Increasing the amount of available serotonin appears to produce changes in certain structures at the nerve endings called *receptors*. Think of the receptors as a "lock," and serotonin as the chemical "key" to that lock. To have proper transmission of energy impulses from one cell to another, there must be a perfect fit between the chemical key and the receptor lock. It is believed that specific serotonin receptors may be abnormal in people with OCD.

Some SSRIs don't provide the right key, so another SSRI may be tried. The SSRIs may also affect other brain chemicals important to a "perfect fit" that is unique for one individual, and no other. This is why someone may respond to one medication and not respond to another one. You may have to try two or more SSRIs before finding one that works for you. If none of the SSRIs sufficiently relieves symptoms, other medications may be used in combination with a SSRI, to give it a boost.

Two or more medications may be combined to get the best results. Other medications are sometimes combined with SSRIs. It is beyond the scope of this book to discuss these. Your doctor should be knowledgeable about the safe combining of medications to help your OCD problem.

Dosages

High dosages of medication are usually needed to relieve OCD symptoms—higher than the dosages typically used to treat depression. Some people, however, are very sensitive to even the lowest dosages. Starting with the lowest dose possible—even breaking pills in half—and gradually increasing the dosage, may be effective. Prozac comes in a liquid form that makes it possible to start at a very low (1–2 mg/day) dose.

Note that a very small number of people who have not seen a reduction of OCD symptoms with large dosages report, for reasons not well understood scientifically, good results with extremely low doses! This result, however, is very atypical and first-time users are best advised to aim for eventually taking the highest dose tolerable.

Medications may take up to twelve weeks to begin working. During the first few weeks, you may experience side effects, but have no relief of OCD symptoms. Even physicians may be tempted to give up on the medication too soon, since it usually takes only four to six weeks for people with depression to improve. Do not stop your medication without consulting your doctor. When these medications are stopped, they often need to be withdrawn gradually.

Dealing with Side Effects

All medications cause side effects, and the medications used to treat OCD are no different. For most people, they are mild and tolerable. For a few, they may be quite severe. If side effects are intolerable with one medication, you may tolerate another medication just fine. Often, the side effects diminish or disappear after you have been on the medication for a while. So give it some time. Many persons with OCD needlessly fear and avoid the medication because of the possibility of side effects. Or they don't give the medication enough time for their bodies to adjust to it. However, most patients who improve and remain on the medication report that the benefits far outweigh problems with side effects.

Be sure to notify your doctor of any uncomfortable side effects or unusual symptoms you have. He will let you know if they are dangerous or if your medication needs adjusting. Adjusting the dosage, dividing the dosage, and changing the time of day that the medication is taken often relieves the side effects. However, these changes must not be made without consulting your doctor. Should you need to stop the medicine, it will probably be discontinued slowly. Abrupt withdrawal, especially of Anafranil, can cause nausea, vomiting, hyperthermia, headache, sleep problems, and malaise.

Don't allow side effects to deter you from taking medication to treat your OCD. Most side effects can be dealt with. If they are severe, your doctor may reduce your dosage or change the medication. Tell your doctor about any symptoms you think may be caused by your medications.

Managing Common Side Effects

Sleep Problems. Medications used to treat OCD may cause some people to have difficulty sleeping. If this happens, ask your doctor if you can change the time of day when you take your medication. In general, "activating" medications are best taken in the morning, and sedating medications are best taken at bedtime. However, everyone reacts to medications differently. A medication that makes some people sleepy may make others feel wide awake.

Restlessness. Some people feel restless or "wired" on medications that treat OCD. Learn some relaxation techniques and practice them daily. If the restlessness and nervousness are severe, your doctor may want to prescribe another medication, temporarily, to help you relax.

Weight Fluctuations. Be prepared for changes in your appetite. Many people gain weight on SSRIs, while others lose weight. Adjust your diet and exercise programs before you start medications that may cause weight gain. If you expect it and take precautions, you are less likely to gain weight. SSRIs sometimes may cause a decreased appetite. Notify your doctor if you have an unwanted five-pound weight loss.

Cherry Pedrick gained about thirty pounds the first two years of her SSRI use. Diet and exercise are helping her to lose the added weight. Was this just due to the medication? Probably not. It seemed also to be related to depression. "When I was real depressed I lost weight. As I began to feel better, I ate more. I also ate when I was nervous and anxious. Like many others on SSRIs, I craved carbohydrates, especially sweets. But, for me, this was partly an excuse. I needed to take back control of my diet. When I did, I lost most of the added weight."

Dry Mouth. This is a common and bothersome side effect of some OCD medications. It is caused by a reduction of saliva. Sipping on fluids helps relieve the dryness. Sucking on hard candies may help. Try sugar-free candies to avoid tooth decay. Saliva helps fight plaque and hardens teeth. The reduction of saliva can lead to dental problems. If dry mouth is more than a bit bothersome, your doctor may recommend an artificial saliva to moisten your mouth.

Nausea. Taking your medication with a small amount of food can help control nausea. Rest a bit after taking medication, but don't lie down as this can induce heartburn.

Heartburn. If heartburn becomes a problem, do not lie down for two hours after eating or taking medications. Heartburn at night may be relieved by adding an extra pillow under your head. If heartburn persists, ask your doctor about medications to relieve it.

Constipation. There are many things you can do to help prevent constipation. Eat a diet high in fiber, fruits, vegetables, and liquids. High-fiber foods include raw vegetables, fruits, and whole grains. Exercise will help too. If these don't relieve your constipation, ask your doctor about taking a fiber supplement or stool softener.

Diarrhea. If you have diarrhea, eat low-fiber foods, such as bananas, and avoid high-fiber foods. Apply petroleum jelly outside of the rectum after bowel movements, if needed. Drink plenty of fluids to avoid dehydration. Notify your doctor of persistent diarrhea, weakness, dizziness, or decreased urine output. These are signs of dehydration. Ask your doctor about taking anti-diarrhea medications.

Dizziness. Diarrhea with dehydration, lowered blood pressure, a fast pulse, or just the nonsymptomatic effects of the medication can lead to dizziness. Notify your doctor to make certain the dizziness is nothing to be overly concerned about. Make sure you are drinking enough fluids. Take precautions to prevent falls or accidents—stand up slowly and wait a few seconds before starting to walk. Do not drive when you are likely to feel dizzy or sleepy.

Sexual Dysfunction. Anafranil and the SSRIs often produce sexual side effects in both men and women. These include lowered sexual drive, delayed ability to have an orgasm, and complete inability to have an erection or orgasm. Some people will have increased interest in sexual activity. Discuss these side effects with your doctor if you experience them.

Some people have been able to reduce sexual side effects and enjoy sexual activity on the weekends by stopping the medication on Fridays and Saturdays. This is not as effective with Prozac because it is longer acting. Do not adjust your medication without your doctor's approval and supervision. Tell your doctor about any problems with sexual function. He will not be surprised because this is common with many medications. He may be able to prescribe a medication to counteract the sexual dysfunction.

Medication Precautions

The medicine you take to treat your OCD is an important part of your recovery plan. A few simple precautions will make it more effective and safer to take. Ask your doctor and your pharmacist to provide you with information about the medication. Use this checklist to remind you what to ask your doctor:

What to Ask Your Doctor

- How does the medicine work?

- How long does it usually take to see positive effects?

- What is the dosage and how often do I take it?

- What are the side effects of the medication?

- Which side effects are dangerous? Which ones should I report immediately?

- What can I do to reduce the severity of side effects?

- Are there any dietary restrictions when taking this medication?

- Do you have printed information about this medication?

Ask your pharmacist too. Many pharmacies give written information with every prescription. Take the time to read it, even if your doctor and pharmacist have explained the medication to you.

- Will I need any tests before starting this medication or while taking it?

Although doctors are obligated to provide information, you also need to give them information that will aid them in making the right medication choices. Notify your doctor if you have any of the following:

- Any known allergies

- Any other medications you are taking, even nonprescription medicines

- If you are pregnant, trying to become pregnant, or breast-feeding

- Any other medical or psychiatric problems

- If you have a seizure or heart murmur

The doctor prescribes the medication, but you are the one taking it. You can take the following further precautions to ensure optimum treatment:

- Make certain the doctor prescribing the medication is a psychiatrist or is very experienced in the treatment of psychiatric disorders.

- Ask your doctor to write out the name of the medication, dosage, and how often you are to take it. When you get the prescription filled, compare it with what the doctor wrote.

- Get a thorough medical examination before starting the medication to make certain you do not have a medical condition that would affect the doctor's choice of medicines.

- Learn all you can about the medication.

- Report any side effects or new symptoms to your doctor. If you aren't sure it is related to the medication, give the doctor a call.

- Know who you should call if your doctor is not available.

- Get any tests your doctor recommends before you start the medication and while you are taking it, for example, blood tests and electrocardiograms.

- Tell all of your doctors what medications you are on.

- Get all of your medications at the same pharmacy. Having one pharmacist who knows what medications you take will help to prevent accidental interactions between the medications.

- Know what your medication looks like. Sometimes you may get the same medicine made by a different company. If the tablets or capsules look different than they usually do, ask your pharmacist about it.

- Do not change the dosage of medication you are taking without consulting your doctor.

- Do not quit or change the dosage of any medication without consulting your doctor.

- Ask your doctor before taking any other medication, even over-the-counter medicine.

- Ask your doctor what you should do if you forget to take your medication.

- Let a family member or friend know what medications you are on. Write them down so you can show your list to doctors and emergency personnel when needed.

- If the medication makes you drowsy or dizzy, adjust your activity. Until you are certain what your reaction will be, don't drive or operate machinery.

- Keep all medications out of reach of children and pets, including children who may visit occasionally.

- Store medications in a cool, dry place. The moisture in bathrooms may decrease the effectiveness of some medications.

- Make sure you have enough medication before vacations and holidays. Always get refills a few days ahead of time because sometimes the pharmacist has to call the doctor for permission to refill the prescription.

- Keep medications in their original bottles with readable labels.

- Develop a system to help you remember when to take your medications. The daily medication containers sold at pharmacies are a great help. There is a pocket for each day of the week. Fill the container at the beginning of the week and, at a glance, you can tell if you have taken your medication. It is easy to forget routine activities that you do every day. If you take many medications, you can get a container with multiple pockets for each day.

- Read the label before taking any medication—even the ones you take every day. It is easy to grab the wrong bottle, especially in the dark.

Alcohol and Medications

Alcohol should be consumed with great caution when taking medications for OCD. It can interfere with the actions of the medication. Combining alcohol with medications used to treat OCD may trigger aggressive behavior. Alcohol is also known to worsen depression. It can have a greater effect on individuals taking medications for OCD—one drink may have the effect of two drinks. If you regularly consume alcohol, be sure and discuss your consumption with your pre-scribing physician. Consider it another chemical that can interfere with the benefits the medica-tion offers you while you combat OCD.

Parts of the previous section were adapted from "Taking Medications Safely" by Cherry Pedrick, R.N., *Mature Years*, Fall. 1999.

Cognitive-Behavior Therapy

Completion of a course of cognitive-behavior therapy (CBT) is an important part of recovery from OCD. Research by Dr. Lewis Baxter of UCLA demonstrated that behavior therapy results in positive changes in brain activity similar to those changes brought about by successful drug treatment (Yaryura-Tobias and Neziroglu, 1997b).

Cognitive-behavior therapy helps by providing the person with OCD the tools necessary to manage their obsessions and compulsions. Continued practice and use of the tools and skills learned in CBT help keep symptoms manageable. Successful behavioral treatment requires moti-vation and daily practice. Initially, it can appear quite challenging, even scary—but obtaining relief from OCD symptoms makes it worthwhile. When used together, medication and behavior therapy complement each other. Medication alters the level of serotonin, while behavior therapy helps modify behavior by teaching the person with OCD the skills to resist compulsions and obsessions. Medication can reduce your anxiety level, thus making it easier to implement cognitive-behavior therapy principles.

Exposure and ritual prevention (ERP) are the principal behavioral techniques for treating OCD. The purpose of exposure is to reduce the anxiety and discomfort associated with obsessions through a process called *habituation*. Habituation is a natural process by which our nervous sys-tem "gets used to" or "bored by" stimuli through repeated, prolonged contact. This is done by prolonged exposure to the real-life anxiety and ritual-evoking situations. This is called in vivo, or "real-life," exposure.

For example, the person may be asked to actually touch or otherwise directly contact some feared object, such as an empty garbage pail or other "contaminated" object, without relieving the anxiety by hand washing. Through repeated practice, the patient realizes that the feared dis-astrous consequences do not occur and the severe anxiety initially associated with that situation decreases. This is the process of habituation.

Exposure is best done in stages, in "baby steps" toward the ultimate goal of complete habituation to the feared object or situation. For example, exposure to a "contaminated" garbage pail may begin by having the patient touch a "safe" corner of the pail with only a fingernail. Eventually, exposure progresses to touching the pail with a finger, and waiting as long as it takes for habituation to occur. Then several fingers are used, then the front of the hand, then the back of the hand. With each step, fear is confronted, anxiety aroused, then habituation is allowed to take place gradually and naturally.

Sometimes, it is either impractical or impossible to recreate the feared situation. An example is the fear of becoming sick or losing a loved one. In these cases, imaginal exposure is used. Imaginal exposure involves prolonged, repeated visualization of the feared image or situation in the mind for as long as it takes for habituation to occur. When combined with in vivo exposure, imaginal exposure is a useful technique for overcoming the "fear structure" of OCD. In the Self-Directed Program you will be instructed in great detail how to devise and implement both in vivo and imaginal exposure to help your OCD problem.

Ritual Prevention

The purpose of ritual prevention is to decrease the frequency of rituals. The person with OCD is instructed to face feared stimuli, experience the urge to do rituals, and then simultaneously block ritual behaviors such as hand washing or excessive checking. At first, the person may be instructed to delay performing a ritual, working gradually toward totally resisting the compulsion. Ultimately, the goal of ritual prevention is the total stopping of all rituals. This sounds frightening, even impossible, to persons with OCD who are considering trying cognitive-behavior therapy. But with regular effort, practice, and the strong support of a "coach," such as a therapist or family member, ritual prevention is one of the most powerful keys for breaking free of OCD.

Cognitive Changes

The cognitive component of cognitive-behavior therapy involves changing distorted thinking and beliefs. There is little controlled research evidence that cognitive therapy alone is an effective treatment for OCD in the absence of behavior therapy. Most people with OCD have already spent a large amount of time trying to correct their faulty thinking. They usually are aware that their thinking is obsessive and abnormal (Pedrick 1997). Cognitive therapy is helpful if it is combined with exposure and ritual prevention.

In cognitive therapy, the person is encouraged to identify inaccurate thoughts and attitudes, and replace them with healthier ones. The following list shows the key cognitive errors of persons with OCD and gives examples of each:

- **Black-and-White, or All-or-Nothing Thinking**

Examples: "If I'm not perfectly safe, then I'm in great, overwhelming danger."
"If I don't do it perfectly, then I've done it horribly."

- **Magical Thinking**

Example: "If I think of a bad, horrible thought, it will certainly cause something bad or horrible to happen."

- **Overestimating Risk and Danger**

Example: "If I should take even the slightest chance, something terrible is likely to happen."

- **Perfectionism**

Example: "Whatever I do, it is intolerable unless I do it perfectly."

- **Hypermorality**

Example: "I'll certainly go to hell (or be punished severely) for even the slightest mistake, error, or miscue."

- **Overresponsibility for Others**

Example: "I must always, at all times, guard against making a mistake that can possibly, even remotely harm an innocent person."

- **Thought/Action Fusion (similar to Magical Thinking)**

Example: "If I have a bad, even horrible thought about harming someone, it feels just as if I've actually done it."

- **Overimportance of Thought**

Example: "If I think of a terrible event occurring, the likelihood that it will actually take place is very high."

- **The Exclusivity Error**

Example: "If something bad is going to happen, it is much more likely to happen to me or to someone I love/care about than to others."

- **The "Nobility Gambit" (also known as the Martyr Complex or Sacrificial Lamb)**

Example: "How noble and wonderful I am! I'll gladly suffer and sacrifice my life doing endless rituals (washing, counting, checking, etc.) all day long as a small price to pay to protect those I love from danger and harm. And since no one close to me has yet died or suffered, I must be doing something right!"

- **"What If" Thinking**

Examples: "In the future, what if I . . . do it wrong?"

. . . make a mistake?"

. . . get AIDS?"

. . . am responsible for causing harm to someone?"

- **Intolerance of Uncertainty**

Example: "I can't relax until I'm one hundred percent certain of everything and know that everything will be okay. If I'm uncertain about *anything* (my future, my health, the health of loved ones) it is intolerable."

In the Self-Directed Program, cognitive restructuring (see chapter 8) directly challenges these dysfunctional thought patterns. Cognitive therapy may concentrate on what makes the consequences of feared events so unacceptable to the person with OCD.

There are some limitations to cognitive therapy. It works best if the person is intellectually able to understand abstract thinking. Unfortunately, anxiety and depression frequently interfere with the person's ability to concentrate on his or her faulty beliefs sufficiently to effectively change them.

Psychotherapy

Obsessive-compulsive disorder appears to be resistant to treatment with traditional psychotherapy or "talk therapy" alone. The disorder was once thought to be the result of life experiences, such as attitudes about cleanliness learned in childhood. The evidence is mounting that the disorder has a biological basis. However, supportive psychotherapy may be helpful in conjunction with cognitive-behavior therapy and medication (Pedrick 1997).

Most competent therapists of all schools of therapy acknowledge a need for a multimodal approach to treating OCD. Psychotherapy may be helpful for strengthening coping mechanisms for dealing with life stresses—stressors that can exacerbate OCD symptoms. By focusing upon obsessive perfectionism, indecisiveness, doubting, and procrastination, psychotherapy may be useful in encouraging compliance with medication and behavior therapy.

Neurosurgery

Medication and cognitive-behavior therapy are the treatments of choice for people with OCD. Most people will get at least some relief from these treatments, but there are a few people who don't obtain adequate relief. Severely treatment-resistant patients are sometimes treated with neurosurgery. These surgeries are performed in just a few centers in the world.

Cingulotomy is the most common neurosurgical procedure for OCD. Other surgeries include anterior capsulotomy, subcaudate tractotomy, and limbic leukotomy. Most of these procedures employ a device called a stereotactic frame to place minute surgical lesions in strategic places.

Possible complications of these surgeries can include infections, hemorrhage, epileptic seizures, weight gain, and hemiplegia (partial paralysis). Seizures are usually controlled with anticonvulsant medications. Neurosurgery doesn't always improve OCD symptoms. Surgeons sometimes create small lesions the first time, leaving room to create larger lesions in a second surgery.

It is also important to realize that treatments that didn't work before surgery might work well after surgery. Cognitive-behavior therapy is an important part of postoperative care. Medication may also be needed. The improvement of symptoms is likely to be progressive rather than immediate, taking several weeks or months to fully manifest.

Who Needs Neurosurgery?

Who should have neurosurgery to treat OCD? Most centers require that patients exhaust all other treatments before undertaking neurosurgery. This includes an intensive trial of cognitive-behavior therapy and adequate trials of most of the available medications (at least ten weeks each, at maximally tolerated doses). The illness must severely affect psychosocial functioning and cause considerable suffering. Most centers require that the patient has undergone intensive treatment for a minimum of five years (Jenike 1998).

Unproven Treatments

Why try unproven, so-called alternative treatments for OCD when there are so many studies supporting medication, behavior, and cognitive therapies? We can think of a few reasons. First, some persons have a basic philosophical objection to the use of synthetic drugs, preferring "natural" treatments. In spite of its proven effectiveness, many patients avoid behavior therapy because they consider it just too difficult. It can be scary at first. Others seek out alternatives because, in spite of the availability of proven treatments, there are still as many as 25 percent of all OCD patients who, for a variety of not well-understood reasons, simply do not benefit much from "proven" treatments. It is tempting to turn to the promise of any alternative that offers the hope of symptom relief.

Finally, some people may try unproven methods because they lack education regarding what helps, and they are vulnerable to exploitation by mental health professionals who are not informed, or who are simply unethical. Relatively few psychotherapists are sufficiently trained in behavior therapy. Behavior therapy is hard work for the therapist in that it often requires leaving the strict confines of their offices to work with patients in the natural environment.

It is important to find a therapist who is trained in behavior therapy or is, at least, willing to study and learn. This book can assist a therapist who does not specialize in OCD. Your therapist can act as your coach or advisor as you work through the program.

Many people with OCD spend years searching for a magical cure, searching for a cause, and blaming themselves for their illness. If you believe you have OCD, stop blaming yourself or those who love you and take control of your illness and your life. The Self-Directed Program is a powerful first step. With the next chapter, you will be embarking on a tremendous journey—perhaps the most difficult journey you have ever taken. Yet, it offers you the promise of the greatest reward you can achieve—relief from the burden of OCD symptoms.

Portions of this chapter were adapted from a continuing education course for nurses, *Obsessive-Compulsive Disorder*, by Cherlene Pedrick, RN. It was published in 1997 by the National Center of Continuing Education, Inc., and is used here with permission.

PART II

CHAPTER 4

Cognitive-Behavior Therapy for OCD: The Self-Directed Program

There are risks and costs to a program of action, but they are far less than the long-range risks and costs of comfortable inaction.

—John F. Kennedy

This chapter introduces the Self-Directed Program for OCD. Over twenty years of research evidence has shown that OCD symptoms improve through a systematically applied intervention called *exposure and ritual prevention* or *ERP:* exposure to feared situations, thoughts, or images, plus ritual prevention, or the voluntary blocking of compulsive behaviors. Sounds simple, doesn't it? In actuality, what you are about to do involves hard work, a high degree of commitment, and courage. Courage, because the images, impulses, and fears seem so real and vivid. The compulsive urges and rituals are so powerful and so persistent that the prospect of change may appear downright terrifying to you. If it didn't, you wouldn't have OCD!

Why ERP Works

Exposure and ritual prevention is based in part on the principle, well-established in scientific research, that fear is overcome by daring to face the very objects or situations that cause anxiety, dread, and avoidance. *Exposure* relies on two important and related learning processes: habituation and extinction.

Habituation

Habituation is the natural tendency of our nervous system to "numb out" from repeated, prolonged contact with a novel stimulus. It has also been referred to as "the remedy of nervous system boredom" (Ciarrocchi 1995). We all experience the process of habituation in our daily lives. One example would be the sudden, jolting chill we feel when we dive into a pool of cold water. Our sensory nerves send a message to our brains, "Boy, this sure is cold!" But if we stay put and don't jump out of the pool immediately, within seconds the chilling sensations gradually diminish and the cold water begins to feel almost warm. What is happening? Certainly the water doesn't become warmer. Instead, our nervous systems "numb out" to the chilly sensations and we become habituated to the cold water.

The same process can also be brought about in situations we fear and dread involving people (the homeless, for example), places (airplanes), and in the case of OCD, even our own thoughts. Through frequent and prolonged confrontation with situations we fear and dread, the human nervous system will automatically "numb out" fear responses to more manageable levels.

A simple example of how habituation works to help overcome fear is demonstrated with the irrational fear, or phobia, of water. The fearful individual is first led to within several feet of the edge of a swimming pool until his/her fear rises to uncomfortable levels, and then waits. Over the next several minutes, his/her original fear gives way to numbing out as nervous system habituation kicks in. When calm, the person next moves within a few inches of the pool. Again, fear rises to uncomfortable levels, and again the person waits until the feelings of dread habituate and diminish to manageable levels. The process is repeated in "baby steps." Gradually one toe is placed in the pool, then the other toe. Then both feet, the legs up to the ankles, and then the knees. Then both legs are entirely immersed. Gradually, the whole body is immersed in water with very little fear accompanying the process. Although extremely simplified, the process of overcoming the fears of OCD takes place in a similar manner, especially when accompanied by the blocking of compulsive rituals, or *ritual prevention*.

Extinction

Another basic principle of learning that provides the basis of ERP is called *extinction*. All behavior—that which you can see, such as eating and driving to work, as well as behavior you can't see, such as thinking and feeling—*is governed by its consequences*.

Consequences shape our behavior. They are either positive—such as praise, hugs, paychecks, delicious tastes, smells, feelings, and attention from someone important to us, or negative—such as punishment, criticism, embarrassment, parking tickets, fines, and jail. Another term for a positive consequence is a *reinforcer*.

Reinforcers work by bringing about feelings of pleasure and satisfaction or by reducing or preventing some unpleasant feeling or experience such as hunger, pain, or tension. Behaviors such as eating, drinking alcohol, or watching TV as an escape are considered reinforcers when they reduce discomfort or unpleasantness. Reinforcers influence all our behavior either by increasing feelings of pleasure and comfort or by decreasing discomfort, uncertainty, pain, or tension.

Extinction is what happens when a reinforcer no longer brings about feelings of pleasure or no longer reduces tension or discomfort. Think of many of the behaviors you engage in that are reinforced or rewarded—working hard for a paycheck or a bonus, buying flowers for a smile or hug from a loved one, playing your favorite sport for fun or relaxation. Now, think of what might happen if these same behaviors, for whatever reason, no longer brought you the reinforcement you want or seek—your bonus is cut despite your hard work, your loved one no longer smiles or gives you a hug when you bring flowers, or your favorite sport is no longer fun or relaxing. Usually, what can be expected to happen is these behaviors become *extinguished*—you stop doing them with the same vigor or eventually you stop doing them altogether.

If behavior is governed by its consequences, then it is not hard to see how compulsive rituals—hand washing, checking, and ordering, for example strengthen or reinforce obsessive worries and fears. Compulsive rituals reinforce obsessions and worries by reducing, at least temporarily, the tension, worry, and anxiety of obsessive thoughts and feelings. In exposure and ritual prevention, blocking rituals with ritual prevention reduces obsessive worries by means of *extinction.* By blocking behaviors that reinforce worries and keep them going, obsessional worries eventually diminish.

Exposure "In Vivo"

In vivo means "in life." Here it is used to mean the prolonged face-to-face confrontation in real-life situations with anxiety-evoking situations, objects, thoughts, or images. Here are some examples of in-vivo exposures for different types of OCD problems:

Washers

- Touch a "contaminated" object, person, or place. Do not wash.

Checkers

- Turn off lights, stoves, and appliances. Do it only once.

- Drive a car slowly through an area where small children play. Do not turn around to check despite powerful feelings that children were struck by the car.

"Pure" Obsessional

- Purposely think distressing thoughts. Record them on a tape or write them down over and over. Do not avoid or counteract these thoughts.

Orderers

- Leave household objects "imperfect"—slightly messy, off-center, not at right angles. Do not straighten, balance, or correct anything.

Effective in-vivo exposures involve the following important elements:

- Exposure must purposefully and vividly reenact the very situation(s) that provokes fear, dread, doubt, and avoidance.

- Exposure must be prolonged, lasting as long as it takes for the anxious feeling to lessen through habituation. This could be anywhere from a few minutes, to several hours before the anxiety reaches tolerable levels.

- Exposure changes the way you appraise or interpret danger and harm in specific situations.

Recall the analogy presented earlier of diving into a swimming pool of cold water. Your brain and central nervous system naturally adapt (or habituate) to the unpleasant sensations within a few minutes, without you having to do anything about it. The water in the swimming pool doesn't change, *your brain's interpretation* of the temperature of the water changes. By doing effective exposure, you are giving your brain the chance to *reinterpret* or *reappraise* the OCD messages:

"It is extremely dangerous to do (touch, think) this."	*Becomes*	"Nothing terrible will happen if I touch this—I can take a chance."
"I must do this many times."	*Becomes*	"I can do it once, and that's OK."
"I must be evil to think such a bad thought."	*Becomes*	"It's just one of those silly OCD thoughts."
"I must turn around to make sure no one was hurt."	*Becomes*	"If I turn around I'm just going to make my OCD worse."

Keep in mind that some fears involve catastrophes that may occur in the distant future, such as getting sick or dying. Such fears are either too complex to confront "in vivo" or they are simply too impractical to reenact in vivo alone. For example, consider the common OCD fears of causing someone's death or going to jail for doing something illegal or immoral. In these situations, *imaginal* exposure will be used in addition to in vivo exposure. People with OCD are instructed to "imagine" or think vividly of the situations that they fear for prolonged periods of time. See chapter 7 for more details.

Ritual Prevention

For exposure to be effective, it is necessary to eliminate, block, or contain all behaviors that neutralize or lessen the feelings of anxiety and discomfort brought about by obsessions. *Ritual prevention* refers to the supervised or self-controlled blocking of the compulsive rituals that lessen or block anxiety and discomfort. Simply put, ritual prevention means preventing yourself from performing your usual ritual. Once the ritual is blocked, your brain then has the opportunity to provide the natural habituation (remember the swimming pool) to the fear-provoking situations. This way more realistic and adaptive interpretations and appraisals of the situations can replace your old, fearful ones.

When blocking rituals, you are purposefully allowing the anxiety to be present. New adaptations can then take place. As with exposure, effective ritual prevention must be prolonged enough to begin to break down previously acquired associations between anxiety-provoking stimuli and rituals. For example, consider the association between a "contaminated" door knob and the urge to immediately wash your hands in order to feel "safe." Doing ritual prevention involves your willingness to tolerate initially high levels of discomfort in the face of powerful urges to relieve your tension and fear through the "tried and true" use of a ritual.

Examples of Ritual Prevention

- Not washing for an entire day or longer after touching something "contaminated"

Note: The word "contaminated" as used in this book means considered dirty, harmful, or to be avoided only to the person with OCD, but which the vast majority of people would not consider dangerous in any way.

- Not receiving reassurance. Have your "significant other" kindly, but firmly, decline your requests for reassurance about obsessions. Reassurance is often sought for obsessions concerning contamination, safety of others, or having done something immoral or illegal. You will be encouraged to live with your uncertainty and doubt until that "gnawing feeling" subsides on its own.

- Not turning around to check that you have hit someone while driving, despite the sensation of having run over somebody. You will allow the fear to rise to uncomfortable levels, then wait and *not* act upon your urge to check. The anxiety will subside to manageable levels.

- Delaying rechecking the door lock (after checking it once) for an agreed upon predetermined length of time—about thirty minutes.

Ritual prevention is one of the key tools you will learn in the Self-Directed Program. You will be making the powerful decision to alter your patterns of rituals in significant ways—by delaying them, shortening them, slowing them down, or eliminating them entirely. This way you choose to feel the feelings of anxiety, doubt, fear, and dread you have been avoiding. If doing ritual prevention does not feel uncomfortable, to some extent, you probably are not blocking enough to make a difference in your OCD. The decision to "feel the discomfort," to just "be with it," or "allow it to be" without acting on it and controlling it will pay off in your progress toward breaking free from the grip of OCD.

Getting Ready for Change

Alan was successfully treated using exposure and ritual prevention after suffering with OCD for forty years. At the beginning of therapy he vividly described the prospect of confronting his fears and rituals: "It's like being asked to do a swan dive off a five-story building into a bucket filled with water." Everyone with OCD feels similarly at the beginning of therapy. Below are some common fears and concerns people with OCD often describe which prevent them from taking the risk of changing. Put a check next to the concerns that apply to you. Note that you may have additional fears and concerns. If you do, write them down in the space provided.

- "If I don't do my rituals, what will I then do to feel safe?" ____

- "If I confront my fear of dirt, germs, AIDS, etc., how can I be guaranteed that the catastrophe I fear (getting sick, losing a loved one, hurting my children) won't happen?" ____

- "Since there is no cure for OCD, why bother?" ____

- "It sounds too easy. I know I'll fail. I've failed at everything else." ____

- "I've already done behavior therapy, and it didn't work for me." ____

- "I'd rather just take medicine . . . this is too hard." ____

- "My rituals are necessary to ward off the dangers I fear." ____

- "I'm too old to try something different." ____

- "I'm afraid I'll go crazy (get sick, harm others, etc.) if I'm prevented from doing my rituals." ____

- "In childhood I was abused (neglected, abandoned, sick, fatherless, motherless, etc.). I'll never get well unless I talk a lot about the *real* problems from my childhood." ____

- "My thoughts are so bad it must mean I have an 'evil seed' inside of me. I don't deserve to get better." ____

- "If I get better or feel happy, then something bad surely has to happen. I don't want to take a chance." ____

- Other _____

- Other _____

- Other _____

The common feature of these fears and concerns is that each can be used as a reason to avoid confronting the OCD problem. Let's look at ways to deal with them:

- *"If I don't do my rituals, what will I do to feel safe?"*

Your *need* to feel perfectly safe is part of your OCD problem. By taking a chance and dealing with your discomfort by not doing rituals, you open yourself to other possible ways of handling the discomfort you feel. You are making progress when you take the "risk" of restraining or eliminating rituals from your life.

- *"If I confront my fear of dirt, germs, AIDS, etc., how can I be guaranteed that the catastrophe I fear (getting sick, losing a loved one, hurting my children) won't happen?"*

You can't be guaranteed a life without risk, pain, loss, hurt, error, or injury. The problem is that your brain has made the mistaken connection between your rituals and feelings of safety and comfort, no matter how temporary. Exposure and ritual prevention can help you break the stranglehold of rituals in your daily life.

- *"Since there is no cure for OCD, why bother?"*

This is the "all-or-nothing" way of thinking typical of persons with OCD. Even modest progress can make a significant difference in the quality of your life—and your family's life.

- *"It sounds too easy. I know I'll fail. I've failed at everything else."*

There is no such thing as failure. The only failure is not trying to succeed with the Self-Directed Program.

- *"I've already done behavior therapy, and it didn't work for me."*

Often what people describe as previous experience with "behavior therapy" was actually some variation on "behavior modification," hypnosis, relaxation training, systematic desensitization, creative visualization, or any number of other techniques, all of which have little or no effectiveness with OCD.

- *"I'd rather just take medicine . . . this is too hard."*

Exposure and ritual prevention is hard, no doubt about it. And certainly, medicine is an important component in the overall treatment of OCD. However, improvement with medicine alone is usually limited. In addition, there are some persons with OCD who simply don't benefit from medicines or who suffer intolerable side effects. To achieve optimum recovery from OCD, the Self-Directed Program should be considered an important element in the overall treatment regimen. There is research evidence (O'Sullivan, Noshirvani, and Marks 1991) to demonstrate that persons who have acquired the skills and tools offered in the Self-Directed Program suffer fewer problems and relapse less should they decide, for whatever reason (e.g., pregnancy, side effects), to discontinue taking OCD medicine.

- *"My rituals are necessary to ward off the dangers I fear."*

The degree to which you *truly* believe your rituals (hand washing, checking, repeating) are necessary—versus knowing they are dumb and make no sense, but feeling that you must do them anyway—predicts how well you are likely to progress in the Self-Directed Program. These are called overvalued ideas. If you have them, they need to be changed first before you will progress in the Self-Directed Program. Refer to chapter 8 for help in changing "overvalued ideas" as well as other "faulty beliefs."

- *"I'm too old to try something different."*

The good news is that treatment for OCD helps no matter when you start. Without treatment, symptoms tend to get worse with age; however, there is no age group that the Self-Directed Program cannot help.

- *"I'll go crazy (get sick, harm others, etc.) if I don't do my rituals."*

In twelve years of working with OCD patients day after day, no one has *ever* become crazy, sick, or psychotic from exposure and ritual prevention. The anxiety experienced may be uncomfortable, but it is never dangerous!

- *"In childhood I was abused (neglected, abandoned, sick, fatherless, motherless, etc.). I'll never get well unless I talk a lot about the real problems from my childhood!"*

Many people with OCD have suffered during their childhood. Many persons without OCD also suffered in their childhood. The majority of people with OCD have loving, concerned parents who did the best they could, possibly dealing with OCD in themselves or other family members. These parents had the added disadvantage of knowing little, if anything, about the disorder. Blaming your parents for your OCD problem only serves to maintain the problem by keeping you stuck in the role of "victim." This leaves you powerless to combat your OCD.

Now that we have addressed many of the fears of getting started, there may still be some that were not addressed here. Write any other fears you may have on the lines provided below. Review what you've written each day for a period of several days until you have either dealt constructively with it or it just no longer bothers you to any great degree. Remember, the important problem is not the fear, but maintaining your freedom and choices in the face of the fear. This is what the Self-Directed Program is designed to do.

_____

_____

_____

_____

Preparing for Change

- Set aside a period of between four and eight weeks during which time you will make the Self-Directed Program the most important priority in your life.

- Be prepared to spend a minimum of two to three hours per day—every day—doing ERP.

- Tell others in your immediate family what you are embarking on and, if you can, get them solidly behind you. Ask family members to read chapter 16.

- Identify a supportive person in your environment who would be willing to "coach" you in carrying out the Self-Directed Program. This can be a close friend, family member, or therapist. It is *vital* that this person be knowledgeable about OCD, accepting, and non-judgmental. This person also should have a sincere interest in helping.

- It is not necessary to delay starting on medication while you are doing the Self-Directed Program. Medication enhances the effectiveness of the program. Likewise, the program enhances the effectiveness of medication. Alert any mental health professional you are seeing that you are beginning a program to reduce your OCD symptoms.

Helping Your Family Get Ready for Change

Living with someone with OCD is frequently painful, baffling, and frustrating. Successfully controlling OCD symptoms requires the support and cooperation of those family members whose lives have been affected daily by the person with OCD. The disorder challenges the patience and compassion of the most benevolent family members. Although most family members wish only the best for the person in the family with OCD, over many years, deep anger and resentments toward the person with OCD may have developed. Negative feelings that are not acknowledged and managed effectively can be destructive to your recovery process. For a detailed discussion of these issues and how to deal with them, refer to chapter 16.

Informed and compassionate family involvement is vital to the recovery process. Family members should educate themselves as much as possible and they should understand how ERP works—and why. They also must understand and confront their own role in perpetuating or "enabling" the OCD problem. For example, one way family members perpetuate OCD symptoms is to do rituals for the person with OCD to "keep the peace." The mother who needlessly launders all the family's clothing several times a week to keep her son with OCD comfortably free of "contamination" is, without intending to, contributing to his OCD problem. Such "enabling" behaviors must eventually be stopped, but *only* in cooperation with the person with OCD.

Family members can help the person with OCD by assisting with the difficult ERP work. Although we are not proposing that family members function as "junior behavior therapists," often they can be very helpful in guiding, coaching, and supporting the person's efforts to overcome his/her OCD problem.

How to Be a Great Coach—Guidelines for Family Members

1. Realize that people with OCD cannot control the powerful urges they are experiencing. It is a chemical imbalance that is ruling their thoughts and behavior. They do not *choose* to have OCD any more than a person chooses to have diabetes or thyroid disease.

2. Family members must never force or impose their wishes upon the person with OCD. The decision to engage in and follow the Self-Directed Program must be solely the choice of the person with OCD.

3. Do *not* criticize or scold if the person with OCD does not fulfill your expectations. Talk about your feelings, but do not blame your disappointment on the person with OCD.

4. The helpful family member should serve as an encourager, guide, monitor, helper, and supporter.

5. Do your best to maintain a nonjudgmental attitude. *Never* judge the person with OCD according to their progress (or lack of progress) with the Self-Directed Program.

6. Expect relapses and backsliding. Progress is often "two steps forward and one step back." Restrain the tendency to become discouraged and negative. Stay positive, keep working at it, and the OCD *will* get better!

7. Use verbal praise to reward progress, no matter how small and seemingly inconsequential it is. Remember, reducing checking from fifty to forty checks may not seem like a big deal to you, but to the person with OCD, it can be a major step.

8. Stop blaming yourself for your child's or spouse's OCD problem. You did not cause the OCD. The causes of OCD are not related so much to the environment as they are to genetic and biological vulnerability. Stop feeling guilty—you did not cause the OCD. Guilt will only drain you of the energy you need to deal effectively with OCD.

9. Expect that OCD symptoms make no sense. They are inconsistent. Dr. Hyman once had a patient who was terrified of germs. He lived in constant horror of the possibility of anyone getting saliva on him. But he loved it when, upon arriving home from work, his dog joyously licked his face. That's the nature of OCD. It makes no sense.

10. Realize the symptoms have little or no *symbolic meaning*. It is useless to interpret the symptoms as having any meaning beyond the impact they have. The symptoms mean nothing other than "it's just OCD."

CHAPTER 5

Preparing for the Challenge—Self-Assessment

You gain strength, courage and confidence by every experience in which you really stop to look fear in the face. You are able to say to yourself, "I lived through this horror, I can take the next thing that comes along." You must do the thing you think you cannot do.

—Eleanor Roosevelt

By now you know what OCD is and you have a general idea of what is involved with recovery from OCD. You are now ready to begin the Self-Directed Program. It is important to your success that you consult a mental health professional before beginning the program. This professional should be at least somewhat familiar with the diagnosis and treatment of OCD. A psychiatrist or psychologist needs to confirm that you indeed have OCD as your primary diagnosis. You probably should *not* undertake the Self-Directed Program if any of the following conditions apply to you:

- Severe clinical depression, bipolar disorder, or schizophrenia is causing more of a problem in your life than OCD at the present time. If not presently under control, these conditions will interfere with your ability to benefit from the Self-Directed Program. Once these conditions are stabilized through proper medication management, you may then benefit from the program. It is especially important to consult with a qualified mental health professional before beginning the program if any of these conditions are the primary problem for you at this time.

- You are in the midst of a major life stressor, change, or transition such as the death or severe illness of a loved one, a job change, or moving. The stress of these life changes will interfere with your progress with the Self-Directed Program. Once your life stabilizes, you will be better able to benefit from the program. Of course, there is no such thing as a life without some stress so don't allow the stress of daily life to delay your taking on the Self-Directed Program.

- Your immediate family is not supportive of your attempts to help yourself. Even the most well meaning of families can sometimes sabotage your efforts. If such is the case, seek family counseling with a mental health professional familiar with OCD before beginning the program. Get together with as many family members who are willing to help as possible. It is important that the key members of your family be on the same page with you.

The guidance and support of an experienced mental health professional can be an excellent source of support for you as you work through this program. If your therapist does not agree with your wish to start the Self-Directed Program at this time, be sure to consider the reasons carefully. If you are still unsure of what to do, consult another qualified mental health professional for a second opinion.

Assessing Your OCD Problem

On the following pages, you will be designing your own Self-Directed Program. The first step is to make a thorough assessment of your OCD problem. This is vital, since the type or types of OCD symptoms you have—ordering, washing, or checking, for example—will determine the specific design of your program. Look back at the OCD symptoms listed in chapter 2. Note the symptoms you checked in chapter 2, then write them down on the lines provided (under "Symptom") in the appropriate section below. Indicate whether each symptom is a past or current one by placing a check in the appropriate box. Then, using the guidelines below, indicate how much of a problem each symptom is presently causing you by marking a 1, 2, or 3 on the blank line below "Disruption Rating." You need to do a disruption rating only on *current symptoms.*

Past = symptom bothered you in the past

Current = symptom bothers you now

Disruption Rating (of current symptoms)

1 = a mild symptom, just a slight nuisance or problem

2 = a moderate symptom, causes some anxiety and disruption in daily life

3 = a severe symptom, causes much anxiety and great disruption in daily life

Obsessions

Remember that obsessions refer to unwanted thoughts, ideas, and impulses that come into your mind. An obsession is usually unrealistic and causes a great deal of anxiety. It has a persistent quality that doesn't let up. Finally, it is usually about trying to prevent something dangerous from happening to you or to others.

Contamination Obsessions (These are the excessive fear or disgust, and/or preoccupation with the avoidance of dirt, germs, contaminants of any kind.)

Symptom	Past	Current	Disruption Rating
Handwashing - germs	☐	☑	1
Avoid objects - cleaning etl	☐	☑	1
Clean house, etc. or Malls	☐	☑	1
Others ell	☐	☐	

Hoarding, Saving, and Collecting Obsessions (These are the acquisition of and failure to discard possessions which appear to be useless or of very limited value.)

Symptom	Past	Current	Disruption Rating
Save sentimental items	☐	☑	1
	☐	☐	
	☐	☐	
	☐	☐	

Ordering Obsessions (These are an excessive preoccupation with symmetry, exactness, or order.)

Symptom	Past	Current	Disruption Rating
Counting	☐	☑	1
Check locks, stove, etc	☐	☑	1
Check writing	☐	☐	
	☐	☐	

Religious Obsessions, Scrupulosity (These are excessive fear, worry, and preoccupation with violating moral and religious laws and rules, such as the fear of being punished for blasphemous thoughts.)

Symptom	Past	Current	Disruption Rating
	☐	☐	
	☐	☐	
	☐	☐	
	☐	☐	

Somatic Obsessions (These involve a preoccupation with the appearance of specific parts of the body, or the possibility of having an illness or incurable disease.)

Symptom	Past	Current	Disruption Rating
_____	☐	☐	_____
_____	☐	☐	_____
_____	☐	☐	_____
_____	☐	☐	_____

Aggressive Obsessions (These involve having excessive thoughts of causing harm to yourself or to others.)

Symptom	Past	Current	Disruption Rating
_____	☐	☐	_____
_____	☐	☐	_____
_____	☐	☐	_____
_____	☐	☐	_____

Sexual Obsessions (These are frequent unwanted, worrisome, and intrusive sexual thoughts, images, or impulses.)

Symptom	Past	Current	Disruption Rating
_____	☐	☐	_____
_____	☐	☐	_____
_____	☐	☐	_____
_____	☐	☐	_____

Miscellaneous Obsessions (These are obsessions that don't fit into any of the descriptions above.)

Symptom	Past	Current	Disruption Rating
Superstitious	☐	☐	_____
fears w/ clothes	☐	☐	_____
_____	☐	☐	_____
_____	☐	☐	_____

Compulsions

Think of compulsions as the "things you do" for temporary relief from an obsession. Another way of putting it is that compulsions "neutralize" the discomfort of an obsession. They are usually physical actions, such as hand washing and checking over and over again. But they can also be "things you do" in your head, in your thoughts. There are three main keys to understanding the compulsions of OCD. First, when you do them, they have the effect of lowering or lessening the anxiety caused by an obsession, but only for a brief period of time. Second, if you don't do them, you feel extremely anxious. Lastly, you tend to do them repeatedly, over and over again.

Past = symptom bothered you in the past

Current = symptom bothers you now

Disruption Rating (of current symptoms)

1 = a mild symptom, just a slight nuisance or problem

2 = a moderate symptom, causes some anxiety and disruption in daily life

3 = a severe symptom, causes much anxiety and great disruption in daily life

Cleaning and Washing Compulsions

Symptom	Past	Current	Disruption Rating
Handwashing	☐	☐	_____
_____	☐	☐	_____
_____	☐	☐	_____
_____	☐	☐	_____

Checking Compulsions

Symptom	Past	Current	Disruption Rating
_____	☐	☐	_____
_____	☐	☐	_____
_____	☐	☐	_____
_____	☐	☐	_____

Hoarding, Saving, and Collecting Compulsions

Symptom	Past	Current	Disruption Rating
_____	❑	❑	_____
_____	❑	❑	_____
_____	❑	❑	_____
_____	❑	❑	_____

Repeating, Counting, Ordering Compulsions

Symptom	Past	Current	Disruption Rating
_____	❑	❑	_____
_____	❑	❑	_____
_____	❑	❑	_____
_____	❑	❑	_____

Miscellaneous Compulsions

Symptom	Past	Current	Disruption Rating
_____	❑	❑	_____
_____	❑	❑	_____
_____	❑	❑	_____
_____	❑	❑	_____

Avoidance Symptoms

Now list all of the situations, persons, places, or things that you avoid because of your OCD. These can also include recurring horrible or disturbing thoughts that you avoid. Indicate the degree to which you avoid each situation on a scale of 0–100:

   0 = I never avoid it.

   50 = I avoid it about half the time.

   75 = I avoid it most of the time.

   100 = I completely avoid this situation, at all costs.

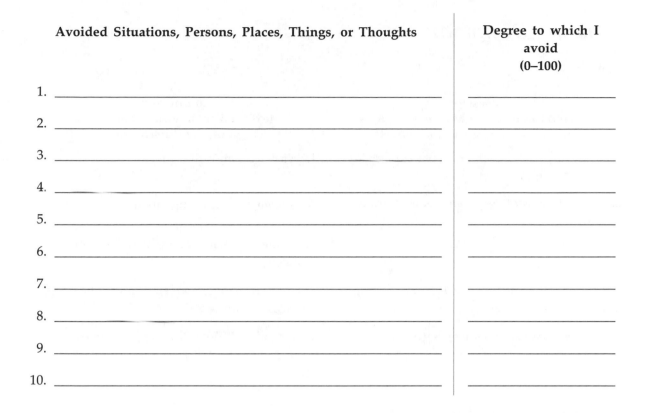

Avoided Situations, Persons, Places, Things, or Thoughts	Degree to which I avoid (0–100)
1. _____	_____
2. _____	_____
3. _____	_____
4. _____	_____
5. _____	_____
6. _____	_____
7. _____	_____
8. _____	_____
9. _____	_____
10. _____	_____

Target Your Symptoms

You have probably noticed that you have several severe symptoms at the same time. This is common among people with OCD. You may be wondering, *How am I ever going to get better with so many symptoms? I must be hopeless!* It can seem overwhelming to think of making improvements with all of your symptoms at once.

The Self-Directed Program will be more manageable if you single out one or two symptoms that are presently causing the most disruption in your daily functioning at work, at home, and in your relationships. Make these symptoms the targets of your initial efforts in the program. Once you achieve success with these, you'll be better able to successfully tackle others that are causing difficulty. Like most challenges in life, success breeds success. As you break free from your worst symptoms, you will gain confidence that you can break free in other areas also. Be patient and work with your symptoms one or two at a time.

Now you are ready for the next step. Write down all the obsessions and compulsions that you marked with a disruption rating of 3. List them in the order of severity, starting with the symptom that disrupts your life the most as number 1. Also, take note of your avoidance symptoms. These main obsessions, compulsions, and avoidances will be the initial target symptoms of your Self-Directed Program.

Target Symptoms

Example:

Obsessions (situations, thoughts images, or impulses that cause discomfort)	Compulsions (external or internal actions that neutralize discomfort)
1. "I must prevent people I love from getting sick or dying."	1. Washing hands 100 times a day
2. "I must prevent harm and danger from germs."	2. Showering with long ritualistic showers
	2a. Avoiding places thought to be contaminated
3. "I must prevent my house from burning down."	3. Checking stove, coffeepot, and other appliances 20 times a day
4. "I must not cause violent harm to my loved ones."	4. Repeating "I love the Lord" 6 times in sets of 3 in my mind

Your Target Symptoms

Obsessions (situations, thoughts images, or impulses that cause discomfort)	Compulsions (external or internal actions that neutralize discomfort)
1. _____	1. _____
2. _____	2. _____
3. _____	3. _____
4. _____	4. _____
5. _____	5. _____
6. _____	6. _____
7. _____	7. _____
8. _____	8. _____
9. _____	9. _____
10. _____	10. _____

Your Target Avoidances

Choose the top five avoidance symptoms that are interfering with your life from the form you just filled out above. Obsessive-compulsive symptoms often lead to the avoidance of numerous situations involving people, places, things and even thoughts. Based on the form you filled out above, think about your avoidances and choose the ones that are the most disruptive to your life:

1. _____

2. _____

3. _____

4. _____

5. _____

As was mentioned previously, many people have OCD symptoms in more than one area. For example, many people with contamination fears have checking compulsions as well. You may have an obsession about contracting AIDS, wash your hands fifty times a day, have intrusive thoughts about harming others, *and* also feel compelled to check the door locks, stove, and appliances several times a day. If this is the case, ask yourself, "Which symptom, if I could be free of it, would make the most difference in the quality of my life?" This is the one to attack first. List this symptom as number 1, then list your other symptoms in the order of their negative impact on your life. Eventually, all of your most disturbing symptoms will be addressed in the following chapters.

CHAPTER 6

Your Intervention Strategy

Don't be afraid to take a big step if one is indicated.
You can't cross a chasm in two small jumps.

—David Lloyd George

Now that you have done a thorough assessment of your OCD symptoms, you are ready to produce your "road map" for doing your exposure and ritual prevention (ERP) work. This road map is called an Anxiety/Exposure List. It is simply a list of situations that you fear and avoid, listed in order of the levels of fear they provoke. Like a road map, your Anxiety/Exposure List shows you where to start, where to finish, and the pathway between. The unit of measurement used to convey and describe the anxiety aroused in various fear-provoking situations is called the SUDS scale. This stands for:

S ubjective

U nits of

D istress

S cale

The SUDS scale is a self-rating system designed to measure the amount of anxiety the person feels. It was invented in the '70s by Edward Wolpe, M.D., a professor of psychiatry at Temple University School of Medicine. The SUDS scale will be useful as you design your own Anxiety/Exposure List. It is a 100-point scale with 100 equaling the most anxiety-provoking situation you have ever experienced in your life. 0 equals neutral or no anxiety whatsoever. A 50 SUDS is neither very high nor very low anxiety. It indicates just medium anxiety.

Now, think of a few situations you have experienced in your life that caused you the most anxiety and fear you have ever experienced. Or think of a very scary situation you hope you never have to deal with. If you find yourself not wanting to think much about this, that's okay. Situations that elicit these kinds of strong feelings of anxiety will earn a 100 on the SUDS scale.

Next, think of a situation that caused you a moderate level of anxiety—not too much and not too little. An example might be seeing your child off on the first day of school. Or having to take a test for which you are very well prepared, but it's still a test. Situations like these tend to provoke moderate feelings of anxiety—around 50 on the SUDS scale.

Now, think of a very neutral or pleasant situation—for example, going to the market, taking a warm bath, or reading a magazine. These situations would be 0 on the SUDS scale. Remember, every person is different as to the specific situations they consider as low, medium, or high on the SUDS scale.

Tips for Writing Your Personal Anxiety/Exposure List

Now that you are familiar with the use of the SUDS scale, you are ready to create your list(s) using the following guidelines:

- Your list should include 10 to 15 specific situations that trigger different levels of fear and anxiety. For some, the most useful place to start is with the list of Target Avoidances you compiled when working with chapter 5.

- The situations or *triggers* in your list should differ from each other by about 5–10 SUDS points each.

- Begin your Anxiety/Exposure List with situations or triggers that provoke about 20–40 SUDS, or low to medium anxiety. Then list situations that trigger higher and higher levels of SUDS.

- For each situation or trigger, rate the SUDS level based on what you think you would feel if you were faced with the fearful situation and *unable or prevented from carrying out the compulsion you would typically use in that situation*. In this way, you can accurately depict your true SUDS level for that particular situation or trigger. For example, for the compulsion to check that the stove is off, rate your SUDS level based upon how it would likely feel if you were, for some reason, prevented from checking the stove more than once. For washers, rate your SUDS based upon how you'd feel if prevented from, say, washing your hands after touching a doorknob in a public bathroom. This is your true SUDS level for that compulsion.

- The last item on your list should be the situation that triggers your highest levels of anxiety and fear.

- From your master list, you can make one or more "mini-lists" that address one situation, trigger, or avoidance behavior. You may list the triggers differing only in their degree of proximity to the feared object or situation. Examples of mini-lists can be found in the text below.

Mary's Anxiety and Exposure List

Let's look at Anxiety/Exposure Lists for Mary. Mary has OCD that began after her oldest son contracted a life-threatening virus five years ago. She has an obsessive fear and avoidance of blood, illness, dirt, and germs. This has resulted in severely disabling hand washing and showering rituals. She washes her hands about fifty times a day, her daily showering ritual takes about one and one-half hours, and she avoids going near specific places in her town because she considers them "contaminated."

Specific triggers for Mary included red-colored spots and objects (red being the color of blood), homeless persons (whom she believed more likely to have open sores and to be disease carriers), and hospitals (lots of blood there!). Mary maintained specific "safe and clean" areas in her household that were off-limits to other family members, especially to her husband, who works for a parcel delivery company that makes daily deliveries to local hospitals. He was therefore considered "contaminated" and was included as an item on her list. Here is Mary's initial Anxiety/Exposure List:

Mary's Anxiety/Exposure Lists for Fear of Contamination by "Illness"	SUDS Level (0–100)
Touching a red spot in book	20
Passing/driving close by homeless person on the street	30
Being visited by someone who went to visit someone in hospital	35
Touching and using public phone	40
Buying groceries from "sickly" looking cashier in market	50
Parking car next to neighbor recently ill	55
Touching mail from mailbox touched by "suspicious looking" mailman	60
Touching red spots on public elevator	75
Husband sitting in "clean" area in living room without having showered	80
Anyone entering her bedroom without prior showering	100

Mary's OCD included avoidance of several "dangerous" situations involving hospitals and homeless persons. She therefore constructed separate mini-lists that addressed those specific situations. The items on each list differed in their SUDS levels based on their degree of proximity to the feared object or situation: persons suspected of having AIDS and everything they might contact; hospitals; and sickly looking homeless persons with "germs."

Mary's Anxiety/Exposure Mini-List for Hospital Triggers	SUDS Level (0–100)
Walking into a hospital known to treat AIDS patients, standing for one minute, then leaving	40
Walking into the hospital, standing in the waiting room	55
Sitting in a chair in the hospital waiting room	60
Touching a chair in the hospital waiting room	70
Standing in a patient room in the hospital	80
Sitting in a chair in a hospital room	90

	SUDS
Touching a chair in a hospital room	95
Sitting in a chair in her own home after returning home from the hospital	100

Here is Mary's list for fear of homeless people. Note that each item on the list describes a scene of getting increasingly closer and closer to her most feared situation (touching the ground that a homeless person has walked on—100 SUDS). Think about how your obsessive fears and avoidance situations might be broken down into similar, smaller pieces/steps.

Mary's Anxiety/Exposure Mini-List for Fear of Homeless People	SUDS Level (0–100)
Driving by area where homeless people congregate, windows down	40
Driving by area where homeless people congregate, windows cracked one inch	45
Driving by area where homeless people congregate, windows open	50
Walking within 25 feet of area where homeless people congregate	60
Walking within 10 feet of area where homeless people congregate	65
Standing directly inside area where homeless people congregate	70
Directly touching the ground where homeless people congregate	80
Handing a homeless person a quarter, making sure to touch his skin	90
Touching the ground where homeless people congregate, and then touching the interior of her own car	100

Anxiety and Exposure Lists for Checkers: Melody's Case

The following are some sample Anxiety/Exposure Lists for Melody, whom you first met in chapter 1. She has extensive checking rituals involving light switches, door locks, and electrical appliances. An important component of her obsession is her fear of being responsible for causing a house fire or a burglary, which intensifies the longer she plans to be away from home.

Melody's Anxiety/Exposure Mini-List for Checking Appliances	SUDS Level (0–100)
Shut refrigerator door once, walk away without checking	50
Shut stove off, walk away without checking	60
Turn off coffee maker, leave plugged in overnight	65
Leave small kitchen appliances plugged in, leave home, return in one hour	70
Leave small kitchen appliances plugged in, leave home, return in three hours	75

Leave small kitchen appliances plugged in, leave home, return in six hours	80
Leave small kitchen appliances plugged in, leave home, return home next day	85
Check door locks only once prior to going to bed at night	95
Leave all small kitchen appliances plugged in overnight	100

Melody constructed the following mini-list involving her compulsion to check door locks:

Melody's Anxiety/Exposure Mini-List for Checking Door Locks	SUDS Level (0–100)
Locking the front door once, check twice, walk away	65
Locking the front door once, check once, walk away	70
Locking the front door once, walk away without checking, stay away for 1 hour	75
Locking the front door once, walk away without checking, stay away for 2 hours	80
Locking the front door once, walk away without checking, stay away for 4 hours	85
Locking the front door once, walk away without checking, stay away for 8 hours	95
Locking the front door once, walk away without checking, stay away overnight	100

Melody's mini-list shows how her SUDS increases the longer she is away from home. This fact will prove useful later in constructing exposure exercises to overcome her compulsion to check over and over.

Anxiety and Exposure Lists for Ordering and Symmetry: Ben's Case

Ben, who has had OCD since childhood, requires that his kitchen pantry items such as cans of food be lined up like toy soldiers, perfectly spaced with labels facing forward. His clothing is hung neatly in closets and organized with surgical precision. Rug tassels must lie perfectly straight. Furnishings and display objects must be placed at perfect right angles to the wall. Linen items are folded and piled with perfect balance. The slightest disorder, disturbance, or misplacement of any object provokes intense anxiety. Here is an example Anxiety/Exposure List for Ben:

Ben's Anxiety/Exposure List for Ordering and Symmetry	SUDS Level (0-100)
Mix clothing so that colored items are not lined up	65
Place throw pillows slightly "out of place"	70

Move cans of food in pantry—so that they are *not* lined up "perfectly straight"	75
Move dining room chairs to "not perfectly straight" position—1 inch off	80
Move dining room chairs to "not perfectly straight" position—2 inches off	85
Place throw pillows moderately "out of place"	90
Place throw pillows extremely "out of place"	95
Move dining room chairs to "not perfectly straight" position—3 inches off	100

Note that, in general, as objects are placed further from their "perfect" position, Ben's SUDS level increases. Along the lines as the cases just discussed, Ben might create mini-lists for specific areas; for example, a list for the dining room, another one for out of place kitchen items, etc. As in Melody's case, these lists will be helpful in constructing exposure exercises to overcome his compulsion for orderliness and symmetry.

Anxiety and Exposure List for Obsessional Slowness: Jack's Case

Jack has obsessional slowness while dressing and showering. These tasks take him as long as two to three hours because he feels that he must perform certain rituals before any piece of clothing feels "right." His rituals include repeating (for example, tying shoe laces three times), counting (e.g., to a "good" number), and straightening the garment until it feels "right." Like Mary, Jack takes excessively long, ritualized showers but with a difference. Whereas Mary showers excessively because she obsessively fears "contamination" from germs and the AIDS virus, Jack's lengthy showers are so long simply because they must be done "just right." For example, body parts must be washed in the "proper" order, and a certain number of "right" times. Contamination is of no concern to him. Here is Jack's Anxiety/Exposure List.

Jack's Anxiety/Exposure List for Obsessional Slowness	SUDS Level (0–100)
Lay clothing on bed "imperfectly"	50
Place left shoe on first (rather than right one first)	55
Tie shoe laces only once	60
Tie shoe laces only once without performing ritual tapping when finished	70
Place shirt in trousers slightly "off" without straightening—do not tap	75
Place foot in pants touching bare feet to inside of pant leg—the "wrong" way	80
Zip up pant zipper only once (rather than a "good number" of times)	90
Leave bedroom with "wrong" foot first	95
Leave bedroom without counting to "8" three times (purposefully "wrong")	100

Here is a sample mini-list for Jack's lengthy showers:

Jack's Anxiety/Exposure Mini-List for Lengthy Showers	SUDS Level (0–100)
While in shower, wash one body part out of "correct" order	55
While in shower, wash two body parts out of "correct" order	65
While in shower, wash three body parts out of "correct" order	75
While in shower, wash all body parts out of "correct" order	85
Wash body parts "wrong" number of times, step out of shower	95
Wash body parts just once, step out of shower	100

Again, note how Jack assessed his SUDS levels to increasing degrees of discomfort should he not complete his ritualized behavior in the "correct" manner. Note that these Anxiety/Exposure lists provide a blueprint for doing your own exposure and ritual prevention work.

Now, using these lists as your guide, construct your own Anxiety/Exposure List for one of your specific target symptoms (see chapter 5). Remember, you can make several mini-lists that cover different fears such as "bathroom list," "AIDS list," or "water faucet" list.

Anxiety/Exposure List for _____	SUDS Level (0–100)
1. _____	_____
2. _____	_____
3. _____	_____
4. _____	_____
5. _____	_____
6. _____	_____
7. _____	_____
8. _____	_____
9. _____	_____
10. _____	_____

Exposure and Ritual Prevention (ERP): Step-by-Step

Now that you have constructed an Anxiety/Exposure List for your trigger symptoms, you are ready to get into the heart of behavior therapy—exposure and ritual prevention (ERP). *Exposure* consists of using situations from your list to create opportunities to change the way you typically respond to these anxiety-arousing situations.

Using Your Anxiety/Exposure List

Step-by-step, you will confront your personal anxiety-arousing situations. You will face these in a manner completely different from your typical way of dealing with them—for example, by excessive showering, hand washing, or cleaning. You will be planting the seeds of your recovery from OCD. Here is the step-by-step process:

Step 1. Choose a mini-list and start with the items that provoke at least a moderate amount of anxiety—about 50–60 SUDS.

Note that it is extremely important that the item you choose for your exposure provokes at least a moderate level of fear. If you do *not* feel any fear or anxiety when doing an exposure, go on to the next situation or trigger on your list. This is done to provide you with firsthand experience of the process of habituation. *Habituation*, as you remember from chapter 3, is your nervous system's natural response to *prolonged* stimuli—with time, the level of fear and arousal diminishes. However, you can benefit from habituation only by bringing on and confronting an adequate level of discomfort. You've heard it many times before: "No pain, no gain!" This is your key to doing ERP! Because it's highly motivational to see your day-to-day progress, use the Daily Exposure Practice Form (on page 84) at the end of this chapter, to keep track of your improvement.

In our example, one of Mary's mini-lists involved the idea of "contamination by a homeless person." Her least anxiety-provoking item was "Driving by an area where homeless people congregate, with the windows down." Mary carried out this exposure by driving through the "contaminated" area. Her beginning SUDS level was moderate, about 45–50. She allowed her feelings of anxiety to emerge.

Step 2. Allow your discomfort to rise, stay with it and do not avoid it!

Begin to feel your SUDS level go up as you encounter a triggering situation. Stay with the feeling and do not avoid or block it! If your SUDS goes up very high, it's okay. The more SUDS you take on now, the better. *Too much SUDS is better than too little!* Try not to fear your discomfort. Although you may feel as if you might, no one has ever died or gone crazy from doing an exposure. In a short while—maybe longer—you are going to notice your SUDS level begin to diminish. This is a sign that habituation is taking place. This can take a few minutes or hours. Hang in there—stick with it, no matter how long it takes!

> ## KEY TO BREAKING FREE!
>
> If you are too uncomfortable starting with even a low anxiety-provoking item on your list, make your exposure a bit easier. For example, if you are afraid of touching a "contaminated" object with your hand, start by touching it with your fingernail, or with the tip of a fingernail. For checking fears, if walking away without checking a faucet is too anxiety-provoking, allow one brief check to start. For ordering rituals, if moving an object out of place one foot is too overwhelming, start by moving it out of place one inch. *It's not so important where you start, but that you start somewhere!*

Exposure Pitfalls: Typical Ways of Blocking or Avoiding Exposure

If your SUDS level is not going high enough, look for ways you may be blocking your experience of the anxiety during the exposure. Some typical ways people block their feelings are as follows:

- Dulling yourself by purposefully becoming "numb" to your experience. It is important to stay alert and connected to the fearful feelings throughout the exposure.

- Relying upon a "safety signal" such as a spouse, therapist, or friend, who excessively reassures you while practicing an exposure. Although a friend/helper can be a source of motivation, be careful that their presence is not serving to neutralize your fears. For example, the friend/helper who, while helping you walk out of the house without checking the door locks and stoves, repeatedly reminds you that "you are perfectly safe, and nothing bad has happened." Or a friend who shows you medical textbooks about how it's impossible to catch AIDS without direct contact. Reliance on this sort of reassurance can become yet another compulsion and can become self-defeating. If you find yourself overrelying on your friend/helper to feel comfortable doing the exposure, eventually try practicing by yourself so that you can obtain the maximum benefit.

- Ritualizing privately by counting, praying, and so forth in order to neutralize the anxiety or discomfort of the exposure.

- Dissociating from the experience—for example, thinking: "It's not me doing this, but someone else." This is a form of "magical" thinking that people with OCD may resort to for handling their discomfort during the exposures.

On the lines below, list some of the ways you may be tempted to block or avoid the exposure(s):

1. _____

2. _____

3. _____

4. _____

5. _____

Step 3. Practice ritual prevention while doing exposure.

As we explained in chapter 3, exposure works only when it is conducted hand in hand with *ritual prevention*. Ritual prevention is the voluntary blocking of compulsive rituals, and it is one of the keys to your progress with the Self-Directed Program. Doing ritual prevention is like refraining from scratching an itchy patch of skin, knowing that if you give in and scratch it, it will only become itchier. If you successfully refrain from scratching, the itch has a chance to go away on its own.

General Rules for Ritual Prevention

- You may have agreed to allow a relative or friend to help as a support person. Instruct this person that should it be necessary to stop you from violating the rules, that you should be told calmly but firmly to follow the rules.

- If you have an urge to ritualize that you are afraid you can't resist, talk to your support person before doing the ritual. Ask this person to remain with you until the urge decreases to a manageable level.

- As a general rule, no one with OCD should be physically restrained from doing rituals. There are, however, certain situations where such restraint may be appropriate. They are:

   The rituals are causing life-threatening harm to the person with OCD.

   You have agreed, *prior* to starting the Self-Directed Program, to a *specific plan* of having your support person (spouse, friend, relative, etc.) physically restrain you.

Facing Your Fears of Doing Ritual Prevention

People with OCD are afraid of not doing their rituals for many reasons. Some typical fears include dying, hurting others, failing to prevent harm to someone else, going crazy, causing someone you care about to get sick, being held guilty for something bad happening, going to jail, and losing one's job.

On the following form, list the consequences you fear might happen if you did not do your rituals. Indicate how afraid you are of not doing your ritual using the SUDS scale. Then rate how much you truly believe that the feared consequence will *really* happen on a scale of 0–100 using the following guidelines:

Feared Consequences of Not Doing Rituals

Rate your degree of belief (third column) using the following 100-point scale:

   0% = Not likely at all, I know it is completely senseless and I have no doubt about that.

   25% = I don't believe it will really happen, but I don't want to take any chances.

   50% = I somewhat believe it will really happen, but I don't want to take any chances.

   75% = I strongly believe it will really happen and I don't want to take any chances.

   100% = I'm completely certain this will happen, I have no doubt whatsoever, and I don't want to take any chances.

Feared Consequence(s) of Not Doing Ritual(s)	SUDS Level (0–100)	Degree of Belief (0–100%)
1. Example: "I or someone I love will get sick and die."	100	50%
2. _____	_____	_____
3. _____	_____	_____
4. _____	_____	_____
5. _____	_____	_____
6. _____	_____	_____
7. _____	_____	_____
8. _____	_____	_____

Step 4. Repeat the exposure task over and over until your SUDS rating goes down to 20 or less. Then move on to the next item on your list.

As discussed in chapter 3, the process of habituation requires *extensive* and *prolonged* contact with the situations, places, and objects that provoke anxiety. In general, habituation occurs when you are in contact with an anxiety-provoking situation and your SUDS level goes down to around 20.

Mary's Exposure and Ritual Prevention

In our example, Mary repeated her first exposure (driving by a homeless person with car windows down) over and over, each time noting the change in her SUDS level. After a while, this situation that had been so fear-provoking became simply boring. She rated her SUDS for this exposure at 20 or less.

Then she was ready to move to the next item on her Anxiety/Exposure List (driving by a homeless person with the windows cracked one inch). Initially, this exposure raised her SUDS level to 60–70. Despite how illogical it seemed, even to her, Mary's OCD caused her to fear that the "contaminated air" around the homeless person might contaminate the inside of her car. Despite her fear, she repeated this exposure over and over until she became habituated to it and felt little, if any, anxiety.

She then gradually moved to the next items on her list and repeated steps 1-4 with each item. By the time Mary was ready to confront her most feared situation (touching the ground where homeless people congregate, and then touching the interior of her own car), she became extremely anxious. Her fearful thoughts included:

- "I'll never be 'clean' again."

- "My whole home will become contaminated."
  (if she went from her car into her home)

- "Everything will become contaminated."

In spite of her fears, she persisted with the exposure, repeating the task by lightly touching all the objects of her car, inside and out. When Mary completed her "homeless" list, she then moved on to her "hospital" list. She lightly dabbed a tiny 1/4-inch corner of a napkin to the backs of chairs in the hospital waiting room (which she thought were contaminated with the AIDS virus). She brought the napkin back to her home and lightly touched many objects there, including the bathroom fixtures, bedroom furniture, and even the kitchen sink, with the "contaminated" napkin.

Mary practiced the exposures for a few hours every day. After a week, she was able to touch nearly all of the items in her home with her napkin and feel very little fear. Her goal was to "avoid avoidances." Any feeling of wanting to protect an object from "contamination" was countered by touching the object to the napkin in spite of that feeling. As she gained confidence that nothing "terrible" would happen to her or her loved ones, her obsessive fears diminished.

Doing ERP for Some Common OCD Problems

Now that you have some familiarity with the basic principles of ERP, you will learn more details about how to apply these principles to some of the most common OCD symptoms, including your own.

Washers

"Fast-Track" Method—Using the Total Water Block

This method, although at first appearing to be the most frightening, if followed rigorously, will produce rapid results for washers within a three-week period.

- For a period of at least three weeks, except for the procedures listed below, you must severely limit, or block, the use of water on your body—limited hand washing, no excessive rinsing, no use of wet towels or pre-moistened towelettes, and no swimming. Showering will consist of *one seven-minute shower for men (ten minutes for women) every three days*–this includes hair washing. Use a timer to limit your showers. Repetitive or ritualistic washing of specific areas of the body—such as genitals and hair—should be limited as much as possible.

- The use of creams and other toiletry articles (bath powder, deodorant, etc.) is okay, except where the use of these items reduces "contamination." Do *not* use antibacterial creams, soaps, or other toiletry items.

- Shaving is done by electric shaver, not with water. Water can be drunk or used to brush teeth. Care must be taken not to get water on your face or hands.

- Restrict your hand washing to the following: before meals; after toileting and after handling greasy or *visibly* dirty things. *Do not exceed* six hand washes per day and do not wash for more than thirty seconds each time. Special considerations may be given to people whose jobs make it necessary to wash their hands more often, such as nurses and other health care workers, and for people who, for medical reasons, need to use the bathroom more frequently than the average person. After you have made progress, you may begin normal hand washing

- People with excessive cleaning rituals, for example, those who use bleaches and other unnecessarily strong detergents to clean their bodies, should remove those cleaning items from the home entirely. Any necessary home cleaning should be done with simple, mild household detergent products (see the discussion of normal washing on page 77).

For washers, the goal of the ritual prevention program is to "recalibrate" your brain's relationship to water and the function of cleaning and washing. In OCD-driven cleaning and washing, water, soap, and detergents are misused as anxiety regulation tools to eliminate "contamination." In contrast, the goal of normal cleaning and washing is merely to achieve the feeling of being "fresh and clean."

Gradual Method for Washers: "Ritual Delay"

If the fast-track ritual prevention method described above seems overwhelming to you, try this gradual procedure using *ritual delay*. It is best done in three phases, proceeding at your own pace.

During Phase One, which can last a few days or as long as a week, you will work on becoming more comfortable with the idea of delaying your washing, while at the same time actually shortening the duration of your washing.

During Phase Two, you will be permitted a brief wash *only* after your SUDS has gone down. You will continue to reduce the length of time *and* the number of times you wash during the day.

During Phase Three, you will expose yourself to increasingly anxiety-provoking situations, and reduce washing to *normal levels*. This means that you will wash *only* at prescribed "normal" times. To help you decide what is "normal," we have included instructions for normal washing (see page 77).

Although you may not progress as rapidly and thoroughly as with the "fast-track" procedure, some people find this procedure easier to manage. Either one can be extremely effective, and either can help you toward your goal of breaking free from OCD.

Week I—Phase I

1. Choose a "contaminated" object or situation from your Anxiety/Exposure List of situations that typically trigger hand washing and/or showering or other neutralizing behaviors (we use the term "neutralizing" to mean "anxiety lowering" or "discomfort diminishing"). Then, decide upon a length of time to refrain from washing that would trigger an anxiety level of around 50–60 SUDS. It may be one, five, ten, twenty, or more minutes. That's up to you.

2. Touch the object until you feel sufficiently "contaminated" (50–60 SUDS). Using a timer, stop watch, or some other timing instrument, wait your chosen amount of time to go without washing, showering, or neutralizing. Experience your anxiety without blocking it.

3. At the end of your predetermined waiting period (five, ten, twenty minutes, etc.), wash, shower, and neutralize as you normally do. But this time, *reduce the length of your washing by one-half*. Each time, work on reducing your washing time by seconds, minutes, or hours, depending upon your baseline level of washing (before you started the Self-Directed Program). If you normally shower for an hour, reduce it to one-half hour. If you wash your hands for three minutes, reduce it to one and one-half minutes. If you neutralize your anxiety in some other way, reduce the length of time it takes by half. Repeat this

exposure three times per day, or as many times as you can, until you get the idea of delaying washing.

Using Mary as an example again, here is her chart showing her ritual delay program for Phase I, lasting one week. Mary's baseline (initial) level of rituals involved washing her hands an average of fifty times per day and taking showers for one and one-half hours. During Phase I, her exposure consisted of sitting in her car in the "contaminated" parking space for five minutes before permitting herself to wash her hands or shower. Mary repeated the exposure situation at least three times a day, on consecutive days until her initial SUDS was reduced to under 20. On day three, she added another item—touching her "contaminated" keys (keys that had touched the "contaminated" car). She work on both exposures at the same time, permitting herself to experience as much discomfort as was tolerable.

Mary set a goal for *Phase I* of reducing rituals (the total number/length of hand washes and the length of her showers) by one-half. Initially, that was what she believed she could handle. However, by the end of the week, she found she could decrease the number and length of hand washes and showers even more! She monitored the number of her hand washes each day using the Ritual Delay Worksheet (on page 75). A kitchen timer was used to time her showers.

Note that for more anxiety-provoking triggers, such as touching the "contaminated" mail box in Phase II, the ritual delay may be shortened for a day or two, if necessary, depending upon the degree of SUDS. The more anxious Mary was, the less time she could delay, at least at the beginning. During Phase I, it is important to keep increasing the length of the delay as much as possible with each successive day of exposure.

Mary's Ritual Delay Worksheet: Phase I

Phase I	Object(s) Touched	Initial SUDS (0–100)	Ritual Delay (minutes/hours)	Length of Shower (% Reduced from Baseline)	Total No. Hand washes (% Reduced from Baseline)
Day 1	Parking car, sitting in "contaminated" parking space	85	5 min.	60 min (33%)	45 washes (10%)
Day 2	Parking car in "contaminated" space	70	10 min.	60 min (33%)	40 washes (20%)
Day 3	Parking car in "contaminated" space	40	20 min.	60 min (33%)	30 washes (40%)
Day 4	Parking car in "contaminated" space	20	30 min.	60 min (33%)	25 washes (50%)
Day 5	Touching "contaminated" keys	90	30 min.	60 min (33%)	25 washes (50%)
Day 6	Touching "contaminated" keys	75	45 min.	45 min. (50%)	25 washes (50%)
Day 7	Touching "contaminated" keys	65	1 hr.	45 min. (50%)	10 washes (80%)

Week II: Phase II

During the second week, you will graduate to Phase II. You are now getting the hang of touching objects and being in places you consider contaminated, and then delaying your rituals by several minutes, even longer. Hopefully, you've reduced your total number and length of hand washes and showers. If you haven't reduced it by much by now, don't worry, you will!

Now you will add one more component to the practices: delay doing your rituals for *as long as it takes for your SUDS level to go down to less than 20*. This requires more time, more willpower, and the ability to withstand some uncomfortable feelings for longer periods of time. You are still permitted to wash, however, but only after your SUDS level has been reduced to a low enough level for your brain to get this message, "If I only wait, the discomfort will go down on its own." Time is on your side. Be patient and wait: the discomfort will diminish!

During Phase II, you still have the "crutch" of knowing that a wash is soon to come. But it comes only after you have become habituated to the anxiety-provoking situation. At that point, be it several minutes or hours, a wash won't seem so vitally important! Repeat the exposures several times per day until you have managed to reduce your initial SUDS level significantly.

Each day, as you master situations that formerly caused you discomfort, introduce new items from your Anxiety/Exposure List while you continue to reduce your rituals. The following worksheet is an example of Mary's Phase II for the fear of AIDS and germs:

Mary's Ritual Delay Worksheet: Phase II

Phase II	Object(s) Touched or Contaminated	Initial SUDS (0–100)	Length of Delay Until 20 SUDS or Less (min./hr.)	Length of Shower (% Reduced from Baseline)	Total No. Hand washes (% Reduced from Baseline)
Day 8	Touching "dirty" mail	95	45 min.	45 min. (50%)	10 washes (80%)
Day 9	Touching "dirty" mail	60	20 min.	30 min. (66%)	10 washes (80%)
Day 10	Touching "dirty" mail	20	5 min.	30 min. (66%)	10 washes (80%)
Day 11	Touching red spots	100	30 min.	30 min. (66%)	10 washes (80%)
Day 12	Touching red spots	75	15 min.	30 min. (66%)	10 washes (80%)
Day 13	Touching red spots	50	5 min.	30 min. (66%)	10 washes (80%)
Day 14	Touching red spots	20	1 min.	30 min. (66%)	10 washes (80%)

Notice that during this phase, the length of time it took before Mary got her SUDS level down to 20 or less was considerably shorter. Mary concurrently decreased her showering and hand washing significantly (66% and 80% below baseline, respectively). Often, she would choose to not wash her hands at all as it began to seem unnecessary.

Week III: Phase III

By now, you should be realizing that although certain situations still cause you anxiety and fear, you have the capacity to withstand the discomfort until the feeling passes on its own without doing a ritual. This means that you'll be going hours without any contact with water, and spending less and less time washing and showering.

During Phase III, the emphasis is on exposures to situations that provoke the most fear, those in the 90–100 SUDS range, with the goal of reducing washing to normal levels. Check the rules for normal washing on page 77. You will notice that at this point, normal washing may leave you with a feeling of being "not quite clean." This is to be expected and will probably persist for some time until your brain adapts to this new, "normal" feeling. Remember, breaking free from OCD means that you are giving up being "OCD clean" for "normal clean" or "just clean enough." This takes time, so be patient.

During Phase III, Mary exposed herself to the situations on her Anxiety/Exposure List that caused her the most fear: people from the outside world sitting on and "contaminating" her living room and bedroom furniture. Several times each day, and for lengthy periods of time, she would have her husband (who worked around "contaminated" people and places) sit in these areas wearing his "dirty" work clothing. He would stay there for as long as it took for her to reduce her discomfort level to 20 SUDS, or to manageable levels. At the same time, she would limit her showering to one shower, only ten minutes per day, and by the end of the week, she would wash her hands only at normal hand washing times (see normal hand washing form on page 78).

Mary's Ritual Delay Worksheet: Phase III

Phase III	Object(s) Touched or Contaminated	Initial SUDS (0–100)	Length of Delay Until 20 SUDS or Less	Length of Shower (% Reduced from Baseline)	Total No. Hand washes (% Reduced from Baseline)
Day 15	"Contaminate" living room with "germs"	95	45 min.	20 min. (78%)	15 washes (70%)
Day 16	"Contaminate" living room with "germs"	80	20 min.	20 min. (78%)	15 washes (70%)
Day 17	"Contaminate" living room with "germs"	40	10 min.	20 min. (78%)	15 washes (70%)
Day 18	"Contaminate" living room with "germs"	20	5 min.	15 min. (85%)	10 washes (80%)
Day 19	"Contaminate" bedroom with "germs"	100	15 min.	15 min (85%)	10 washes (80%)
Day 20	"Contaminate" bedroom with "germs"	50	5 min.	10 min. (90%)	5 washes (90%)
Day 21	"Contaminate" bedroom with "germs"	20	0 min.	10 min. (90%)	5 washes (90%)

Now, make copies of the Ritual Delay Worksheet below to plan your own three-week ritual delay strategy.

Ritual Delay Worksheet: Washers

Phase ____	Exposure	Initial SUDS (0–100)	Ritual Delay (minutes/hours)	Length of Shower (% Reduced from Baseline)	Total No. Hand washes (% Reduced from Baseline)
Day —					
Day —					
Day —					
Day —					
Day —					
Day —					

Rules for "Normal" Washing

For the purposes of exposure and ritual prevention, normal washing consists of the following:

1. One hand wash (less than thirty seconds) just prior to eating a meal, and one hand wash after meals (less than thirty seconds).

2. One hand wash (less than thirty seconds) after toileting.

3. One hand wash (less than thirty seconds) after changing a diaper, emptying a cat litter box, taking out the garbage, or doing the laundry.

4. One hand wash (less than thirty seconds) after handling greasy or *visibly* dirty things.

5. One shower per day, seven minutes only for men, ten to twelve minutes for women.

6. No rituals whatsoever are to be performed during showering.

7. After vigorous activities, such as playing sports, working out, or gardening, brief hand washing and showering (using the above guidelines) is okay.

8. In general, other than at the times prescribed above, hand washing should be done *only* if there are *visible* signs of dirt on hands. If not, do not wash.

9. Be aware that OCD is tricky! It can create the sensations on your body of being dirty even if you are not. Be as honest with yourself as possible regarding the presence of dirt. *When in doubt, don't wash.*

10. Do not use anything to clean hands other than plain soap such as Ivory, Dial, or other plain commercial soap. Do not use any "antibacterial" soaps, whatsoever.

11. Special considerations may be given to people whose jobs make it necessary to wash their hands more often, such as nurses and other health care workers, and for people who, for medical reasons, must use the bathroom more frequently than the average person.

12. Of course when ill, proper hygiene should always be observed.

Additional Procedures for Washers

• As in Mary's example, it is a good idea to create a "contamination towel" (it could be any small piece of cloth or napkin) that you will use as a tool for doing exposures to feared objects such as doorknobs or toilet seats. Lightly touch a small edge of a small hand towel to a feared object and then touch the towel to objects you live with daily in your car and your home. It is only necessary to "contaminate" the tiniest edge of the towel to feel fully "contaminated." While doing exposure with your towel, you may find that after some time (a few minutes to a few hours) the towel no longer feels "contaminated" (this means that you've become habituated to the towel). It is therefore necessary to "recharge" the towel by retouching it to the original "contaminated" object. You are then ready to resume your exposures.

• Should you slip up and wash when you were not supposed to, "recontaminate" yourself with your "contamination towel" *immediately* after washing. Then continue on track with exposure and ritual prevention exercises.

• Often people with contamination OCD do not distinguish between "unpleasant" and "dangerous." They worry excessively about touching an object merely because it is unpleasant to do so. By going ahead and touching an "unpleasant" object, the fearful feelings associated with the object eventually will subside to manageable levels.

Reducing Washing Rituals with the Self-Monitoring Method

If you are just too fearful of doing any type of exposure whatsoever, try this useful method for reducing washing rituals:

1. Make a copy of the following chart and tape it to an area above the sink. Use it to keep track of how many times you wash your hands every day. Keep a pen or pencil nearby for immediate use.

2. Each time you wash your hands, mark it down on the chart, immediately. Include baths and showers as well. Even if the washing is for a valid reason (before meals, after using the toilet), mark it down. If you try to justify whether or not it needs to be marked, you will be making excuses every time, so mark *every* time you wash your hands. No exceptions.

3. To wean yourself from soap and water, you may begin to *temporarily* substitute nonalcohol baby wipes or wet wipes such as Diaperene brand baby washcloths. These are much less harsh and avoid towel rubbing, which irritates the hands.

4. Mark a wet-wipe washing on the chart as a hand washing as well, using the code letter "W." The first goal is to have as few total marks as possible. The second goal is to have as

few "soap and water" washings as possible (code S). Do not cheat! The OCD knows when you are lying, and feeds off it!

5. Use dry napkins to clean your hands after a meal rather than washing them.

6. Schedule activities that will get your hands dirty close together, then wash at the end of the last activity, rather than after each activity.

Daily Washing Monitoring Form

S - Hand wash with soap and water

Sh - Shower

W- Hand wash with wet wipes

B - Bath

HO - Hand wash—other location

Date	Washing Event	Total No. Washes for Day

Checkers

When doing exposure and ritual prevention for checking, work toward the goal of checking only once in situations where most people might do so. For example, door locks, faucets, appliances, etc., should be checked only once before leaving the house or going to bed. The stove, oven, and appliances should be checked only once after using them. Work to refrain from checking items in situations where they are not normally checked, for example, repeatedly checking a check you've written to pay a bill to make sure that you wrote the proper amount on the check.

Strict ritual prevention for checking is very challenging. Try using the following techniques to help strengthen your efforts to deal with the powerful urges to check:

- Instead of checking a door lock over and over, check it once; then plan to check it once every five minutes for an hour. This "overcorrection" makes the checking more cumbersome and thus may inhibit it.

- Use procrastination as part of your ritual prevention. In other words, make a "deal" with yourself to check it later. Often, by the time "later" comes, the urge to check will have passed.

- The urge to ritualize during ritual prevention is powerful! It is like a strong magnet that tries to pull you back to the area not checked. Coach yourself to "resist the magnet" by taking your mind off the urge. Focus on another activity. Do a chore, make a phone call, or do a vigorous physical activity, such as walking or strenuous exercise.

- Because checking often involves fears and images of catastrophic future events and consequences, use imaginal exposure along with ERP (see chapter 7).

- Fight the urge to check by using self-talk techniques, as explained more fully in the section of chapter 8, "Correcting Faulty Beliefs."

Ordering and Symmetry

These compulsions involve an intolerance for objects in the home that are not placed in perfect order and position, or are even slightly asymmetrical. Exposure and ritual prevention consists of the gradual habituation to the purposeful placement of objects in "wrong," imperfect places. Ritual prevention involves the management of the compulsive urge to restore these objects to their previous "perfect" positions.

Proceed with exposure to the items on your Anxiety/Exposure List(s) that produce the least anxiety-provoking SUDS level and gradually move up. After purposely moving an object out of its "perfect" position, maintain ritual prevention by not re-straightening. Allow your discomfort to rise, and continue blocking the urge until it lowers to manageable levels.

If you are unable to tolerate even the slightest ritual prevention, use the "ritual delay" technique outlined above on page 73, but as applied to your ordering problem. For example, each day for one week, try "messing up" an item or several items in the house, such as a bedspread or throw pillows. Then try to delay straightening for a predetermined period of time that raises your SUDS up to at least 50 or 60. Fifteen minutes, a half hour, or more is fine. Again, it's up to you.

Repeat this two or three times each day for a few days until you've begun to habituate. Then, increase the "waiting time" to two hours. After a period of time, as you've habituated, increase the wait time even more until you are able to "mess up" and not straighten for a whole day with little discomfort. Don't worry, your family won't mind the house not being "perfect." They'll likely appreciate your efforts to help yourself!

Note that family members sometimes believe they are being helpful by purposefully "messing things up" around the house that are normally kept straight and symmetrical by the person with OCD. Unless this "messing up" is requested by the person with OCD, it is of little help and is likely to antagonize that person and make matters worse.

Many people with ordering and symmetry compulsions fear that if they are "cured" of their problem they will change into disorderly, sloppy, or unorganized people. Nothing of the sort is going to happen. Rather, as you break free from this tyrannical form of OCD, you will develop a much healthier, more flexible relationship with the environment in which you live.

Obsessional Slowness

This common feature of OCD involves taking an extremely long time to complete the most basic daily tasks such as dressing, bathing, and grooming. Obsessional slowness is a by-product of pathological perfectionism and the intolerance of not doing a task "just right." Often, the activity must be performed in a strict, rigid order and accompanied by various counting, repeating, tapping, or other rituals in order to arrive at the feeling of "just right." Usually the person becomes so absorbed in the ritual activity that he or she loses the "forest for the trees," in other words, the goal of getting the task done and moving on to the next becomes secondary to getting it "just right."

Slowness is often made worse by "trying harder." The more pressure you put on yourself to speed up, the worse the slowness tends to become. When working on slowness, exposure and ritual prevention should focus on confronting the feeling of "doing it wrong."

People with slowness OCD may benefit from procedures that involve monitoring the length of time it takes to do various tasks. For example, first decide on a goal for the length of time it should take to complete various activities of daily living, such as dressing or showering. Then set a goal of decreasing that time to complete the task by two to five minutes per day. Use a simple watch timer or countdown alarm timer, or have a friend or family member act as a "helper," to time your completion of the task. Monitor the task on a daily basis using Jack's Activity Monitoring Form on this page as a model.

Jack's Activity Monitoring Form

> **Target Activity:** <u>Showering</u>
>
> **Goal:** <u>Reduce time to complete shower</u>
>
> **Baseline:** <u>2 hour showers</u>
>
> **Goal Time:** <u>15 min.</u> or reduce by <u>25%</u> per day/week

Date	Time Start	Time End	Total Time	Date	Time Start	Time End	Total Time
3/13/99	8:30am	10:30am	2 hrs.	3/22/99			
3/14/99	8:25am	10:15am	1 hr. 50 min	3/23/99			
3/15/99	8:30am	10:35am	2 hrs. 5 min	3/24/99			
3/16/99				3/25/99			
3/17/99				3/26/99			
3/18/99				3/27/99			
3/19/99				3/28/99			
3/20/99				3/29/99			
3/21/99				3/30/99			

Your Activity Monitoring Form

Target Activity: _____

Goal: _____

Baseline: _____

Goal Time: _____ or reduce by _____ % per day / week

Date	Time Start	Time End	Total Time	Date	Time Start	Time End	Total Time

 **KEYS TO BREAKING FREE!**

1. To break free from all forms of OCD, it is necessary to stretch your limitations somewhat. You must go to "reasonable extremes" when doing exposure and ritual prevention. What this means is that you must be willing to take some reasonable risks to engage in activities (such as touching an object thought to be "contaminated") that by "OCD standards" may appear unsafe, even a bit risky. OCD feeds upon the fear of risk and it demands perfect safety and control in living life. Breaking free requires accepting the possible risks and, therefore, the rewards in living life. Take a chance for a change!

2. Remember that it's okay and normal to feel afraid at various times while doing ERP. Don't be alarmed if your fears and worries increase temporarily. It is only a sign of the progress you are making. They will diminish with continued exposure and ritual prevention work.

3. Get mad at the OCD! Anger can be a great motivator as you continue to face your fears.

4. Note that if you rated your belief in the feared consequence of not doing your ritual at 70% or higher, research on OCD predicts that you may not be successful doing exposure and ritual prevention (Steketee 1993). In this case, it is suggested that you skip both this chapter and chapter 7 for the time being and move on to chapter 8. That chapter deals with modifying the strength of your belief in these feared consequences. If you are able to modify your beliefs enough to rigorously do the ERP exercises, it is highly likely you'll benefit from them.

5. Use the behavioral learning principle of "modeling" to gain the courage to do exposures that seem disturbing. Ask yourself, "Would a reasonable person *without* OCD scrupulously avoid touching this object merely because it is *unpleasant* to do so?" If you answer "no," then to break free you should consider touching the object. Then ask yourself, "Would a reasonable person *without* OCD consider the touching of this object to be *dangerous*?" (Dangerous = having a high probability of causing *immediate* harm to yourself or others.) If your answer is "no," then you should consider touching the object and doing the exposure.

6. If doing exposures to feared/avoided situations seems scary to you, make a distinction in your mind between *"possibly harmful/dangerous"* and *"probably harmful/dangerous."* According to the American Heritage Dictionary, "possible" means "capable of happening, existing, or being true without contradicting proven facts, laws, or circumstances." "Probably" means simply, "most likely."

    Realize that many more things are "capable" of going wrong than are "likely" to go wrong. For example, walking outside on a rainy day in Florida, one can "possibly" be hit by lightning. But "probably," you won't be. Likewise, touching a doorknob and not washing can be "possibly harmful," yet in reality, it is "probably harmless." Walking out of the house and checking the door locks just once can appear to be "possibly dangerous" but in reality, it's "probably harmless." When OCD is strong, there is little or no distinction made between "possibly harmful/dangerous" and "probably harmful/dangerous." They appear to be one and the same. As you confront more and more fear-provoking situations, it is helpful to ask yourself: "while (this situation) is *possibly* harmful/dangerous, is it *probably* harmful/dangerous?"

7. Be careful to "avoid avoidance." Realize that any exposure you avoid doing will persist as a fear and eventually erode your progress. Be rigorous with yourself!

8. Make exposure and ritual prevention a daily part of your life. As you make progress, you will find opportunities to practice going beyond your previous limitations.

Daily Exposure Practice Form

Exposure Task: _____

Ritual Prevention: _____

Initial SUDS (before starting ERP): _____

Goal SUDS Level (after ERP): _____

Goal Length of time (minutes/hours) per Exposure _____

Frequency of exposures (days, weeks): _____ times per _____ day

	Length of Time		SUDS (0–100)		
Day/Date	Start	Stop	Beginning	End	Comments

CHAPTER 7

Imaginal Exposure

We are healed of a suffering only by experiencing it to the full.

—Marcel Proust

Exposure and ritual prevention (ERP) is the core of the Self-Directed Program. It can be enhanced and made more powerful with additional techniques. People with OCD are afflicted by the presence of powerful images of possible future dangers. The images are often triggered in relatively harmless situations, yet are often highly charged and frightening. This imagery about future disastrous events fuels obsessive worry and compulsive rituals.

The object of doing ERP is to free your mind from needless worry about possible dangers and disasters. In vivo ERP involves confronting the situations you fear in real life, so you can learn that which you fear *will* happen, is highly unlikely to happen. There are situations, however, that are either impossible or just too impractical to re-create in real life for the purpose of exposure and ritual prevention. Mary, for example, needed to go beyond in vivo ERP.

Mary's Experience

You met Mary in earlier chapters. Her biggest fear was of contracting the AIDS virus and then possibly transmitting it to others she cared about. She was well versed in accurate knowledge of how the AIDS virus is actually spread. But she could not shake the feeling that everyday activities, such as using a public rest room, shaking hands, or being in the range of an errant cough or sneeze, could endanger her.

Mary washed her hands as many as one hundred times a day and took one-hour showers. Her fear of getting sick from AIDS involved images of increasing incapacity to take care of her family. The thought of not living up to her responsibilities as a wife and mother was particularly distressing. She also had images of being responsible for the illness of others, and the attendant shame from disappointing her immediate and extended family.

Exposure and ritual prevention to such feared situations as using public bathrooms and shaking hands was very helpful, but it also proved necessary to do ERP to counter the feared images of future disaster involving contracting the AIDS virus. This is where *imaginal exposure* helped.

Doing Imaginal Exposure

Imaginal exposure will enable you to think uncomfortable, fear-provoking thoughts and hold them briefly in your mind without excessive discomfort. It can help you become less anxious when you have a bad thought and to learn to accept such thoughts for what they are—just thoughts. In time, anxiety-provoking thoughts are likely to lessen in intensity.

Other examples of fear-provoking images of future harm and danger include being held responsible for a crime, being rejected by others, going to jail, losing a loved one, and going crazy. The goal of in vivo exposure is to provide real-life opportunities to become habituated to feared situations, but the goal of imaginal exposure is to provide opportunities to become *habituated to your own thoughts.*

Step 1

Write a three to five-minute narrative in the first person, present tense ("I am . . ."), describing the feared situation that would arise if you were not to check or carry out a compulsive ritual or behavior. Include all relevant fear triggers and avoided situations. Write it as if you were describing a scene from a movie, frame by frame. Make it as vivid as possible. You can even enlarge the scene and your fear triggers to the point of absurdity.

Like exposure in vivo, your imaginal exposure should create an initially high SUDS (Subjective Units of Distress Scale) level. The higher the SUDS you can tolerate in your narrative, the better the overall effect. However, some images (the death of a loved one, for example) may seem much too scary to include in a narrative, especially in the beginning. In this case, describe a situation that provokes medium levels of fear—60–75 SUDS. When you have habituated to that situation, do another narrative with more frightening images—in the 80–90 SUDS range.

Step 2

Record the three- to five-minute narrative on a cassette tape and listen to it over and over for a minimum of forty-five minutes a day, for one week. An endless loop tape works best; then you won't have to keep stopping and rewinding. It will play the narrative continuously. A regular sixty-minute cassette tape works just fine, but you will need to rewind it after each replay of your narrative.

It is helpful to monitor your SUDS level after each replay of the narrative using the Imaginal Exposure (IE) Monitoring Form below. Your goal is to play your narrative over and over until your SUDS lowers to twenty or less. This indicates it is likely that habituation has occurred. It often takes about forty-five minutes, but as each individual with OCD is different, the habituation may take less or more time. When the images from this narrative no longer evoke excessive discomfort, write other narratives using more fear-provoking situations until all of your frightful imaginings have been neutralized.

Imaginal Exposure (IE) Monitoring Form

For each IE session, rate your SUDS (0–100) after each repetition of the narrative.
You may make copies of this form for daily use. You will need one form for each session.

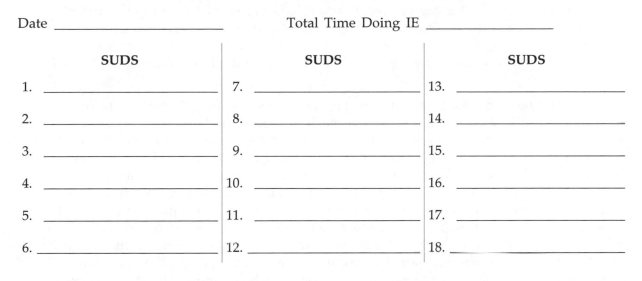

Date _____   Total Time Doing IE _____

SUDS	SUDS	SUDS
1. _____	7. _____	13. _____
2. _____	8. _____	14. _____
3. _____	9. _____	15. _____
4. _____	10. _____	16. _____
5. _____	11. _____	17. _____
6. _____	12. _____	18. _____

Average SUDS level for this session (total SUDS ÷ number of times listening to the tape) _____

Mary's Experience with Imaginal Exposure

Because Mary found images of death to her immediate family too scary to begin with, her initial imaginal exposure taped narrative consisted of frightening images intended to create moderate anxiety (about 75 SUDS). She imagined causing someone who was well-known to her to become sick and then to die a long, painful death from AIDS. She chose a neighbor who is a single mother. Her narrative describes a situation (which she is aware is extremely unlikely, even preposterous) of her "negligence" resulting in the neighbor becoming "contaminated." It involves her having to shoulder the sole responsibility for her neighbor's illness and death, and images and expectations of future ridicule from her family, extended family, and community. Mary listened to the three-minute narrative for one and a half hours daily for the first week, evoking powerful feelings of pain and dread.

Mary's Fear Narrative

I'm sitting at my kitchen table and the doorbell rings. It's my neighbor who's come over to borrow some sugar. I hand her a glass bowl of sugar, but as my hands are wet from cooking, the bowl is slippery and it slips out of my hands. It falls to the floor, shattering on the ground into a hundred pieces. Some sharp pieces of glass cut my neighbor's skin, puncturing it and causing bleeding. I grab a napkin to wet with water to wash the cuts, and while she turns her gaze away, the neighbor walks over to my husband's "contaminated" chair and sits in it to tend to the cuts on her leg.

Upon realizing what's happened, I'm frozen in terror! The open cuts will surely result in her catching AIDS! I take care of the neighbor's cuts and she eventually leaves. Six months later, upon paying a visit to my neighbor's apartment, the neighbor tearfully discloses that she was just diagnosed with AIDS, and the cause was something that happened six months ago, in my apartment. I'm totally devastated. I caused this mishap and now my neighbor is going to die from it! I'm so careless and irresponsible!

Over the next few months I notice a deterioration in my neighbor's health. She is becoming thinner and weaker. I know she is going to doctors every week to obtain treatment for her disease. She has four small children who will now be deprived of a mother thanks to my negligence! Over the next several weeks she becomes sicker and sicker. She becomes unable to take care of herself. I can't bear to look into the eyes of those poor children. My family shuns me for my irresponsible behavior. I can't bear that I must live with this mistake for the rest of my life.

At first, Mary was resistant to listening the tape, even terrified. It was as if merely hearing these thoughts said aloud would somehow magically cause the terrible events to occur. After hearing the narrative repeated around thirty times, she'd distract herself from the horrific images by numbing out or by thinking about innocuous events that just popped into her mind. Each time her mind wandered, she'd make an effort to focus on the images on the tape.

During the second week, Mary reported that listening to the tape was becoming slightly less disturbing. She reported being able to recite the narrative by heart, like a move script she'd memorized. By the end of the second week, Mary reported an overall SUDS level of around 30–40, having become bored with it. The images were having much less impact than in the beginning. She then devised another narrative, this time using images of herself becoming ill with the AIDS virus from contact with a homeless person. She reluctantly infused the narrative with painful images of not being around for her children as they grew and of being scorned by her family.

Upon repeated listening to the tape, over and over again, the fearful imagery although disturbing, began to lose its painful charge and intensity. It became less believable that such a thing could "just happen." With further repetition, her "logical brain" was better able to overcome the irrational OCD images. After another week of daily exposure to these images, she was able to tolerate them with much less discomfort.

Melody's Experience with Imaginal Exposure

Remember Melody from chapter 1? She is the woman whose need to check the door, stove, windows, and appliances was taking up more and more of her time. The fear that she may have harmed someone overwhelmed her. She was diagnosed with OCD and her symptoms improved with medication. Ten years later, as a single thirty-three-year-old successful attorney, she was still struggling with OCD.

Melody's symptoms included compulsively checking her car at night. She feared her car might not function in the morning because of a flat tire, leak, or other mechanical failure. She woke up every night and spent one to two hours checking her car for leaks and flat tires. Rain, sleet, and snow did not deter her from her nightly ritual.

What was she afraid might happen if in the morning she discovered her car could not run? She described feelings of horror at the thought of being late for work, of being fired from her job for lateness, and losing her career. Her ultimate fear was being a disappointment to her parents. Here is her imaginal exposure narrative:

It is the first day of the start of my new job as an attorney for a prestigious law firm. I am getting ready to go to work. I leave my apartment, walk downstairs, and look at my car. Suddenly, I become shocked and horrified at what I am seeing. A tire is completely flat.

I wonder how in the world I'm going to get to work! I can feel the sweat starting to pour out of my pores . . . I walk around the car and I'm horrified to see that there's a puddle of oil beneath the engine compartment! . . . I open up the hood of the car and am shocked to see there is oil splashed all over the engine compartment—on the engine, the electrical system, all over the radiator, throughout all the wiring—everything is coated with the thick, slippery substance.

I get into the car to start it, but it won't start . . . I look at the passenger side and my heart pounds even louder as I see a puddle of oil on the floor of the passenger side . . . I'm feeling hopeless and helpless . . . I go upstairs to call a garage for help, but they tell me they are backed up with calls and won't be able to come look at my car for several hours, if at all . . . I call another garage, and they tell me the same story . . . I call another, and still another . . . They are all busy and can't help me now.

The sweat is pouring from my body now, my heart is beating so fast I think I will now have a heart attack . . . I call my boss to tell him it will be several hours before I can get to work, if at all today . . . He answers me in a cold, harsh, and critical voice: "If that is the way you act as a professional, then perhaps you really don't deserve to work in the law profession! How could someone so irresponsible, someone so careless, be a fine lawyer?" I beg him to take into consideration that something unexpected happened, something beyond my control, but to no avail! My boss replies that as far as he is concerned, I should look for another job, but probably no legal firm in this town would hire someone so irresponsible, so careless in her professional responsibilities as me!

I feel rejected, hopeless, discouraged, and angry . . . How will I ever find another job in this city? Maybe I'll never get another job . . . Someone so careless and irresponsible doesn't deserve to work with people in trouble! . . . Word gets out that I am irresponsible and after ten different job interviews, nobody hires me for anything . . . I can't find any job, anywhere . . . And no man will want to be with someone so irresponsible . . . I eventually become a burden to my parents and society. I wind up homeless—living on the street.

Melody recorded this imaginal narrative on a cassette tape and listened to it over and over for one hour every day. She was able to vividly picture the images in her narrative. Her SUDS level following her initial listening was 85. The images provoked intense anxiety, even tears at the thought of being reprimanded by her boss and becoming unemployed. After a week of repeated listening, her SUDS level dropped down into the 60–80 range.

But, by the middle of the second week, she reported that the repetitive narrative had become monotonous, even boring. Her SUDS level reduced to the 20–30 level. By this time, after repeated listening, she was better able to access her "rational" mind and thus reassure herself that her job performance had been deemed excellent by her boss.

Although the thought of catastrophic harm to her career still bothered her, the idea of actually being fired from her job because of a possible tardiness became an absurd and remote possibility. One additional benefit of listening to her imaginal exposure tape was an increased awareness of her excessive perfectionism and how it pervaded her life. The exercise bolstered her ability to block her nightly car checking rituals. After five weeks of listening to the tape, she was no longer getting up at night to check her car.

Robert's Experience

Robert, a thirty-two-year-old salesman, had a six-month history of OCD. His symptoms involved the obsessive concern and preoccupation with the possibility of harming someone while he was driving. He lived a nightmare of guilt, fear, and dread every time he got behind the wheel. A simple bump in the road, an unexpected noise, or shadow, or flash of light triggered a heart-pounding, tire-screeching turnaround back to the scene to make certain an accident had not happened. To relieve his feelings of panic and dread, Robert had to return to the location where he thought the accident might have happened.

As soon as he felt reassured no accident took place, his anxiety was relieved, but only briefly. Feelings of intense doubt and fear would recur, compelling yet another U-turn back to the "accident" scene. Driving near schools, children, and bicyclists was especially nerve-wracking. Potholes and speed bumps felt like dead bodies lying in the road, triggering his compulsion to check for signs of his having injured someone.

In doing imaginal exposure, Robert described his worst nightmare—that of being held responsible for a driving-related accident that results in his incarceration. Included are images of guilt, shame, and loss of freedom:

> *I'm out with a couple buddies . . . we're blowing off some steam watching a football game at a local watering hole. I have a beer, then a snack, and when the game ends, I leave to drive back home. I stop at a gas station a half a mile from my house to get some gas. I go in, pay for the gas, get back in the car. As I pull out of the parking lot onto the main road, I suddenly feel a strong bump . . . a jolt to the car . . . I pull over, stop the car, and get out to see what happened.*
>
> *Sure enough, there is the body of a child lying on the ground, bloodied. My heart begins to pound, my stomach turns as I view this horrible, gruesome sight. The child looks to be about seven years old and is unconscious. Blood is everywhere. I see the bloodstains on my fender. I hit this poor innocent child! I look up and see a police car with its flashing lights on, then ambulances gather around the scene. The emotional pain is unbearable. Due to my reckless and careless behavior, this innocent child's life is now hanging on a thread! If I had been more careful, more responsible, this never would have happened!*
>
> *The child is transported to the nearest hospital. The parents, terribly distraught and in shock, come into the emergency room. They look at me with contempt. They ask me why I did what I did. I am speechless. I feel like my world, too, is coming to an end. After a few hours, I am notified that the child is dead. The sickest feeling of all comes over me. I feel like vomiting. The grief and remorse are overwhelming.*
>
> *After a few days, I am notified by the sheriff's office that I am being charged with vehicular manslaughter and reckless driving. If convicted, I face a prison sentence and years of probation. Rather than fight the charges, I plead guilty as charged. In a brief court appearance I am sentenced by a judge to ten years in prison. I am escorted out of the courtroom, into a county prison. There, I face living the next ten years of my life with a variety of criminals, who have done all kinds of violence to people. The feeling of being confined, of losing my freedom, of my life going down the drain, is too painful to bear.*

Robert recorded this narrative on a cassette tape and listened to it for forty-five minutes daily for ten days. His initial SUDS level was 95. Although it was extremely uncomfortable at first, upon repeated listening he found his SUDS level lowering to about 50 by the second week of listening. In addition he combined the imaginal exposure with practice using in vivo exposure and ritual prevention (see chapter 6 for more on how to do this). Overall, with the combined use of imaginal and in vivo exposure, Robert was able to get his OCD symptoms under control.

When Imaginal Exposure Doesn't Work

A word of caution is in order here. There are some people who should *not* try imaginal exposure without the supervision of a qualified therapist. These include people who have severe OCD combined with having a strong belief that their obsessive thoughts are real and make sense (also called "overvalued ideas"), a history of psychosis, or borderline personality disorder.

Listed below are some common problems that may arise while doing imaginal exposure and some possible solutions:

- **If you can't tolerate the anxiety levels of your imaginal exposure:**

Make your narrative shorter, less anxiety-provoking. Have your imaginal exposure generate about 50–60 SUDS rather than 90–100 SUDS. If you can make the narrative really absurd, even ridiculous, it will take the edge off. However, some images (the death of a loved one, for example) may seem much too scary to include in a narrative, especially in the beginning. In this case, describe a situation that provokes medium levels of fear—60–75 SUDS. When you have habituated to that situation, do another narrative with more scary images—in the 80–90 SUDS range.

- **If your imaginal exposure doesn't arouse much anxiety:**

Your narrative may be too generalized. Make it more vivid, and include specific disturbing images of situations you fear. For example, if you fear being ill in the future, describe a specific image of being in a hospital hooked up to IVs and a breathing machine, or of being left alone and unable to call for a nurse, and so forth. Also, you may be blocking the full emotional impact of the experience while listening. You may be distracting yourself, thinking about other things while listening to the tape. Try to get into the words, feelings, and images as much as possible.

- **If just imagining the scary scene is not enough to provoke anxiety:**

Some people are just not imaginative and they have difficulty imagining scenes vividly. They simply must experience "the real thing" to arouse an appropriate level of anxiety. If this is the case for you, you would benefit most from exposure in vivo and ritual prevention.

CHAPTER 8

Challenging Your Faulty Beliefs

When I look back on all these worries I remember the story of the old man who said on his deathbed that he had had a lot of trouble in his life, most of which had never happened.

—Sir Winston Churchill

Although the structure and functioning of the brain has been an important focus for scientists studying OCD, there has also been considerable interest in the role played by patterns of thinking in persons with OCD. Scientists (Salkovskis 1985; Freeston, Rheaume, and La Doucher 1996) have concluded that faulty beliefs about the risks of danger and harm play an important part in the fear, anxiety, and dread suffered by people with OCD.

Imagine yourself walking through a densely wooded forest with some friends. It's a beautiful day, and you're enjoying the sights and sounds all around you. You're relaxed and calm as you enjoy the sounds of birds and wildlife. Suddenly, your friend tells you he thinks he just saw a poisonous snake.

Now, an image of a snake crawling in the grass suddenly attacking you triggers your body to prepare for danger. You become edgy, fearful, and anxious. Your heart pounds, your muscles tighten, and your walking pace picks up as you think of the fastest way to leave the forest. Slight movements of the bushes and the sounds of rustling tree leaves—that just moments ago you ignored or were pleased by—now cause you to feel fear. You won't relax until you exit the forest safely.

When you finally leave the forest unharmed, you breathe a sigh of relief. Although you never actually saw a snake, your brain didn't care. You reacted anxiously solely to your *appraisal* of the situation—your *belief* about the presence of the snake! Whether there was a snake nearby didn't matter. Such is the power of a belief to trigger powerful bodily sensations and reactions.

People with OCD possess strong beliefs about the likelihood of a given situation being dangerous to them or others. Often the belief is not supportable by facts. This makes the belief a faulty one. Here are some typical faulty beliefs of people with OCD with examples.

Overestimating Risk, Harm, and Danger

- "I must protect myself (or others/loved ones) even if there is only the remotest chance of something bad happening. A tiny, one-in-a-million chance of something bad happening is exactly the same as a huge, 99.999 percent chance of something bad happening."

Black-and-White or All-or-Nothing Thinking

- "If I'm not perfectly safe, then I'm in great, overwhelming danger."

- "If I don't do it perfectly, then I've done it horribly."

- "If I don't perfectly protect others from harm, I'll be severely punished."

- "If I don't perfectly understand everything I read, it's as if I don't understand anything."

Overcontrol and Perfectionism

- "I must maintain absolute control over my thoughts and actions, as well as control over all the circumstances that occur in my life. Unless I do everything perfectly, it is intolerable."

- "Extreme harm and danger can come to me, my loved ones, or innocent others if I don't protect them perfectly."

- "If it doesn't look or feel 'just right,' it's intolerable."

Persistent Doubting

"Maybe I . . .

- wasn't careful enough and therefore something bad will happen

- harmed/molested/injured/cheated someone

- stole/plagiarized/did something improper/immoral/bad

"even though it makes no sense and doesn't agree with the facts."

Crystal Ball or "What if" Thinking

"In the future, what if I . . .

- do it wrong?"

- get AIDS?"

- am responsible for injuring someone?"

Magical Thinking

- "Thoughts are very powerful. Merely thinking a bad, horrible thought will certainly cause something horrible to happen."

Superstitious Thinking

- "By doing my ritual (washing, tapping, repeating, touching, spinning, etc.), I can ward off bad things from happening to me and protect those I love."

- "There are bad numbers and good numbers. Bad numbers cause bad things to happen and good numbers cause good things to happen or they can stop bad things from happening."

Thought/Action Fusion (Similar to Magical Thinking)

- "If I have a bad, even a horrible thought about harming someone, it feels just as if I've actually done it."

- "If I think about something bad happening, I'm implicitly responsible should it actually happen."

Overimportance of Thoughts

- "If I have a bad thought, it means I'm bad, dangerous, or crazy."

- "My thoughts are the true indicator of who I am and what I'll do. If I have a bad thought, it means I'm bad, dangerous, or crazy."

- "I'm judged as much by my thoughts as for what I actually do."

Intolerance of Uncertainty

- "I must be 100 percent certain of everything, and I must be 100 percent sure that everything will be 'right.' If I'm the slightest bit uncertain about *anything* (my future, my health/loved ones' health) it is intolerable."

Catastrophizing

- "An open sore on my arm means I'll *definitely* get AIDS."

- "If I get into arguments with my mother . . . it must mean I'm *definitely* a violent person."

Overresponsibility

- "Maybe I caused something bad to happen. My failure to prevent it must mean that I'm certainly a bad person."

- "I must always, at all times, guard against making a mistake that can possibly—even remotely—harm an innocent person."

Extraordinary Cause and Effect

- "Objects have the ability to defy the forces of nature . . . for example, stoves can spontaneously turn on, refrigerators can open, locks can unlock—all without human intervention. Germs and viruses can leap long distances—even across city streets—and thus contaminate me and others."

Pessimistic Bias

- "If something bad is going to happen, it is much more likely to happen to me or someone I love/care about than to others. This occurs for no other reason than it's me."

Intolerance of Anxiety

- "I can't stand being anxious for even a short period of time . . . I'll do anything to feel better, now."

The ABCDs of Faulty Beliefs

The role of faulty beliefs in maintaining OCD symptoms can be understood by using the "ABCD Method." This is an adaptation for OCD patients of the original "ABC" method of cognitive therapy used by Ellis (1962) and Beck, Emery, and Greenberg (1985). The anxiety, emotional discomfort, and resulting compulsive behaviors of OCD take place in the following sequence:

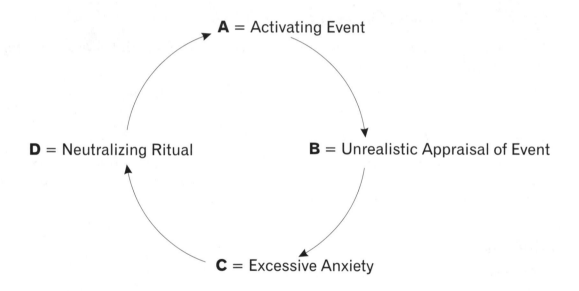

A = Activating Event

B = Unrealistic Appraisal of Event

C = Excessive Anxiety

D = Neutralizing Ritual

A: Activating Event

An event, such as touching a doorknob, checking that the stove is turned off, stepping on a crack, or thinking an embarrassing or horrifying thought takes place.

B: Unrealistic or Dysfunctional Appraisal of the Event

After the activating event, an automatic, unrealistic appraisal or interpretation of the activating event occurs *in a split second, beyond your awareness*. This interpretation or appraisal involves an unrealistic sense of impending harm, damage, danger, or catastrophe that could result from the activating event. It causes you to feel extremely anxious. Look at the list on pages 94–96 above to identify specific types of faulty beliefs. Then, in the table below, read the examples of events/situations that typically activate faulty beliefs and their accompanying unrealistic appraisals in those who have OCD.

Common Faulty Beliefs

A: Activating Event (Situation or event that triggers anxiety)	B: Unrealistic Appraisal (Automatic irrational thought)	Faulty Belief(s) (Choose from the list above)
Door didn't sound "right" when I shut it after the twentieth time.	*"It's dangerous to leave the house unless the door shuts perfectly. Maybe I'll be blamed if there is a break-in."*	Overcontrol and Perfectionism Overestimating Risk, Harm, and Danger Persistent Doubting
Touched doorknob of public bathroom without tissue paper.	*"For sure, I'll get catch a horrible disease and die from it."*	Intolerance of Uncertainty Overestimating Risk, Harm, and Danger Persistent Doubting
Seeing silhouette of naked child in shower stall.	*"What if I enjoyed what I saw? Maybe I'm a child molester." "My bad thought is a sign of an evil seed inside of me."*	Magical Thinking Thought/Action Fusion "What if" Thinking Overimportance of Thoughts
Seeing pillows on couch in living room not lined up in perfectly symmetrical order.	*"If the pillows are not perfectly straight, something bad will happen to me and my children."*	Superstitious Thinking Overcontrol and Perfectionism
Looking in a mirror, making sure every hair is perfectly even.	*"I must keep cutting it more and more (for hours and hours) until it looks perfect. If my hair isn't perfect, people will ridicule me."*	Overcontrol and Perfectionism Persistent Doubting
Seeing a banana peel on a sidewalk across a busy street.	*"I'll be guilty of negligence and punished unless I remove the banana peel and prevent others from slipping and breaking their necks on it."*	Overresponsibility Overcontrol and Perfectionism
Switching off light switch	*"I must do it five times in a row or something bad will happen to my parents."*	Superstitious Thinking Overcontrol and Perfectionism
Twisting the tops of food jars closed, extremely tight.	*"I must make sure the top of the jar will not 'fly open' and everything spoil."*	Extraordinary Cause and Effect "What if" Thinking Persistent Doubting

C: Excessive Anxiety

The unrealistic appraisal triggers high levels of anxiety. The feelings of anxiety are, in turn, unrealistically appraised as intolerable, unacceptable, and dangerous. For a person with OCD, the anxiety spins out of control. There is a powerful urge to relieve that anxiety however possible.

D: Neutralizing Ritual

A compulsive action or set of actions such as excessive washing, checking, and ordering brings the anxiety under control for a while, until the next activating event occurs.

Correcting Faulty Beliefs

Cognitive restructuring is the technical phrase for the process of directly challenging the faulty beliefs that underlie OCD behaviors. This process doesn't make you stop your dysfunctional thinking. Rather, it helps by encouraging you to become a better observer of your own thoughts, bringing in what Dr. Jeffrey Schwartz (1996) calls "the impartial observer."

By learning to challenge your automatic beliefs you make the sequence of obsessions and rituals less habitual and automatic. Challenging your automatic belief system is like throwing gunk into the gears of the well-oiled engine of your OCD thinking. In this way, you will have more control over the impact that your thoughts have upon you and your behavior.

Step 1. Write Down Your Unrealistic Appraisals and Faulty Beliefs

It is important to know exactly what situations/events activate a specific unrealistic appraisal, and what the actual belief is. Write the activating situation or event in the first column of Your Own Faulty Beliefs Assessment chart below. Write the unrealistic appraisal in the second column; and then in the third column, using your own words, write what your faulty belief is.

Refer to the Common Faulty Beliefs table on page 97 for examples of unrealistic appraisals common to many people with OCD. Then, using that table, write your own faulty belief(s). Often, there is more than one such belief operating for each obsessive thought. This exercise will help you to see the various unrealistic appraisals that you make in response to an activating event.

Your Own Faulty Beliefs Assessment

A: Activating Event (Situation or event that triggers anxiety)	B: Unrealistic Appraisal (Automatic irrational thought)	Faulty Belief(s) (Choose from the list on pp. 94–96)
_____	_____	_____
_____	_____	_____
_____	_____	_____
_____	_____	_____
_____	_____	_____

Step 2. Challenge Your Unrealistic Appraisals with Realistic "Self-Talk"

Now, begin to challenge the unrealistic appraisals of your "OCD brain" by applying more realistic appraisals to these trigger situations. Note that many people confuse this step with so-called positive thinking. The goal, however, is not to be a "positive thinker," but an "accurate thinker." Accurate thinking means that you identify your OCD-based thoughts and label them as such. Then you can identify the true facts about the situations that trigger anxiety and rituals.

OCD images and ideas can be very strong and are almost always based on negative feelings concerning future harm and danger. The Coping Self-Talk table below provides ways to fight against your OCD-caused unrealistic appraisals with self-talk strategies designed to help you cope.

Coping Self-Talk

Faulty Belief	Unrealistic Appraisal (Automatic, Irrational Thought)	Fight Back with Realistic Appraisals (Coping Self-Talk)
Overestimating Risk, Harm, and Danger	"I must protect myself (or others/loved ones) even if there is only the remotest chance of something bad happening."	*"I must learn to take a chance in order to get better."* *"What would a prudent person (someone who didn't have OCD) do?"*
Overcontrol and Perfectionism	"I must maintain absolute control over my thoughts and actions, as well as control over all the circumstances of my life. It is intolerable unless I do it perfectly." "If it doesn't look or feel 'just right,' it's intolerable."	*"This is so exhausting . . . It's hard, but I think I'll take a chance on being imperfect for a change."* *"I'm afraid of change, but it's just my OCD brain playing tricks on me."* *"For a change, I'll try being perfectly imperfect."*
Catastrophizing Black-and-White All-or-Nothing Thinking	"Unless I'm sure everything is perfectly safe, I'm certain I or my loved ones are in terrible danger."	*"What is and where is the evidence of harm? There is no proof that something bad is inevitably going to happen."*
Persistent Doubting	"Maybe I harmed/molested/ injured/cheated stole/plagiarized, etc."	*"It's my OCD brain playing tricks."* *"I know logically what's what."* *"I'm not buying into these dumb messages!"*
Magical Thinking Thought/Action Fusion Overvaluing Thoughts	"Merely thinking a bad thought will cause something bad to happen."	*"It's only a thought. I am not my thoughts. It's just an OCD thought, and therefore means nothing. Only actions can harm, not thoughts."*

Faulty Belief	Unrealistic Appraisal (Automatic, Irrational Thought)	Fight Back with Realistic Appraisals (Coping Self-Talk)
Superstitious Thinking	"By doing my ritual I can ward off bad things from happening to me and protect those I love."	*"These rituals are so tiring . . . I must take the chance that even if I don't do my rituals, nothing bad will happen to me or my loved ones. My rituals do nothing except torment me and those around me."*
Intolerance of Uncertainty	"If I'm even slightly uncertain about *anything* (my future, my health, and the health of my loved ones) it is intolerable"	*"I can remain calm in the face of uncertainty. Since I can't control everything, why try? By trying to control everything, I only make my OCD worse"* *"By not acting upon my need for absolute certainty, the urge to do a ritual will diminish after a while."*
Overesponsibility	"Maybe I will cause something bad to happen, and if I fail to prevent it, that will mean that I'm a very bad person."	*"I'm only human . . . my responsibilities end where others' responsibilities begin."* *"I can be a 'good citizen' without having to be everyone's guardian angel."*
Pessimistic Bias	"If something bad is going to happen, it is much more likely to happen to me or to someone I love/care about than to others."	*"The probability of something bad happening to me or my loved ones is no greater than the probability of bad things happening to anyone else. I'm just not so special!"*
"What-if" or the Crystal Ball	"What if I . . . do it wrong/make a mistake/get cancer/get AIDS/cause someone harm?"	*"The torture I put myself through by worrying about the future is certainly worse than anything that could possibly happen. I'll deal with it when it happens."* *Living my life in terms of "What-ifs" only wastes my time"* *"What are the true odds of getting cancer or AIDS, or causing someone harm? The odds are much smaller than my OCD-brain wants to believe."*
Intolerance of Anxiety	"I can't stand being anxious for even a short period of time . . . I'll do anything to feel better, *now*."	*"I can handle the discomfort . . . I don't have to do a ritual now. My anxiety level will go down if I just wait it out."*

Now that you have some idea about how you might fight your faulty OCD beliefs, try it on your own using the beliefs you wrote down on Your Own Faulty Beliefs Assessment table on page 98. Make copies of the Challenging Your Faulty Beliefs Form below for various activating events and complete it, using the following instructions:

1. Write down an activating event that regularly triggers your anxiety. Choose one event to begin, and then move on to others.

2. Rate the level of your discomfort using the SUDS scale (0–100).

3. Write a description of your unrealistic appraisal of the situation that results in anxiety and discomfort.

4. Using a percent rating of the SUDS scale (0–100%), assess the degree to which you believe your appraisal is an accurate description of the situation (for example, that by counting to 8 six times you will keep your loved ones safe from harm).

5. Then, decide which faulty belief or thinking error you are using to make your appraisal. There may be more than one faulty belief involved, and if you are not sure, that's okay, too.

6. Then, write a realistic appraisal using "coping self-talk" that you could apply in this situation to "talk back" to your OCD. You should write the exact words that your "logical brain" comes up with. Use the "Realistic Appraisals" column from the Coping Self-Talk chart above to guide you.

7. Using a percent rating, indicate the degree to which you truly believe in this realistic appraisal *right now*.

8. Repeat this exercise for as many different activating events as you can.

Challenging Your Faulty Beliefs Form

Activating Event _____

_____

Discomfort Level (SUDS Level: 0–100%) _____

Unrealistic Appraisal (automatic irrational thought): _____

_____

How much do you believe this appraisal is true (0–100%)? _____

Which "Faulty Belief(s)" is/are at work here (choose from the list above)? _____

_____

_____

Realistic Appraisal or Coping Self-talk: _____

_____

_____

How much do you believe this appraisal is true (0–100%)? _____

Additional Challenges to Faulty Beliefs

In the previous section, you challenged your faulty beliefs by changing your self-talk when an OCD thought occurs. This requires consistent practice. Another way to challenge the faulty beliefs of OCD is through the use of "behavioral experiments." These exercises provide an opportunity for you to dispute your OCD predictions of potential harm and catastrophic danger. By testing out the faulty beliefs in the real world, you will further weaken the grip of the faulty belief on your thinking.

Thought/Action Fusion and Overvaluing Thoughts

The following exercises are to be used to test the faulty beliefs that thoughts can cause bad events to occur and that thoughts are the same as actions (Freeston, Rheaume, and LaDoucheur 1996).

Think and Win

Purchase a lottery ticket on Monday and think about winning the grand prize for half an hour every day (the typical odds are 27,000,000 to one). In your mind, create as vivid an image of yourself winning as you can. At the time of the drawing for the big prize, note the outcome. Then, ask yourself, "To what extent did my repetitively thinking these thoughts influence the outcome of the lottery? What was the effect of all my thinking on what actually happened?"

Think and Break

Choose an old small appliance (like a toaster) that is known to be in good working order. Every day for one week write on a piece of paper: "The toaster will break." Write it one hundred times and picture it in your mind each time. After one week, examine the outcome. Did your thoughts affect the operation of the toaster?

Think Dying Goldfish

Buy a goldfish and a fish bowl from a local pet store. Set it up at home and provide normal, proper care for the fish. For fifteen minutes twice daily, vividly imagine the fish dying. First imagine it gasping. Then imagine it dead and floating on the surface of the water instead of swimming in the bowl. Repeat this every day for a week. Observe the effect on the fish. According to your belief, the goldfish should die because merely thinking something bad causes bad things to happen! Can you alter your rigid belief?

While these "experiments" may sound silly to OCD sufferers and nonsufferers alike, by testing your prediction that your thoughts will cause harm against the outcome, you can begin to challenge your faulty beliefs about the "magical" power of your thoughts.

Overresponsibility for Harm to Others

As a person with OCD, you often fail to consider the numerous factors that may contribute to a negative event such as losing your job or the illness of a loved one. Even when it clearly doesn't make sense, you tend to assume the entire burden and responsibility for preventing negative events on your worried shoulders. The "pie technique" is intended to help you attribute responsibility for negative events more accurately and appropriately.

Pie Technique

To demonstrate the Pie Technique, consider Michael's situation. He has an obsessive concern with the possibility of harming others through his own carelessness. He checks constantly that he has not injured others by acting carelessly; for example, by spilling water on the floor and causing someone to trip and injure himself or herself. He usually keeps his car windows rolled up for fear that something in his car might fly out and cause an accident.

His present obsession is that a piece of paper that *did* fly out of his car window *did* obstruct another driver's view and *did* result in an auto accident. (He had briefly rolled down the window to get some fresh air.) The wind blew a folder on the passenger seat open and a piece of paper flew out. It wasn't an important paper, but it did have his name and address on it.

Now he worries constantly about that piece of paper and the accident it *may* have caused. Despite the complete lack of evidence of any mishap ever having happened, his obsessive thinking places his actions as the primary cause of an unfortunate chain of events. He ignores all other possible factors that could result in auto accidents, aside from his "carelessness." Using the downward arrow technique, let's look at the sequence of thoughts that make up Michael's obsession:

Paper blew out of car.

↓

Paper flew onto the windshield of another driver's car; accident occurs.

↓

Driver and passengers seriously injured.

↓

Paper traced to my car.

↓

I'm held responsible for accident by judge. Found guilty of crime.

↓

I'm punished, fined, sent to jail.

↓

I must live with the perpetual guilt of causing harm to someone through my irresponsible act.

Now, with Michael's case in mind, do the following exercise to learn how to plot percentages of possible events in order to work on your own faulty assumptions of guilt and responsibility

1. Describe in detail your obsessive concern regarding your responsibility for the safety of others and the possibilities of their being harmed. Write a scenario where someone is injured as a result of your negligence. Write this in the space below:

_____

_____

_____

_____

2. Then, try to identify every conceivable factor that could have contributed to the accident, in addition to your contribution.

In every mishap, there are a number of factors that could have influenced the cause. For example, in Michael's case, some of the possible conditions that might contribute to an auto accident (in addition to his negligence) include another driver's state of mind (possibly impaired, sleepy, or drunk), the condition of the roads (slippery), the automobile (bad tires or brakes), the weather (dark, wet, or windy), etc.

Following is a list showing the imagined percentage of other causal contributions to a *possible* auto accident in addition to Michael's piece of paper flying onto the road (all the various factors are made to add up to 100 percent):

Possible cause of an accident	Probability of contribution to an accident (0–100%)
1. Driver carelessness	20%
2. Defective car	15%
3. Poor road conditions	10%
4. Other driver's poor vision	5%
5. Other driver upset by an argument with spouse	5%
6. Driver emotionally upset over parent's illness	5%
7. Bad weather conditions	20%
8. Poor driving skills—bad driver education	15%
9. Paper flying out of my car, onto road	5%
TOTAL	100%

Pictured as a pie chart, all of the competing factors would look like this:

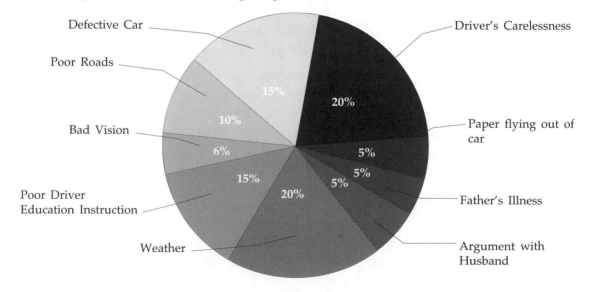

Now, think of your own obsessive worry that you might harm another, and list all the possible factors that could result in the consequences you fear. For each cause, make an estimate of the percent of the cause's contribution to the overall imagined accident. There are no right and wrong responses. Don't worry if it doesn't add up to 100%—an approximation is fine.

Possible cause of the mishap	Probability of contribution to the mishap (0–100%)
1.	
2.	
3.	
4.	
5.	
6.	
7.	
8.	
9.	
10.	
	TOTAL = 100%

Now ask yourself the following questions:

1. Based solely on the chart above, if you knew an accident actually had happened, and you knew nothing more about its specifics, what is the *likely* cause of the accident?

2. What is the evidence for your decision?

3. Is your decision based on your feelings about what might have happened or on the "facts"?

4. What else might have caused the accident/mishap? _____

_____

_____

5. Are you certain about your decision? _____

6. If you are not certain, how uncomfortable are you with not knowing for sure? _____

_____

_____

7. How strongly do you rate your responsibility for the accident/mishap (0–100%)? ____

8. If you rated your responsibility higher than 50%, is this consistent with the facts of the accident/mishap in light of all the other factors that could possibly cause it to happen?

_____

_____

Now, having completed this exercise, you may have a clearer idea that, for *any* accident/mishap, it is possible that many factors could be responsible, in addition to your own contribution. Assigning responsibility for something going wrong is not easy. People with OCD make the assignment of blame so overly simple that it defies both logic and the facts. In the absence of perfect certainty, people with OCD just automatically assume, "It's all my fault! I'm going to be punished for it!"

Defense Attorney Technique

The Defense Attorney Technique is a helpful role-play exercise that can be used in conjunction with the Pie Technique. You can practice this with a support person or your therapist. In this role play you are to playact being your own defense attorney. Your job is to vigorously argue your innocence in a courtroom where you are on trial for causing some serious mishap/crime that resulted in someone's injury. The crime/mishap is to result from your main obsession of being responsible for causing harm to others—i.e, causing an auto accident or illness, or failing to be cautious enough in protecting others.

It's a good idea to start by doing the Pie Technique exercise, like the one you did above, thus familiarizing yourself with all of the possible alternative explanations for the crime/mishap. This list will be the basis of your "defense."

On the other side, there is the "prosecuting attorney" (the OCD), who will argue that you are guilty of the crime/mishap and should be condemned to harsh and certain punishment—going to jail, and/or being condemned to a "living hell" of guilt and so forth. You, as your own defense attorney, are going to argue vigorously that there is no way you can be found guilty because it can't be proven—there are just so many other explanations for the crime/mishap. Some other factor(s) than your carelessness caused it! As your own defense attorney, you are to staunchly defend and fight for your innocence.

Here is a sample dialog of the Defense Attorney Technique using Michael's case as an example:

Prosecuting Attorney: *Michael, did you allow a piece of paper to fly out your car window onto the street while driving near the corner of twenty-fifth and Main?*

Defense Attorney (you): Yes, I was driving by there, my window was open, and the piece of paper accidentally flew out of the car.

Prosecuting Attorney: *Are you telling me that you did not turn the car around to retrieve the paper from the street?*

Defense Attorney: Nope . . . I was in a hurry, and there was no time to turn around. Besides, what harm could possibly come from a piece of paper?

Prosecuting Attorney: *Do you realize how much damage you did with that piece of paper? A family is devastated because of your recklessness and irresponsibility!*

Defense Attorney: I'm sorry they've suffered, but why should I take the heat? You can't prove anything! The driver could have been drunk, or just a bad driver! The paper could have had nothing to do with the accident.

Prosecuting Attorney: *A piece of paper with your name and address on it was found ten feet from the accident scene. There's your proof!*

Defense Attorney: That's no proof! What about the car? It might have had something mechanically wrong with it, and that caused the accident!

Prosecuting Attorney: *The car was in perfect shape prior to the accident!*

Defense Attorney: What's the evidence?

Prosecuting Attorney: *We have the auto shop's repair records from three weeks prior to the accident.*

Defense Attorney: That doesn't mean the car was safe that day! What about the weather? It was rainy, and the slippery roads may have had a lot to do with it, not my piece of paper!

Prosecuting Attorney: *There was a paper caught in the windshield wiper that obviously startled the driver, who lost control of the car. You should be ashamed of yourself!*

Defense Attorney: Did you get the blood/alcohol levels for the driver? Have you considered that he might have been drunk and because of his drunken state couldn't control the car. . . .

Notice how your OCD creeps in at times, and causes you to feel anxious and to doubt your position. That's okay—keep strongly making your point(s). When you feel as if you've successfully argued your innocence, or even swayed the prosecution, the role play is over. Then try this exercise with another obsessive worry. Having the experience of actively "talking back" to your obsessive worries and concerns can help to loosen their grip on you.

Challenging "What if?" Thinking

Obsessional worries most often involve a catastrophic view of the future and persistent feelings of doubt. These thoughts always start with "What if?" For example, "What if I get AIDS?" or, "What if I didn't turn off the stove?" or, "What if I ran someone over?"

A helpful way to deal with "what-iffing" is to go one step beyond "What if?" and ask your-self, "*So What!?*" Then go to the next step and ask yourself what you'd reasonably do if the situation you fear actually occurred. The third step is to ask yourself, "What might be a positive result should the feared situation actually happen?" Finally, ask yourself what you might be able to do now to be prepared should the feared situation actually occur. Here is how this exercise might be done in Michael's case:

What if? a piece of paper flies out the window and causes an accident? *So What?*

Then I will accept the consequences, possibly pay a fine or go to jail. *So What?*

Then I will still have my life and three meals a day. My family will visit me there. I can catch up on my reading and write a book while in jail.

What is the worst that can happen? I could run out of reading material.

What is the positive result of the What-if? fear? I could become more knowledgeable due to the knowledge I'd acquire while in jail, improve my letter writing skills, and learn the virtue of patience.

How can I prepare now for the possibility? Construct an exhaustive reading list, purchase writing implements.

If this sounds like an exercise in absurdity, it certainly is! But then, so many of the obsessive fears of OCD are exercises in absurdity! Now, do the exercise with your own obsessive fears and worries:

What if? _____ *So What!*

Then I will _____ *So What!*

Then I will _____

What is the worst that can happen? _____

_____

What is a possible positive result of the "What if?" fear? _____

_____

How can I prepare for the possibility now? _____

_____

"What if" I Lose Control?

The "What if I lose control" theme of "What if?" thinking involves the obsessive preoccupation with the idea that anxiety, fear, anger, and aggression are dangerous and should be avoided at all costs. Robert, a salesman with OCD, avoided all social situations for fear of getting angry and losing control in public places. His typical fear sequence goes as follows:

What if I'm in a restaurant and scream at you, calling you a jerk?

↓

I would become extremely anxious.

↓

Being anxious, I could lose control of myself.

↓

If I lose control and call you a jerk, I could go on to call you lots of other names.

↓

I'll be embarrassed in front all of the other customers.

↓

Everyone will stare at me with contempt/hatred.

↓

I'll go crazy.

↓

They'll take me away in a straightjacket.

↓

I'll be locked up in a psychiatric ward.

↓

I'll go even crazier from being locked up.

↓

I'll never escape the shame of it all.

"What if?" thinking combined with the notion that anger is dangerous results in extreme avoidance and isolation from any public or social situation where anger or anxiety could possibly be triggered.

One helpful strategy is to construct an imaginal exposure using a scenario like the one above. Chapter 7 describes the steps in carrying out an imaginal exposure. By repeatedly confronting the feared situation in your imagination, the imagery of danger becomes less and less potent.

Another strategy is to devise an "experiment" in getting angry or "losing control." Try the following practice situations as "mini-experiments":

1. Using a cassette tape recorder, record a five-minute role play of a situation that typically or potentially arouses your anger. It can be an ongoing situation from your life, or one that typically irks you, such as a salesman you perceive to be purposely trying to cheat you. Allow yourself to argue vigorously with your role-play partner/salesman. Allow the dialog to become more and more heated. Allow your language to become stronger as your temper rises. You may even start yelling. Punch a pillow . . . really let go!

2. Now, rewind the tape and listen to the role play. If you think you can make it even more dramatic, rerecord it. Listen again to the finished product. Observe your anxiety level as

you listen. Does it go up? If it does, listen again and again until your anxiety lowers to a SUDS level of less than 20.

3. If your anxiety level doesn't go up, try practicing your role play "argument" in public with a partner. It could be in a restaurant, a park, a store—anywhere you have a strong fear you'd be embarrassed and lose control. Practice your "argument" for five minutes. Note your SUDS level. Do the role play in different public places that evoke anxiety until you "habituate" to the worry and are reasonably comfortable having your "argument."

What If My Beliefs Aren't Changing?

In people with OCD, the process of changing obsessive worries and beliefs can be difficult. As the powerful cycle of obsessive fears and compulsive rituals becomes locked into place, it becomes extremely difficult to change beliefs about what is harmful and dangerous and what is not. If your beliefs seem extremely resistant to change, try using the following approaches:

- Work extra hard to change what you actually *do* in the face of the obsessional beliefs. In other words, one key to changing entrenched obsessional beliefs is to do the *exact opposite* of what your OCD beliefs direct you to do. For example, the best way to change the faulty belief that you must avoid sitting on "contaminated" furniture and touching "contaminated" objects to be safe from getting AIDS is to do the opposite: take the chance, face your fears and sit on the feared furniture and touch the feared objects (see chapter 6). Just do it! Even though your OCD brain is sending messages of impending illness and death! By consistently acting directly opposite to what your OCD beliefs direct you to do, these entrenched beliefs will gradually change.

- Although it may seem scary, work on giving up and letting go of being in total control of your worries. A useful approach to letting go of an obsessional fear or worry is to shout to yourself: *"I'm in Charge Here, and I'm Not Going to Do This Anymore!"* and then walk away without doing your ritual.

- Acknowledge that though the faulty beliefs of OCD may cause you pain, you may, without realizing it, be holding on to your faulty beliefs and be reluctant to change them. This is because for some people with OCD, these beliefs provide a way of feeling safe and in control of a world that often seems scary and unpredictable. Ask yourself if the price you are paying for this feeling of control and safety is worth the impact the faulty beliefs are having on your life.

- Consider starting or changing OCD medications. The proper medicine for OCD can help to lessen the grip of obsessional thoughts significantly. When the medication is effective, changing your thoughts, rituals, and beliefs becomes easier to accomplish.

PART III

CHAPTER 9

Breaking Free from Pure Obsessions

To want to forget something is to think of it.

—French proverb

The most typical forms of OCD involve obsessive thoughts, feelings, or urges combined with compulsive rituals such as hand washing or checking. There is a form of OCD, however, that mainly involves thoughts—intrusive, horrific thoughts and images of causing danger or harm to others. The thoughts are experienced as part of one's own mind (rather than as originating from outside one's mind), and cause great distress, fear, and shame. Because people with this type of OCD feel especially alone and ashamed, they tend to keep their thoughts secret.

We call this type of OCD *pure obsessions*, or *"Pure-O."* It was once the thinking among behavioral scientists that people with pure obsessions had no compulsions or rituals. Recent studies of pure obsessions, however, reveal that while some people have no overt compulsions, many others, in fact, have mental rituals (Steketee 1993; Freeston and LaDoucheur 1997). These are thoughts to counteract and neutralize the discomfort of their unwanted, intrusive thoughts. For our purposes, we will consider Pure-O to be both OCD with obsessive thoughts alone and OCD with obsessive thoughts and accompanying mental rituals. Following are some examples of pure obsessions.

Paula, age twenty-five, was playing with her beloved cats while smoking a cigarette. Out of the blue, the thought popped into her mind of burning a cat with the cigarette. The thought horrified her, prompting intense feelings of guilt. She wondered over and over, "How can I think such thoughts. . . . Maybe I don't really love my cats. I must be a horrible person to think of doing that!" From then on, caring for her cats was nerve-wracking because she felt that her cats were in some danger being near her. She avoided touching her animals except when it was absolutely necessary.

Anthony, a twenty-three-year-old business student, while sitting in a large lecture class, had the intrusive thought that should he open his mouth to ask a question, he would lose control and vomit in front of the entire class. Not normally a shy person, Anthony had always participated actively in school classes from a young age. However, the intrusive thought so frightened him that he now avoids asking questions in class and dreads being called upon by his professors.

Steve is a forty-eight-year-old, devoutly religious teacher, who has had disturbing, intrusive thoughts involving images of Jesus and the Virgin Mary. Often his thoughts involved sexual encounters with them. The images were embarrassing and humiliating. He felt extremely guilty, especially since they tended to increase when he was in church. Feeling unworthy, he avoided church.

Robert, a thirty-three-year-old physician, had been married a year when his wife gave birth to their first child. One night, while watching his baby girl sleeping peacefully, the intrusive image of touching the child's genitals popped into his mind. Feeling guilty, embarrassed, and ashamed, he avoided any physical contact with the child. His wife began to wonder why he refused to change the baby's diapers or even hold her.

The Nature of Pure Obsessions

Here are some general observations about Pure-O:

- **People with Pure-O have an abnormal reaction to basically normal thought processes.**

Research studies of normal adults (those with no OCD symptoms), reveal that everyone experiences unwanted, intrusive thoughts at some time (Steketee 1998). The difference is that people with pure obsessions seem to have an extreme oversensitivity to these normally occurring "weird" thoughts. The obsessive-compulsive cycle arises from striving to alleviate the guilt and discomfort of having the thoughts. This results in attempts to avoid, suppress, or escape the intrusive thoughts. These attempts amplify and strengthen the thoughts, making them worse and worse. The person becomes locked into an endless obsessive-compulsive loop.

- **People with pure obsessions are highly unlikely to carry out the horrific acts and urges that pop into their heads.**

Regardless of whether the thought involves violent or sexual images, *people with pure obsessions are not in danger of acting out these horrible thoughts.* People who do act on such thoughts may have what is known as antisocial personality disorder. They are people lacking a conscience. Unlike people with OCD, they tend not to worry much about their bad thoughts. Their lack of conscience makes their actions seem not so terribly disturbing to them. On the other hand, people with pure obsessions tend to be excessively rule-bound and concerned with doing things "right." Likewise, they obsessively fear and avoid doing things "wrong." They tend to be perfectionists who apply overly rigid, unforgiving standards to everything they think, do, and say. Clearly, people with pure obsessions suffer from a problem with worry and fear of their own thoughts, rather than a problem with antisocial personalities, doing bad things, or committing crimes.

- **Rituals make it worse.**

To control the anxiety and discomfort produced by horrific thoughts, people with pure obsessions often carry out subtle neutralization strategies that are not obvious to others. Examples are repeating a silent prayer over and over or subvocalizing a statement such as "I don't really want this to happen." These are compulsive thoughts meant to magically undo the negative thought.

- **The intrusive thoughts mean *nothing*.**

Intrusive thoughts tell us nothing about a person's character, true desires, or intentions. All they mean is that the person with the thoughts has a disease called OCD. Attempts to find "hidden meanings" or some "root cause" of the thoughts—neglect or child abuse, for example—are most often futile and only make the thoughts worse.

Anatomy of a Pure Obsession: Overview

Pure-O begins with an uncomfortable thought that is appraised in a particularly negative way. In the person's mind, the thoughts are experienced as having the same reality as actions. Then, attempts are made to avoid or suppress the thought. This leads to various "overcontrol strategies" to reduce anxiety, including mental rituals. Discomfort is reduced, but only temporarily. Then the cycle begins again.

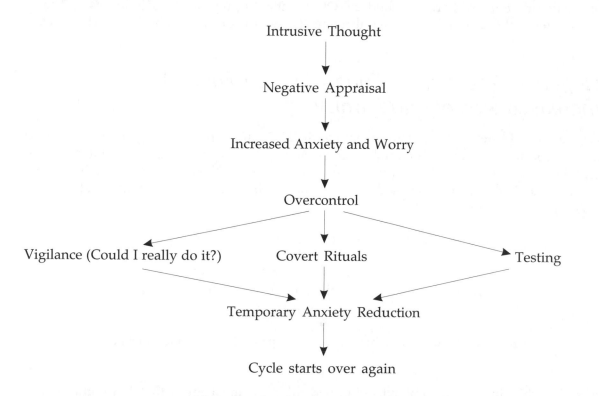

Now, let's examine in detail how a pure obsession happens.

Intrusive Thought → Negative Appraisal

A thought, image, or urge pops into the mind that is disturbing, humiliating, embarrassing, even horrifying. It is most often of sexual or aggressive content and causes guilt, shame, and embarrassment. Because OCD is the "doubting disease," it can cause you to doubt aspects of yourself that lie at the core of what kind of person you believe yourself to be.

For example, if you are a lover of children, it is likely that your OCD may result in the intrusive thought of "What if I actually harmed my children . . . ?" The thought may include a strong mental image or impulse to do something embarrassing or humiliating. If you are an especially religious or moral person, your intrusive OCD thoughts may involve "blasphemous" religious themes with strong sexual or aggressive content. If you tend to be nonviolent, your OCD's themes are likely to be aggressive and hostile. If you pride yourself on being an extremely responsible person, intrusive thoughts and urges are likely to be of committing irresponsible acts, such as setting a house on fire or pushing an innocent pedestrian into oncoming traffic. If you are secure in your heterosexual gender identity, OCD may fill your mind with images of homosexual activity. Needless to say, this may be very exasperating.

The content of the thoughts often reflects the normal anxieties everyone experiences as they move through life. Where a particular issue of self-development is most commonly apparent, the content of the thoughts may reflect normal anxiety about those points in the life cycle. For example, preteens who are becoming more aware of their autonomy and independence are likely to have unwanted, intrusive thoughts regarding doing violent or immoral acts to their parents. Young adults seeking to settle down with a mate may have intrusive thoughts regarding their sexuality. A newlywed, overwhelmed with the prospect and responsibility of parenthood, may have intrusive thoughts of harming children. OCD seems to prey on the self-doubts and fears that people normally have as they move through the typical phases of the human life cycle.

Negative Appraisal (Thought/Action Fusion) → Increased Anxiety and Worry

As mentioned in chapter 8, many people with OCD suffer from the cognitive error called "thought/action fusion" in which thoughts are experienced and felt as if they were the same as actions. Likewise, many people with pure obsessions experience their intrusive thoughts as evidence of the likelihood of their having performed the horrific act they were thinking about. The OCD logic goes something like this:

"I'm having a bad thought—that must mean I'm bad."

↓

"I wouldn't be having these thoughts if I wasn't truly bad!"

↓

"The more bad thoughts I have, the more proof I have that I'm bad."

↓

"Because I'm thinking so much about doing bad things, it must mean that I'm highly likely to do something bad."

↓

"If I don't try hard to prevent harm from happening, it is as bad as doing something bad on purpose."

↓

"Since it is likely that I'm going to do something bad, I'd better watch out for it. I may even have to make sure that others are protected from my bad actions."

Increased Anxiety and Worry → Overcontrol

Having labeled their thoughts as potentially dangerous, people with pure obsessions attempt to avoid, suppress, or neutralize their anxiety about their thoughts by using the following strategies:

- **Vigilance**

After experiencing a number of intrusive thoughts, the mind goes "on guard" for the presence of the intrusive thoughts. Like a sentry in a watchtower or a cop on the beat, the mind becomes nervously preoccupied with "catching the bad thought." The effect is that the thoughts become overly important. The mind ruminates about the next occurrence of the thoughts and more and more energy is tied up in preventing and controlling them. Attempts to suppress or stop the thoughts become more and more elaborate.

The effect of thought suppression is not unlike what happens when someone is given the instruction: "Don't, under any circumstances, think about pink elephants!" Try it—don't think about pink elephants for five minutes. How many times did the thought of pink elephants pop into your head? As you can see, attempts to suppress thoughts only increase their occurrence (Stekelee 1993; Wegner 1989).

- **Covert Rituals**

Covert, or hidden, thinking may be developed to "undo" or neutralize the thought, such as:

> Silent praying—"Forgive me God for having that thought."

> Undoing rhymes or phrases—"I really don't want to do that."

> Balancing the thought with a "correct" thought or image

> Silent counting, using "good" numbers

- **Testing**

Many patients develop "testing" strategies to reassure themselves about their intrusive thoughts. These are persistent, repetitive, and sometimes odd behaviors. For example, Paula, the woman with the intrusive thought of harming her cats (whom she adores) "tests" herself by holding a knife near a cat's neck for several minutes to reassure herself that she doesn't *truly* wish to harm her beloved cats. Only when she feels reassured that she wouldn't harm her cats, can she put the knife down.

A heterosexual married man with the intrusive thought, "I'm gay," purposefully looks at pictures of naked men to "test" whether he is aroused by such pictures. He can relax only when he is reassured that he is not aroused by them.

Testing is considered a neutralization strategy that brings only temporary relief from the anxiety of the thought. However, it only serves to continue keeping the person locked in an endless obsessive-compulsive cycle.

Four Steps to Breaking Free from Pure Obsessions

"When I let the thoughts be, they let me be."

—Recovering Person with Pure-O

Step 1. Write It Down

Writing down your obsessive thoughts will probably be embarrassing, even nerve-wracking, but do it! On the Intrusive Thoughts Worksheet on page 118, rate the degree of disturbance using the SUDS scale of 0–100. (Remember the Subjective Units of Distress Scale from chapter 6?) Then note what happened just before the thought occurred. This is called a *triggering event*. Some examples of triggering events could be holding a child in your arms, getting mad at your brother, or entering a church. Often, however, there is *no* triggering event preceding an intrusive thought.

Now think about any neutralizing strategies you may be using to lessen your anxiety about your thoughts. These include testing strategies or compulsive rituals you may be using, such as countering a bad thought with a good thought, phrase, or prayer.

Intrusive Thoughts Worksheet

Intrusive Thought	SUDS (0–100)	Triggering Event (What happened just before the thought?)	Neutralizing Strategies (Testing, reassurance rituals)
1.			1.
2.			2.
3.			3.
4.			4.
5.			5.
6.			6.
7.			7.
8.			8.

Step 2. Remind Yourself: "I Am Not My OCD Thoughts!"

Try on the belief that the OCD thought is senseless and means nothing about what you are likely to do or not do. How much do you truly believe that you will act out the thought? List your intrusive thoughts on the Intrusive Thought Rating Worksheet. Rate your beliefs using this 8-point rating scale:

0	1	2	3	4	5	6	7	8

0 = no chance at all
4 = pretty strong chance
8 = I'm extremely likely to act upon my intrusive thoughts

Intrusive Thought Rating Worksheet

Intrusive Thought	Likelihood of Acting on Thought
1. _____	_____
2. _____	_____
3. _____	_____
4. _____	_____
5. _____	_____
6. _____	_____
7. _____	_____
8. _____	_____

Most people with pure obsessions initially will rate their beliefs between 4 and 8. This indicates the presence of thought/action fusion and the tendency toward doubt, which are hallmarks of OCD. Remember, thought/action fusion is the belief that just thinking a bad thought, will cause bad things to happen.

Step 3. Accept the Presence of the Thought and Resist the Urge to Perform Avoidance/Neutralization Strategies

Accepting the presence of the thought requires that you allow the thought to be there without judgment. Judgment is defined in Webster's dictionary as: "the capacity to form an opinion by distinguishing and evaluating; the formation of an opinion after consideration or deliberation." As human beings we feel compelled to create meaning out of our experience, to make judgments. Ceasing all judging of your intrusive thoughts takes effort, but it will enhance your ability to be an objective observer of your thoughts without getting too caught up in them.

Step 4. Confront Your Thought: Do Exposure Exercises to Habituate to the Thought's Presence

Intrusive thoughts are frequently experienced with the accompanying emotions of fear and dread. All the classic physiological responses to fear may be present, including a racing heart, sweaty palms, and dry mouth. The process of "desensitizing" your brain to the thoughts involves deliberately exposing yourself to the bad thoughts until the brain has a chance to "habituate," that is, to have the thought without the accompanying discomfort.

To demonstrate how this works, say your name or the name of someone you have a strong feeling about—or attachment or reaction to your child, spouse, parent, or boss, for example. Now, pay attention to your internal "feeling" reaction to this name. Then repeat the name, over and over again. Keep repeating the name a minimum of fifty times.

Observe how your reaction to the name changes after about the fiftieth repetition. Pay attention to your internal "feeling" reaction to the name now. Notice how the name no longer has the same emotional impact. It is even likely to sound like a mere garble of syllables with no particular meaning! This is the by now familiar process of habituation at work. Because of the constant repetition, your nervous system has become "bored" with the originally felt "meaning" you had attached to this name. This is how it works: By repeating a feared thought, it loses its power and impact over you.

Thought Habituation Exercises

The goal of the following exercises is to help you hold an uncomfortable thought in your mind without feeling undue discomfort.

Exercise 1. Written Exposure

1. Get a pad of lined paper and divide the paper in half so that there are two columns. On the left side, write the thought down. Note your SUDS level (0–100) and write it across the page in the right column.

2. Resist avoiding, distracting, or ritualizing away the anxiety of the thought.

3. Go back to the left column, go down to the next line and write the identical thought again. Rate your SUDS level in the right column again.

4. Repeat steps 1–3 until your SUDS level diminishes down to 20–30. You may have to write the thought down fifty or more times before your SUDS level starts to reduce. When this happens, go on to another thought, and repeat steps 1–3.

Exercise 2. Taped Exposure

1. Using a cassette tape recorder, record the thought(s) by saying it over and over about thirty times.

2. Rewind the tape and listen to the thought repeated over and over. Be aware of your tendency to avoid listening or to distract yourself from listening.

3. Note your SUDS level after each listening. Write it down. Rewind and listen again.

4. Repeat steps 1–3 until your SUDS goes down to a level of 20–30.

The goal of these two exercises is to help you begin to coexist with your frightening thoughts with less discomfort. No one ever died or lost control merely from the presence of a thought! *It is the interpretation of the meaning of the thought that determines how people behave and what they actually do.* Although it is unrealistic to expect your intrusive thoughts to go away magically, you will experience significant relief once you have understood that a thought is just a thought! Nothing more!

Remember the following well-worn phrase, *"Whatever you resist, persists!"* This means that the OCD feeds off your persistent attempts to avoid, suppress, or create excessive meaning out of your intrusive thoughts. *When you give up trying so hard to control the activity in your head, the OCD will lessen.*

Exercise 3. Self-Talk Strategies

Dr. Jeffery Schwartz, in his book *Brain Lock* (1996), discusses the concept of the "impartial observer," which is that capacity *all* human beings have to observe their own thoughts, feelings, and behavior. You can be an impartial observer of your own thoughts too. Try to pay attention to your inner conversation with OCD. Allow the intrusive thoughts to be there, but don't give them control. Take an *active approach* and *talk back* to the intrusive thoughts! Replace your negative self-talk with more positive statements. For example:

When You Catch Yourself Saying:	Talk Back to Your Brain:
"These bad thoughts mean I'm bad."	*"It's only my overactive brain chemicals."*
"Maybe I'll act on these bad thoughts."	*"It's not me, it's only my OCD."* (Thanks to Dr. Jeff Schwartz.)
"These bad thoughts must mean that I'm bad."	*"It's just an OCD thought, and means absolutely nothing."*
"Maybe this time it's not OCD."	*"This is even more evidence that it's just OCD."*

By learning some self-talk strategies (see additional exercises in chapter 8), you will have some valuable tools to "talk back" to the intrusive thoughts. By reinterpreting their meaning, they become less disturbing.

Exercise 4. Intensive Taped Exposure for Thought/Action Fusion

This exposure is very useful for people who overestimate the likelihood of their doing harm to others. Because this exposure can be highly stressful, it is advised that it be done in the presence of a qualified mental health professional. A portable cassette tape player such as a Walkman with headphones is the most useful for this exercise.

1. Prepare the taped exposure exercise as described in Exercise 2 above.

2. Put the headphones on, and listen to the tape in the presence of the person who is the target or object of the feared harm or danger, your spouse or parent. If it is a child, actually place the child on your lap.

3. Listen to the tape in the presence of this person. Allow your anxiety to rise. Resist avoiding, suppressing, or ritualizing. Stay in the exposure situation for at least forty-five minutes to one and one-half hours. Your goal is to reduce your SUDS level to below 20 through habituation to the frightening thought. Use the Daily Exposure Practice Form on page 84 in chapter 6 to monitor your daily progress. Use this exercise to gain some sense of the very limited power of your thoughts to cause harm.

Dealing with Covert Rituals

But what about the *covert* or *thinking rituals*? These are mental compulsions performed internally that include repetitious prayer, phrases, words, counting numbers, recalling the past, and thought balancing (balancing a good thought against a bad thought). They are compulsive, repetitive thought patterns done as a direct response to an obsessive thought. Their purpose is to neutralize the discomfort of obsessive thoughts. In addition to the exercises in this chapter, use the ritual prevention exercises in chapter 6 to reduce your covert rituals. Deal with covert rituals just as you would with any other compulsive behaviors and rituals. Some helpful techniques include the following:

- **Ritual Delay**: Put off the performance of the covert ritual. Put it off for a few minutes, or hours, or days.

- **Thought Stopping**: Picture a large red traffic stop sign in your mind while yelling "STOP" subvocally as loudly as possible *before* the performance of the mental ritual. This has the effect of "short circuiting" the automatic use of a ritual to relieve the discomfort of the intrusive thought. (This is *not* intended for use to "stop" the intrusive thoughts. If used for that purpose, the thought stopping technique only increases them. It is intended only as a tool to help prevent you from doing your compulsive mental rituals.)

You may be confused over the difference between *obsessive thoughts* and *mental compulsions*. To tell the difference, ask yourself these questions:

- Does this thought cause anxiety? If your answer is "yes," it is an *obsessive thought*. The overall self-help strategy is to confront, invite, encourage, and face the discomfort of this thought.

- Does this thought relieve anxiety? If your answer is "yes," it is a *mental compulsion*. The overall self-help strategy is to block, reduce, or change this thought in any way possible. Any way to alter the "automatic" quality of a compulsion is progress in the right direction.

For years, it was widely believed that pure obsessions were much more difficult to help than obsessions with overt compulsions. From our experience and background, we have found that this is not necessarily true. We believe that by using the techniques described above, combined in many cases, with the right medications, you can break free from pure obsessions. And the reward is great; relief from the frustration of dealing with the constant noise in your mind.

Will your pure obsessions go away completely, and forever? Probably not. They tend to flare up during times when life becomes stressful. But overall, you can learn to live more comfortably with your annoying thoughts. They can become mere occasional background noise as you learn to enjoy life once again.

CHAPTER 10

Scrupulosity: When OCD Gets Religious

Avoiding danger is no safer in the long run than outright exposure. The fearful are caught as often as the bold.

—Helen Keller

What Is Scrupulosity?

Webster defines *scrupulous* as:

> 1. a) extremely careful to do the precisely right, proper, or correct thing in every last detail; most punctilious b) showing extreme care, precision, and punctiliousness 2. extremely conscientious 3. full of scruples, hesitant, doubtful, or uneasy, esp. constantly and obsessively, in deciding what is right or wrong.

Over the past twenty years scrupulosity has come to be viewed as OCD with a religious theme. It alludes to the condition of "seeing sin where there is none" (Ciarrocchi 1998). Scrupulosity has a very long history. The writings of some major figures in the Roman Catholic and Protestant churches reveal individuals who struggled with scruples, the historical predecessor of what we now call "scrupulosity." For example, the writer John Bunyan, author of *Pilgrim's Progress*, the Protestant theologian Martin Luther, and St. Ignatius Loyola, founder of the Jesuit order, were all tormented by unacceptable thoughts, images, and impulses that sound eerily like OCD symptoms as they are described today (Ciarrocchi 1998; Seuss and Halpern 1989).

What It Is Like to Have Scrupulosity

People with religious obsessions and compulsions are ruled by an overly strict and rigid code of religious, moral, or ethical conduct. Rather than subscribing to religious precepts and laws as guides for living a richer, more peaceful and spiritually fulfilled life, people with scrupulosity become victims of their own beliefs. Their scrupulous behavior robs them of peace of mind. They live in a relentless, tortured state of vigilance, always alert to the possibility of committing some immoral or blasphemous act and being punished harshly for it.

Some examples of scrupulosity are given below:

- Repeatedly attending confession to request forgiveness for sins and transgressions for which one has already been forgiven

- Excessively worrying about having a sexual thought while looking at another person's spouse for fear of violating the commandment "Thou shalt not covet another man's wife"

- Repeatedly reciting the Lord's Prayer over and over until each word is pronounced "perfectly," without experiencing even the slightest distraction. If concentration is broken and distraction occurs, or if the words are not pronounced perfectly, the prayer must be repeated

- Constantly checking the ground to make sure one has not stepped on an object resembling the sign of the cross and thus desecrating an important symbol

- Meticulously avoiding swallowing one's own saliva in order to follow the requirement to abstain from eating or drinking during the Jewish celebration of Yom Kippur

Differentiating Between Strong Religious Beliefs and Scrupulosity

The psychiatrist David Greenberg (1984) described five essential principles for distinguishing normal religious beliefs and practices from pathological or overly scrupulous beliefs and practices:

1. Practices that go far beyond the requirements of religious law and custom, when members act "more Catholic than the Pope." For example, if a ritual requires abstaining from food or drink, the scrupulous person may feel that swallowing saliva is sinful.

2. Beliefs or practices that have an overly narrow, trivial focus, or excessive attention paid in prayer to "saying it right" or "perfectly," rather than as a way of developing a relationship with God.

3. Healthy religious beliefs don't interfere with the normal practice of the religion. Scrupulosity OCD, on the other hand, frequently interferes with practice of the religion, for example, when a person with blasphemous thoughts avoids going to church altogether.

4. The person with scrupulosity spends excessive time and energy on minute, trivial aspects of religious observance, often ignoring more important aspects of spiritual life such as charity for the less fortunate.

5. The excessive preoccupation with doing religious rituals until they are "just right," repetitive praying, and unnecessary confessing seen in scrupulosity resemble the typical symptoms of OCD, such as checking, repeating, and asking for reassurance. Like the typical behaviors of OCD, overly scrupulous behaviors are repetitive, persistent, and unwanted.

Does having strong religious beliefs increase the likelihood of having scrupulosity OCD? Our basic model of OCD as a neurobehavioral disorder holds that there must be a biological predisposition to have OCD. Strong religious beliefs are not the cause of OCD. They are only the grist for the OCD mill in a person who is biologically predisposed to it. Remember that OCD is "the doubting disease." As such, it attacks, undermines, and wreaks havoc with the very foundation of who you are and who you know yourself to be. If strong religious beliefs were not present in the individual, the OCD would surely take a different form, such as contamination fears or checking compulsions, for example. Scrupulosity OCD takes well-intended beliefs and precepts and blows them out of proportion. The true moral and spiritual aspects of the individual's character become fused with the OCD, and thus become distorted and corrupted.

Hypermorality and Hyperresponsibility

Hypermorality and hyperresponsibility are major behavioral characteristics of people with scrupulosity OCD. *Hypermorality* involves an excessive preoccupation with the fear of doing something morally wrong, reprehensible, and/or condemnable. These individuals set excessive, unrealistically rigid and narrow standards in the areas of their lives touched by the OCD.

Here are some examples of hypermorality:

- Checking sales receipts laboriously to make sure an error wasn't made in your favor, for fear that this is the equivalent of stealing from the merchant.

- Reviewing conversations you had with others over and over in your mind to be absolutely sure that you did not inadvertently tell a lie.

People who are *hyperresponsible* have an overly unrealistic sense of accountability in particular areas of their lives. Such people take on responsibilities that realistically belong to others, or take responsibility for things that are beyond anyone's reasonable control. Here are some examples of hyperresponsibility:

- Constantly checking the ground for stray sharp objects that others might possibly step on and thus hurt themselves.

- Checking every piece of garbage to make sure recyclable items are separated, then carrying them by hand individually to a recycling landfill to ensure they are not lost, thereby contributing to pollution.

- Taking many stray animals into your home to "protect" them, to the point of endangering your health and your family's.

Hyperresponsibility/scrupulosity OCD is *not* to be confused with being virtuous or extremely compassionate about the welfare of others. Although certainly not lacking in compassion for others, these individuals are driven to extremes of worry and anxiety mainly out of the fear of possible condemnation. For example, they are afraid of going to hell, angering God, or living with perpetual feelings of guilt for their failure to protect others from harm or endangerment. They have little time or energy left to concern themselves with the well-being of others because of living in constant fear for their own fate.

The Self-Directed Program for Scrupulosity

Step 1. Find a Spiritual/Religious Advisor

You will probably feel reluctant to do some of the Self-Directed Program's exposure and ritual prevention exercises proposed in this chapter, feeling that they are morally, ethically, or spiritually wrong. Or you may fear that changing your behavior will do damage to your spiritual identity and beliefs. To help deal with these issues, choose a trusted, prudent person to serve as your moral, ethical, and/or spiritual advisor and as your guide through the changes that you will experience while doing the Self-Directed Program. This person should have religious beliefs similar to yours and a basic understanding of scrupulosity OCD. You may choose your counselor, pastor, rabbi, or other spiritual advisor. Or, it could be your spouse, parent, relative, or a close friend. For the time being, you will need to follow your advisor as a "sheep follows a shepherd."

If you are doing the Self-Directed Program with a therapist, ask if you can bring the advisor to your counseling sessions to assist the therapist in your treatment. A trained behavior therapist knowledgeable about OCD will welcome this collaboration. Discuss each exposure task and ask about each, "Is this morally acceptable for me to do?" Adjust the tasks until you find those that are morally, ethically, and spiritually acceptable both to you and your advisor.

Agree to make a sincere attempt at completing your personalized Self-Directed Program. Model your behavior after your advisor's example. Expect there to be times when you will doubt your advisor's guidance. However, with time, the OCD will weaken and your true moral and spiritual self-identity will emerge. Trust your advisor to guide you as you move ever closer to that time.

Now, write the name(s) of persons you know who might serve as your advisor for these exercises and make a commitment to choose one of these people to act as your advisor as soon as you can.

Step 2. Keep a Daily Record of Your Obsessions and Compulsions

To the scrupulous person, excessive time, effort, and energy is expended warding off thoughts, images, or urges considered dangerous, unacceptable, offensive, repulsive, or disgusting. These are the obsessions, and they cause intense anxiety and shame. For one week, keep an ongoing record of your obsessions, using the Scrupulosity Daily Monitoring Form on the next page. Make a copy to carry with you. Then record the date and describe each situation that triggers the obsessive thoughts or worries. Rate the degree of distress these thoughts cause you on a SUDS scale of 0–100. Then write down the compulsive behaviors, including repetitive thoughts, images, or behaviors you use to relieve anxiety and to neutralize the distress of your thoughts. Immediately following the Scrupulosity Daily Monitoring Form, there is an example of how to use it.

Scrupulosity Daily Monitoring Form

Date	Situation that triggers discomfort	Discomfort level (0–100)	Obsession: Thought(s), image(s) or impulse(s) that increase anxiety	Compulsion: Excessive thoughts, images, or behaviors that reduce anxiety

Scrupulosity Daily Monitoring Form (Example)

Date	Situation that triggers discomfort	Discomfort level (0–100)	Obsession: Thought(s), image(s) or impulse(s) that increase anxiety	Compulsion: Excessive thoughts, images, or behaviors that reduce anxiety
9/21/00	Thought about attractive person other than my spouse	95	*I'm having an impure thought and God will punish me.*	Prayed for 75 minutes, or until it felt "right"
9/21/00	Looked at my infant's genitals	85	*Maybe I'm enjoying looking and I will go to hell for that.*	Avoided touching baby or going into baby's room
9/22/00	Went for a walk.	90	*I must never step on any living thing. That would violate God's commandments.*	Kept my eyes on the ground, watching everything I walked upon
9/23/00	Sitting in church, looked up at the image of Jesus	75	*I feel like shouting obscenities at the image of Jesus.*	Attended confession three times this week to confess my blasphemous thoughts

Step 3. Make a Target Obsessions List

Using your monitoring form, make a list of your obsessions and rank them in order of the amount of distress they cause you. Here is an example list of target obsessive thoughts:

Target Obsessions List (Example)

Obsessive Thoughts (Thought, image, or impulse)	SUDS level (0–100)
1. I'm having an impure thought and God will punish me.	70
2. Maybe I'm enjoying looking and I will go to hell.	80
3. I must never step on any living thing. That would violate God's commandments.	60
4. I feel like shouting obscenities at the image of Jesus.	90
5. Maybe I told a lie without knowing it. That would certainly mean that I'm a bad person.	95
6. Maybe I don't understand this particular passage of scripture and I won't go to Heaven after all.	100

Target Obsessions List

Obsessive Thoughts (Thought, image, or impulse)	SUDS level (0–100)
1. _____	_____
2. _____	_____
3. _____	_____
4. _____	_____
5. _____	_____
6. _____	_____
7. _____	_____
8. _____	_____
9. _____	_____
10. _____	_____

Step 4. Make a Target Compulsions List

Again, using your monitoring form, make a list of your compulsive behaviors and rank them in order of the amount of distress you would feel if you *did not* carry out your compulsions. If the compulsion is an avoidance behavior (such as not going to church), indicate so. Include in your assessment an estimate (it doesn't have to be exact!) of the amount of time (in hours) your compulsions take up in an average day (if they are not practiced every day, estimate your average for an entire week).

Target Compulsions List (Example)

Compulsive Behaviors (Compulsive behaviors, including thoughts, actions—including avoidance—that neutralize or contain anxiety)	SUDS level if you *do not* do the compulsion (0–100)	Average amount of time per day (or week, if applicable)
1. Praying for long periods, until it feels "right."	100	Most of the time
2. Avoiding touching baby or going into baby's room.	90	About 4 times per week
3. Keeping my eyes on the ground, watching everything walked upon.	85	90 minutes/day every day
4. Attending confession frequently to confess blasphemous thoughts.	95	All the time when outside
5. Repeating "God forgives me" 24 times.	100	4 hours per day
6. Repetitively reading the same scriptures over and over until they are "perfectly" understood.	95	2 hours per day
7. Holding my breath when walking by a non-kosher butcher so I won't inhale the scent of non-kosher meat.	80	Avoided daily

Target Compulsions List

Compulsive Behaviors (compulsive behaviors, including thoughts, actions—including avoidance—that neutralize or contain anxiety)	SUDS level if you *do not* do the compulsion (0–100)	Average amount of time per day (or week, if applicable)
1. _____	_____	_____
2. _____	_____	_____
3. _____	_____	_____
4. _____	_____	_____
5. _____	_____	_____
6. _____	_____	_____

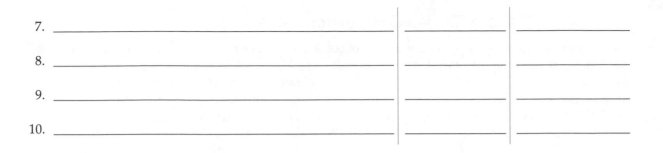

7. _____ | _____ | _____

8. _____ | _____ | _____

9. _____ | _____ | _____

10. _____ | _____ | _____

Step 5. Devise an Exposure and Ritual Prevention Strategy

You will now devise a strategy for doing exposure and ritual prevention based on your lists of target obsessions and compulsions. Your strategy will be to first target those items on your lists that cause a lower level of distress. When you master those, you will gradually move up to dealing with more difficult items.

Remember, exposure and ritual prevention works best when the following elements are present:

1. Exposure must be prolonged and repeated—between one and a half hours and three hours per day, for four to seven days or longer. While there are no definitive lengths of time one must do an exposure, you must remain in the anxiety-provoking situation long enough to promote *habituation,* or what Joseph Ciarrocchi (1998) calls the *remedy of nervous system boredom.*

2. The exposure must be acceptable to you and not oppose your core religious beliefs. This is the tricky part. Remember that OCD behaviors are excessive, unwanted, persistent, and not based on the true requirements of religious or spiritual practice. It is important to separate out what are OCD behaviors from the behaviors that are appropriate expressions of true religious or spiritual belief. Use the authority and guidance of your advisor/therapist to assist you in sorting this out and to help you find the courage to take the bold steps of confronting your OCD-based scrupulous ideas and behaviors.

3. For obsessions regarding feared situations that are difficult to replicate (for example the fear of going to hell), use imaginal exposure. The imaginal exposure method can be found in chapter 7. Remember that the goal of imaginal exposure is to be able to hold uncomfortable or frightening thoughts in your mind with less discomfort.

4. As you expose yourself to anxiety-provoking situations, work to reduce your compulsive rituals gradually on a day-to-day, week-to-week basis. Review chapter 6 for how to do ritual prevention and read the examples in the following tables.

5. If you are feeling unsure or unsafe when blocking a ritual, the general rule is *"do the opposite"* of whatever scrupulous idea your OCD mind tells you to do. St. Ignatius Loyola, the founder of the Jesuit order, gave the same advice 400 years ago to his scrupulous followers (Ciarrocchi 1995).

6. Make copies of the Scrupulosity Exposure and Ritual Prevention Planning Form and use it to help you plan your ERP strategy on a day-to-day or week-to-week basis.

Scrupulosity Exposure and Ritual Prevention Planning Form

Target Obsessive thought(s), image(s), or impulse(s): _____

_____

Target Compulsion(s): _____

_____

Exposure and Ritual Prevention Strategy: _____

_____

SUDS before starting ERP: _____

How long (minutes/hours) per exposure: _____

How often (days, weeks): _____

Target SUDS level: _____

Avoidances to be stopped: _____

Additional Instructions: _____

_____

Exposure & Ritual Prevention Daily (Weekly) Plan

Day (Week) 1: _____

_____

Day (Week) 2: _____

_____

Day (Week) 3: _____

_____

Day (Week) 4: _____

_____

Imaginal Exposure Plan

Day (Week) 1: _____

_____

Day (Week) 2: _____

_____

Day (Week) 3: _____

_____

Day (Week) 4: _____

_____

Scrupulosity Exposure and Ritual Prevention Planning Form (Example 1)

Target Obsessive thought(s), image(s), or impulse(s): <u>"Never step on any living thing or I'll be punished."</u>

Target Compulsion(s): <u>Check, recheck and retrace steps while walking outside.</u>

Exposure and Ritual Prevention Strategy: <u>Become more comfortable taking reasonable and prudent risks while walking. Gradually reduce checking behaviors.</u>

SUDS before starting ERP: <u>95</u>

How long (minutes/hours) per exposure: <u>30 minutes</u>

How often (days, weeks): <u>Three times per day</u>

Target SUDS level: <u>20</u>

Avoidances to be stopped: <u>Walking outside is not to be avoided</u>

Additional instructions: <u>Discuss exposures with advisor before proceeding!</u>

Exposure and Ritual Prevention Daily (Weekly) Plan

Day (Week) 1: <u>Walk 30 paces (or about ½–1 minute) without looking down or checking. Repeat five times per day.</u>

Day (Week) 2: <u>Walk 60 paces (about 1–2 minutes) without looking down. Repeat five times per day.</u>

Day (Week) 3: <u>Walk 120 paces (2–4 minutes) without looking down. Repeat five times per day.</u>

Day (Week) 4: <u>Walk 160 paces (3–6 minutes) without looking down. Repeat five times per day.</u>

Imaginal Exposure Plan

Day (Week) 1: <u>Do Imaginal Exposure with the image of accidentally stepping on an ant. Hold image in mind until SUDS level goes to less than 20. Repeat daily.</u>

Day (Week) 2: <u>Do imaginal exposure of image of accidentally stepping on frog or snake and killing it. Repeat until SUDS less than 20. Repeat daily.</u>

Day (Week) 3: <u>Do imaginal exposure of image of accidentally stepping on a frog or a snake, killing it, and being tried in court for "cruelty to animals." Found guilty and punished. Repeat until SUDS level is less than 20. Repeat daily.</u>

Day (Week) 4: Not applicable to this example.

Scrupulosity Exposure and Ritual Prevention Planning Form (Example 2)

Target Obsessive thought(s), image(s)or impulse(s): <u>Intrusive thought/impulse to shout obscenities at the image of Jesus.</u>

Target Compulsion(s): <u>Attend confession repeatedly; repeat the Lord's prayer four times.</u>

Exposure and Ritual Prevention Strategy: <u>Expose self to horrific thoughts for increasing amounts of time until horrific thought habituates. Reduce confessions and reassurance.</u>

SUDS before starting ERP: <u>90</u>

How long (minutes/hours) per Exposure: <u>45–90 minutes per day</u>

How often (days, weeks): <u>once a day</u>

Target SUDS level per session: <u>0–20</u>

Avoidances to be stopped: <u>Must attend church regularly</u>

Additional instructions: <u>Discuss exposures with advisor before proceeding! Discuss guidelines for appropriate use of confession and prayer with advisor</u>

Exposure and Ritual Prevention Plan

Day (Week) 1: <u>Reduce confessions to two per week, reduce Lord's Prayer to twice per day.</u>

Day (Week) 2: <u>Reduce confessions to one per week, reduce Lord's Prayer to once per day (maintain normal prayer schedule).</u>

Day (Week) 3: <u>Stop all obsessional confessing.</u>

Day (Week) 4: <u>Stop all obsessional confessing.</u>

Imaginal Exposure Plan

Day (Week) 1: <u>Hold thought of shouting obscenities at the image of Jesus in mind for 1 min. Repeat every 10 minutes for one hour.</u>

Day (Week) 2: <u>Hold thought of shouting obscenities at the image of Jesus in mind for 2 min. Repeat every 7 minutes for 1½ hours.</u>

Day (Week) 3: <u>Hold thought of shouting obscenities at the image of Jesus in mind for 4 min. Repeat every 5 minutes for 1½ hours.</u>

Day (Week) 4: <u>Hold thought of shouting obscenities at the image of Jesus in mind for 8 min. Repeat every 5 minutes for 1½ hours.</u>

KEYS TO BREAKING FREE FROM SCRUPULOSITY

1. You are not planning to act on your bad thoughts, only to think about them. Discuss with your advisor the relationship between thoughts and actions. You will progress further once you can accept that *thoughts do not equal actions.*

2. If you have difficulty resisting a ritual, try postponing, delaying, or changing it. If you do a ritual very quickly, do it very slowly. If you are reciting a phrase like "Jesus loves me" to yourself, sing it to yourself, or change it in some other way, for example, leave out one word.

3. Daily, find the courage to place yourself in the very situations that will trigger symptoms. *Avoid avoidance.*

4. Tell your advisor, friends, and relatives to give you reassurance that you are doing the right thing *only once.* Rephrasing a question or asking a second person to get another reassuring answer is not helpful. Think about your questions before you ask them. Be honest with yourself—if you already know the answer, *don't ask!*

5. When you want to avoid a situation or activity, *do it anyway*. If you feel an urge to do something to alleviate your anxiety, *don't do it.* Consult your advisor if you aren't sure what you should do. Ask yourself, "What would a reasonable, prudent person do?"

6. When you are not doing ERP tasks, occupy yourself with the activities of the present. Notice your surroundings and pay attention to conversations around you. Observe details. Allow bad thoughts to pass through your mind, as if seeing them from a distance. Ignoring obsessive thoughts weakens them while fighting against them strengthens them, causing them to grow and multiply.

7. When doing ERP, expect, even invite anxiety. Don't expect to feel good while you're doing ERP—you won't! You will begin to feel good, even great, from small, gradual successes letting go of obsessions, eliminating rituals, and reclaiming your true spiritual self.

8. If you find an exposure too threatening, break it down into smaller steps that are easier to manage and master.

9. Let go of your need for certainty. Religious belief requires faith. If you had total certainty in your life, you would have no need for faith.

10. Let go of outdated or extreme religious rituals and develop a more personal faith. The standards and beliefs of people with scrupulosity OCD often go beyond those of the most devout members of their own religion.

11. Find ways to replace religious rituals with sincere spiritual practices. Spend more quality time with your children, do volunteer work, spend time with a lonely person, or help a neighbor, for example.

CHAPTER 11

Hyperresponsibility: Hit 'n Run OCD

I believe that anyone can conquer fear by doing the things he fears to do, provided he keeps doing them until he gets a record of successful experiences behind him.

—Eleanor Roosevelt

One of the more crippling forms of OCD involves the obsessive preoccupation with the possibility of being held responsible for hitting, injuring, or killing someone while driving a car. "Hit 'n run" OCD was aptly named by a long-suffering patient with the disorder. People with this form of OCD live a nightmare of guilt, fear, and dread every time they get behind the wheel.

A simple bump in the road, an unexpected noise, shadow, or flash of light can trigger a heart-pounding, tire-screeching foray back to the site where a crime/accident was thought to have happened. Feeling reassured that no accident took place, the anxiety is relieved—but only briefly. Feelings of intense doubt and fear recur, compelling yet another U-turn back to the "crime" site. The pattern may be repeated many times until the person feels "right" and drives on. However, the feelings of doubt and anxiety may persist for hours, even days.

Driving near schools, children, and bicyclists can be especially nerve-wracking. Potholes and speed bumps may feel like bodies lying in the road, triggering the compulsion to check for signs of injury. Checking behaviors may go to such extremes as routinely looking up accident reports in the local police department columns in the newspapers, watching TV news programs specifically for local accident information, and chasing ambulances to accident scenes. Some people with hit 'n run OCD repeatedly check the surfaces of their vehicles for dents or bloodstains.

Some people may actually endanger themselves by getting out of their cars in traffic to check underneath the car for signs of injured pedestrians. It is not known how many people suffer from hit 'n run OCD, but from the anecdotal experience of mental health professionals who treat OCD, it appears as a symptom at some time in as many as 20 percent of patients with OCD. It seems to occur equally in males and females.

"Hit 'n run" patients suffer a particular sense of shame and humiliation about their problem. Like most people with OCD, they are aware their behavior is irrational and makes no sense—but they can't control it. Many resort to driving only with a suitable "witness" in the car, and some avoid driving altogether.

Self-Directed Program for Hit 'n Run OCD

Step 1. Assess the Hit 'n Run Problem

Describe the problem in detail by answering the following questions:

How often do you feel anxious while driving? (All the time? Some of the time? Rarely? Only when anxious about other things? When driving alone?) _____

_____

What places and driving situations cause you the most anxiety and fear? _____

_____

_____

What are the specific triggers for anxiety? (Bumps in the road, pedestrians passing by? Children walking by? Emergency sirens?)_____

_____

Overall, how anxious do you feel when driving? (Indicate your average SUDS level when driving.) _____

_____

What other factors affect how anxious you are? (Fatigue, alcohol, or a "witness," for example.)

_____

How much do you avoid driving? (All the time, some of the time, rarely, or not at all?)

_____

Are there any special circumstances in which you avoid driving? Places or situations you avoid?

_____

_____

What do you do to relieve the anxiety when it occurs? (Neutralization strategies: turnarounds, asking for reassurance, checking the car for signs of blood or dents, checking accident reports, or calling the police department, for example.) _____

_____

_____

For the next seven days, use the following form to monitor your actual driving situations. Make note of the specific anxiety-provoking situations, your SUDS level when driving, thoughts that trigger anxiety and worry, and the compulsive rituals/behaviors you use to neutralize anxiety (like checking). Below is a Hit 'n Run Daily Monitoring Form, followed by an example of how to complete it.

Hit 'n Run Daily Monitoring Form

Date	Driving Situation That Triggers Obsessive Thought	Discomfort (SUDS) Level (0-100)	Obsessive Thought (Thought, image that triggers anxiety)	Compulsion (Excessive, repetitive behaviors that reduce or neutralize anxiety)

Hit 'n Run Daily Monitoring Form (Example)

Date	Driving Situation That Triggers Obsessive Thought	Discomfort (SUDS) Level (0–100)	Obsessive Thought (Thought, image that triggers anxiety)	Compulsion (Excessive, repetitive behaviors that reduce or neutralize anxiety)
2/3/99	Driving by bicyclist next to car	95	*Maybe I hit him*	Checked in mirror Returned to area to check to see if accident occurred
2/3/99	Switching lanes	75	*Maybe I forced someone off the road, causing an accident*	Returned to area to check to see if accident occurred Asked passenger for reassurance ("Did I hit anyone?")
2/4/99	Driving over bump in road	90	*Maybe I ran over someone*	Turnaround, returned to place where bump occurred—checked for signs of an accident, harm, or injury
2/4/99	Pulling out of parking space	85	*Maybe I ran over a child behind the car*	Got out of car, checked to make sure no one behind car
2/4/99	Hear police siren, see police car racing to accident scene	100	*Maybe I caused that accident*	Checked police reports of accidents in area where I'd driven
2/5/99	Turning head while driving	75	*Maybe I didn't see what was in front of me and I hit someone*	Checked in mirror to make sure I hadn't caused an accident
2/6/99	Parking and getting out of car	80	*Maybe I injured someone—I'd better make sure*	Checked around car for signs of dents, blood
2/7/99	Driving by an elementary school with children walking	95	*I'm likely to cause an accident and injure a child*	Went out of way to avoid driving near school

Step 2. Make an Anxiety/Exposure List

After you have compiled a record of the situations that cause you distress while driving, use your chart to list them in order, from the most distressing to the least distressing. Refer to the example.

Anxiety/Exposure List

Situation That Triggers Distress	SUDS Level (0–100)
1.	
2.	
3.	
4.	
5.	
6.	
7.	
8.	
9.	
10.	

Anxiety/Exposure List (Example)

Situation That Triggers Distress	SUDS Level (0–100)
1. Hear police siren, see police car racing to accident scene	100
2. Driving by elementary school with children walking	95
3. Driving by bicyclist next to car	95
4. Driving over bump in road	90
5. Pulling out of parking space	85
6. Parking and getting out of car	80
7. Turning head while driving	75
8. Switching lanes	75

Step 3. Do Exposure and Ritual Prevention to Situations on Your Anxiety/Exposure List

Remember, the key to overcoming the anxiety of driving is through exposure to fear-provoking driving situations, combined with blocking of the behaviors typically used to neutralize anxiety, such as doing turnarounds, checking the car, and checking accident reports. Now, starting with the situation on the bottom of your list, practice the driving situation repeatedly without doing any anxiety neutralizing rituals or compulsions. Practice the situation a minimum of ten times per day for one week. Or practice until you can drive in the situation at a level of 20 SUDS or less. Below are examples of exposure and ritual prevention with situations from the Anxiety/Exposure List example.

Exposure and Ritual Prevention Planning Form—Hit 'n Run

(Example 1)

Target Driving Situation: <u>Driving over bump in road</u>

Target Obsessive Thought: <u>"It was probably a body that I ran over."</u>

Target Compulsion: <u>Turnaround to the scene of the accident</u>

Exposure and Ritual Prevention Strategy: <u>Repeatedly drive over bumpy objects on the road, delay turnarounds for first few weeks, or limit to one and only one per incident. By the third week, stop all turnarounds.</u>

SUDS before starting ERP: <u>95</u>

How long (minutes/hours) per exposure: <u>One to two hours</u>

How often (days, weeks): <u>As often as possible for four-five weeks</u>

Target SUDS level: <u>20 or less</u>

Avoidances to be stopped: <u>Stop avoiding driving in heavy traffic</u>

Additional instructions: <u>Put all mirrors out of position during practice</u>

Exposure and Ritual Prevention Daily Plan:

Day 1–3: <u>Drive over speed bump in apartment complex at 25 mph. Do not do turnaround for fifteen minutes.</u>

Day 4–6: <u>Drive over two speed bumps in apartment complex. Do not do turnaround for thirty minutes.</u>

Day 7–10: <u>Drive over three or more speed bumps in apartment complex. Do not do turnaround for one hour.</u>

Day 11–14: <u>Drive over all speed bumps in apartment complex—do not do turnaround.</u>

Exposure and Ritual Prevention Planning Form—Hit 'n Run

(Example 2)

Target Situation: Driving by elementary school with children walking

Target Obsessive Thought: "I've run over a child and I'll be punished for it."

Target Compulsion: Checking car all around to make sure child was not run over

Exposure and Ritual Prevention Strategy: Expose to situations of driving around areas where children congregate. Park, walk away without checking. Delay checking car for first week, or limit to one and only one check. By the second week, stop all checking of car.

SUDS before starting ERP: 95

How long (minutes/hours) per exposure: One to two hours

How often (days, weeks): As often as possible for two-three weeks

Target SUDS level: 20 or less

Avoidances to be stopped: Stop avoiding driving around and near elementary schools

Additional instructions: Resist urge to ask others for reassurance ("Did I run over anyone?")

Exposure and Ritual Prevention Plan:

Day 1–3: Drive by elementary school when children are not outside. Park, get out of car, walk away, do not check car for fifteen minutes.

Day 4–7: Drive by elementary school when children are not outside. Park, get out of car, walk away, do not check car for thirty minutes.

Day 7–10: Drive by elementary school when children are walking outside. Park, get out of car, walk away, do not check car for thirty minutes.

Day 11–14: Drive by elementary school when children are walking outside. Park, get out of car, walk away, do not check car for sixty minutes.

Exposure and Ritual Prevention Planning Form—Hit 'n Run

Target Obsessive Thought: _____

_____

_____

Target Compulsion: _____

_____

_____

Exposure and Ritual Prevention Strategy: _____

_____

_____

SUDS before starting ERP: _____

How long (minutes/hours) per exposure: _____

How often (days, weeks): _____

Target SUDS level: _____

Avoidances to be stopped: _____

Additional Instructions: _____

_____

_____

Exposure and Ritual Prevention Plan

Day 1–3: _____

_____

Day 4–7: _____

_____

Day 8–10: _____

_____

Day 11–14: _____

_____

Self-Talk Strategies to Deal with Obsessive Thoughts and Urges to Check

Anxiety-Provoking Thought	Alternative Self-Talk
I can't stand it if I don't check.	*I can resist the magnet and not check.* *If I just wait, the urge will go away.*
Maybe I hit or ran over someone. I'll surely go to jail.	*It's just my OCD brain giving me false messages.* *It's just ghosts and goblins—hey look real, but are not.*
I'll have to give in and check later.	*If I check, it will only make my OCD worse.* *Instead of checking, I can do something different now.*

 **KEYS TO BREAKING FREE**

1. When starting ERP, expect your urges to do neutralizing behaviors, such as checking and turnarounds, to be very strong at the beginning. You will likely feel worse before you start feeling better. With repetition, the urges will lessen over time. *Persistence and resistance are the keys*.

2. It is helpful to make use of props to simulate the actual sensation of hitting or driving the car over a large object. Use twenty-five-pound sacks of Sackrete, sand, or mulch to simulate driving over bumps in the road. Deflated tires and two-by-four pieces of wood are also useful. To simulate hitting a body, use a padded department store mannequin or a rolled up piece of heavy carpet. Have a friend or helper toss the mannequin or carpet at the car while it is moving to simulate the feeling of the car hitting a heavy object.

3. Be sure to repeat all exposure exercises over and over daily, as often as necessary to lower SUDS to less than 20.

4. If the urge to neutralize is too strong during your exposures, shorten the driving distance, or make the exposure task simpler and easier to accomplish. When you master an easy task, graduate to a more difficult task.

5. Beware of the overuse of and overreliance on mirrors as a "safety signal."

6. If you tend to neutralize anxiety with the use of a "witness," do exposure practices alone whenever possible.

7. Record a five- to ten-minute motivational tape in your own voice. See chapter 8 for more instructions about how to do this. Play the tape in your car's cassette player while you are driving to keep you mindful of the need to relabel your obsessive thoughts and to resist checking compulsions.

"This is _____ , and I have OCD. I live in fear that I will be punished severely and perpetually for a mistake I'll make while driving—a mistake that will cost someone their life. This fear has prevented me from living life freely. I accept that to live life free of fear, I must confront and face the things I fear. I'm committed wholeheartedly to this. As I drive down the street now, I'm aware of the tension throughout my body. I'm releasing this tension now, breathing deeply, relaxing my muscles in my hands, arms, shoulders, neck, and legs. I'm taking a deep breath now, exhaling slowly. I'm in total control of the steering wheel of my vehicle.

Continued on the Next Page

Keys to Breaking Free Cont.

Due to the OCD, I'm extremely aware of everything around me, of every noise, of everyone I pass as I drive by. This awareness is excessive and causes tension. As an obsessive fear jumps into my brain, I can relabel the idea as only an obsessive thought! The thought is only the result of my out-of-whack brain chemicals and nothing more! It is coming from my OCD brain, not from my logical brain. Logically, I sense that nothing bad has happened. Knowing this is an obsessive thought, I can react to it differently. I can outsmart the OCD message when I treat it as merely a false message, my OCD brain sending me 'ghosts and goblins.' This way I give them no power over me!

If I let the OCD trick me and I react to the images and messages as if they were real, my OCD wins and gets bigger and bigger. If I give in to this monster, I'll only be feeding it, making it bigger, stronger, more in control. I win when I courageously resist the magnetic pull of the compulsive urge. And although there is great discomfort in not giving in to a compulsive urge, if I wait, and hang on through the discomfort, the urge will eventually diminish on its own. I am willing to fight the battle of my life and be victorious against this monster! I hate this OCD so much, and my commitment to my recovery is so very strong, that I'm willing to risk everything, to put everything on the line and not check. I'm willing to take a chance that this is nothing more than my OCD, and that I don't need to check anything. I have a choice to not give in to it. I am gaining the strength and courage to begin to take charge of my OCD."

The Role of Hyperresponsibility

Hit 'n run OCD has *hyperresponsibility* as an important component. As such, it is very similar to other types of hyperresponsibility OCD—scrupulosity and checking compulsions involving preventing harm and danger to others, for example. At the heart of hyperresponsibility OCD is the feeling of a dark cloud always hanging overhead. It is a feeling that unless one is constantly "on guard," at any moment disaster will strike and life will inevitably turn into a horror show of guilt and retribution.

Driving, because it is an activity that places you in a machine that is well-known to inflict pain and death, is a perfect breeding ground for hyperresponsibility OCD. Progress with hit 'n run, as well as all types of hyperresponsibility OCD, requires acceptance of the risks inherent in living life fully. Being in charge of one's life can be stifled by fear and the need to overcontrol events we have little control over. Only by letting go of the need for control do we truly gain it.

CHAPTER 12

Hoarding OCD

By perseverance, the snail reached the ark.

—Charles Haddon Spurgeon

Compulsive hoarding is a widely recognized symptom of OCD. It is defined as the acquisition of, and failure to discard, possessions that appear to be useless or of limited value (Frost and Gross 1993). While everyone is familiar with someone whom they consider a "pack rat" or chronic saver, people with hoarding OCD distinguish themselves by the sheer quantity of objects collected, and by their strong emotional attachment to items most would clearly consider useless. The objects of hoarding can be almost anything, but often include such things as newspapers, clothing, food stuffs, books, papers, junk mail, and old appliances. One person with hoarding OCD aptly described her apartment as "something between a wastebasket and a suitcase" (Griest and Jefferson 1995).

People with hoarding OCD seem to overvalue the importance of these objects, and therefore they develop an overattachment to them that prevents them from discarding the objects. Often, the rationale is, "What if I should need it in the future? I'd better not throw it out." With piles of clutter stacked to the ceiling and only a little space for walkways through the house, meandering through the cluttered home of a person with hoarding OCD can be challenging.

Estimates of hoarding behaviors range from between 18 percent and 31 percent of all OCD patients (Damecour and Charron 1998; Frost and Steketee 1998), with the onset occurring most often in the patient's early twenties (Greenberg 1987). Gender differences in hoarders have not been noted. Although many theories exist about the cause of hoarding, for years psychologists have theorized that compulsive hoarding develops from the perfectionist striving for control over the environment (Salzman 1973).

People with hoarding OCD are often extremely resistant to changing their behavior. They tend to ignore the impact their behavior has on themselves and others, preferring to see their hoarding as necessary to feel in control of their lives. Attempts by family members to discard possessions may be met with intense anger and threats of violence. An effort to remove clutter is likely to occur when it becomes intolerable to family members, or when a health hazard emerges thus prompting an emergency situation. Should a move from the property become inevitable, it is likely the hoarding will only continue in the new environment.

The following five features characterize persons with hoarding OCD (Frost and Steketee 1998):

Indecisiveness

The simplest decisions of everyday life, such as what to wear in the morning, what to eat for dinner, and where to take a vacation, are troublesome for compulsive hoarders. This indecisiveness appears to be related to the perfectionistic fear of making mistakes. Hoarding useless objects may therefore be a means of avoiding making bad decisions, or decisions that may be regretted later. If every object, even seemingly useless ones, is hoarded, there can never be any regrets or pain over having lost or discarded the object (Frost and Steketee 1998).

Categorization Problems

People with hoarding OCD have difficulty sorting objects into useful classifications for efficient use or discard. One object seems as important and vital as another. A gum wrapper may have as much importance as a recent tax return. Decisions over keeping and/or discarding objects become exceedingly complicated by the inability to differentiate between what is truly valuable, and what is not.

Beliefs about Memory

Despite little objective evidence of their having memory problems, people with hoarding OCD typically display obsessional concerns about the reliability of their memory. They fear that their "faulty" memory will prevent them from having access to all their possessions. This lack of confidence in their own memory renders the compulsive hoarder reluctant to put items away and out of sight. They fear that if an object is out of sight, it will be forgotten. Therefore, useless objects are everywhere within sight of a person their home, contributing to the extreme clutter.

Excessive Emotional Attachment to Things

People with hoarding OCD regard their "stuff" as part of themselves. They attach much more sentiment to objects than nonhoarders do and they find an extreme degree of emotional comfort in their possessions (Frost and Gross 1993). Taking great delight in "things" also results in a marked tendency toward excessive purchasing—that is, "shop-aholic" behavior.

Control of Ownership

People with hoarding OCD have an exaggerated need to feel in control of their possessions, to protect the items from harm or irresponsible use. Hence, the person with hoarding OCD will feel extreme discomfort or even feel personally violated should the objects be touched or moved by anyone other than the himself or herself.

Self-Directed Program for Hoarding OCD

For some people, hoarding is the major symptom of OCD. It is so severe that it greatly interferes with maintaining healthy living standards. More commonly, hoarding is just one more type of

OCD symptom. Either way, the Self-Directed Program for hoarding OCD can help you to break free from hoarding.

Step 1. Set a Realistic Goal That You Are Willing to Achieve

Most often, people with hoarding OCD will feel overwhelmed and therefore resist the goal of ridding their homes of all of their collected "stuff." If you feel this way, instead of thinking that you will try to get rid of all of your possessions, start small and set more realistic goals—that of becoming less indecisive and living in a better organized, uncluttered living space.

Step 2. Make an Assessment of Your Hoarding Problem

Answer the following questions to gain a better understanding of your hoarding problem (thanks to Frost and Steketee 1998):

How much of the house is cluttered? Which rooms? _____

_____

How much discomfort does the problem cause you? Your family members? _____

_____

How severe would you describe the clutter problem? (Very bad, somewhat bad, not too bad)?

_____

What types of items do you save?_____

_____

For each type of item, what are your reasons for saving it? _____

_____

_____

_____

Do you have any form of organization for the stuff in your home? How do you decide what item goes where? _____

_____

_____

How does the problem affect your relationship with family members? _____

_____

Step 3. Put a Moratorium on All Accumulating

For the duration of time you are working on the Self-Directed Program, temporarily suspend accumulating all but the most essential items for your household. This will enable you to see progress faster, and lead to greater success as you gain control over your hoarding problem.

Step 4. Develop an Organization Plan for Your Home

Using the chart below, list all the areas of your home, including the kitchen, dining room, family room, closets, bathrooms, garage, and so forth. Write down exactly how the space is presently being used. Then, estimate approximately what percent of the usable space is presently cluttered. In the fourth column, indicate your goal for the functional use of the space (for example, to entertain guests, watch TV, or eat meals). Indicate your goal for the amount of clutter allowed in that room. Be sure to include in your plan ample areas for storage.

Organizational Plan

Area of Home	How Presently Used?	How Cluttered? (% of usable space)	Goal for Use: Function	% Clutter
Living room				
Kitchen				
Dining room				
Family room				
Master bedroom				
Second bedroom				
Third bedroom				
Fourth bedroom				
Hallway				
Closet— master bedroom				

Closet— 2nd bedroom	_____	_____	_____	_____
Closet— 3rd bedroom	_____	_____	_____	_____
Closet—Hallway	_____	_____	_____	_____
Bathroom	_____	_____	_____	_____
_____	_____	_____	_____	_____
_____	_____	_____	_____	_____

Step 5. Decide Where to Start First

This decision about where to start is often the hardest to make. Choose an area that if it were uncluttered would provide a high degree of satisfaction. For example it might be a kitchen table, hallway, or corner of the living room. This is the best place to start. Another way to start is to pick a type of item that you have many of in one small area, such as books, clothing, or types of papers, and work only on that class of item first. Since it is easier to sort and store large groups of similar objects, the job will go faster and provide faster satisfaction.

Step 6. Establish a Few, Simple Rules for Placing, Storing and Discarding, and *Stick to Them*

Place three empty large boxes in the area to be worked on. Label one box "Store," the next box "Sell" or "Donate," and the third box "Discard." One helpful rule for uncluttering (Frost and Steketee 1998) is called the OHIO rule: *Only Handle It Once*. This means that once an item is touched or picked up, it cannot be returned to the clutter pile. It *must* be placed in one of the three boxes.

As the act of discarding causes the most anxiety, discard items that provoke the least anxiety first. Using the SUDS scale, rate your level of discomfort (on a scale of 0–100) when you discard items in a specific area. First discard the items provoking the least SUDS score, say, between 0 and 40. Then move to more anxiety-provoking items in the 40–80 SUDS range. Finally, discard items in the 80–100 SUDS range. If discarding an item is much too distressing, place the item in the "Store" box. Be sure to find a place to store the "Store" box.

Establishing the following rule for the "Discard" box is helpful: If you don't have a specific use for the object now—such as displaying it—or you don't foresee a specific use for the object in the next six months, discard it. Keep only items that you know for a fact have a distinct use and function within your home.

Perhaps you feel particularly paralyzed by the fear of making a mistake. You may feel that you will mistakenly discard something you could use later. Ask yourself, "What is the worst thing that could happen if I never saw this object again?" Chances are, after your initial discomfort you'll forget you discarded it! It is helpful to make a distinction between what you "feel" you'd use, and what you *know for a fact* will be used for a distinct purpose within the next six months. Basing your decision on what you "feel" you "may" use someday (that almost always never comes) will only cause you to perpetuate your hoarding problem. A helpful change would be to base your decision on the facts only. Memorize this saying: *"When in doubt, throw it out!"*

Remember, your goal is to create *usable living space*, not a "museum of past memories." If you have a particular attachment to an item that takes up too much space, or you can't find a place for it, consider selling or donating it. Donating it will give you the satisfaction of knowing that someone else can enjoy it as you have! If the item is useless to everyone but you, remember that letting go of it does not erase it from memory. The memory will always be there. It is the clutter resulting from that item (and all the other items) that you truly don't need!

Step 7. Pace Yourself

Don't overdo it. This is a marathon, not a sprint. Don't wear yourself out. Pace yourself. Try the "30/30 system": First, identify a small area that you would like to work on—for instance, the sofa seats, the corner of a room, or the kitchen table. Set a kitchen timer for between 15 and 30 minutes, and then work on your identified area for that period of time. At the end of the 15 to 30 minutes, do something fun or relaxing for the next 15 to 30 minutes. Play on the computer, cross-stitch, play with your children, or enjoy a cup of coffee and read a magazine article you've been wanting to read.

Then, set your timer and continue uncluttering for another 15 to 30 minutes again. Continue in this way until the area is uncluttered. Some alternate time frames that work just as well are 15/15, 5/5, 5/30, and so forth. Work daily, but every few days take a day off so that you can look forward to a break. Reward yourself when you get over a big hurdle.

Step 8. When an Area Is Clear, Decide How the Cleared Space Is to Be Appropriately Used

Is the space to be used for work? Relaxation? Sleep? Entertainment? Storage? Decoration? Set about preparing the area for its intended use. If you can't decide, delay the decision until you get a clear idea of the manner in which the space will be used. But be sure to not clutter the area again! Establish a "no clutter" rule for the particular space should you be tempted to clutter the area again, and stick to it!

 **KEYS TO BREAKING FREE**

1. All decisions about saving, discarding, and organizing are to be made *only* by the person with the hoarding problem. Family members can be most helpful by letting the person with hoarding OCD make the decisions he or she needs to learn to make. Making decisions for the person with the hoarding problem won't help.

2. Family members should involve themselves only to the extent that they are invited to do so by the person with the hoarding problem.

3. During each uncluttering session, stay focused on one small area. Do not move into another area until you have completed the area you started. This way, you are more likely to see the positive effects of your efforts.

4. Play soothing, pleasing background music while uncluttering. It can make the job seem to go faster.

5. Severe hoarding behavior is associated with a number of neurological/psychiatric disorders, besides OCD (Damecour and Charron 1998). If you are unable to progress with the Self-Directed Program, obtain a thorough evaluation by a qualified neurologist or psychiatrist. Then, the proper help can be tailored to your specific hoarding problem.

CHAPTER 13

Two Steps Forward, One Step Back: Maintaining Your Gains and Managing Relapse

One of the things I learned the hard way was that it doesn't pay to get discouraged. Keeping busy and making optimism a way of life can restore your faith in yourself.

—Lucille Ball

As you work through the Self-Directed Program, you will have good days and bad days. As time goes on, you will have more and more good days. But what about the bad days? And what about those persistent OCD symptoms that just seem to linger no matter what you have tried to do?

It's Not Working: Common Problems

When you find yourself not progressing with your OCD problem, here are some common issues to explore.

Denial: "Maybe It's Not OCD"

People with OCD frequently lack a basic sense of trust in other people and their motives. Therefore, you may doubt your family members. You may doubt your doctor. No wonder OCD is called the *doubting disease!* It may even cause you to doubt that you have OCD! In some cases, denial may be due to overvalued ideas or having other illnesses in addition to OCD that affect your ability to view your problem objectively.

Righteous Denial, or The "Martyr Complex"

This type of denial is a form of self-deception that enables those with OCD to avoid change by rationalizing their symptoms to themselves and others with the notion that "I'm doing it for everyone's good." It shields sufferers from the painful impact of their OCD upon themselves and those around them. Secretly, their OCD becomes a source of pride and provides feelings of uniqueness, and superiority. The rationale goes something like this:

"How noble and wonderful I am! I'll gladly sacrifice my life doing endless rituals (washing, counting, checking, etc.) all day long as a small price to pay to protect those I love from danger and harm. And since no one close to me has yet to die or suffer, I must be doing something right!"

Overvalued Ideas

Do you really believe your obsessions are unreasonable? Do you feel the compulsions are necessary to prevent misfortune or tragedy? If so, you have attached too much importance to your obsessions and compulsions. List any overvalued or faulty beliefs you still hold on the blank lines below and refer to chapter 8 again to help you confront them.

_____

_____

_____

_____

Ritual Substitution

OCD can be sneaky in its persistence to re-invade your life. Sometimes people substitute one ritual with another one. Or they change a ritual by speeding it up or performing it differently. The new one is likely to be less obvious than the old one was. Instead of checking the locked door a second time, you may tap the door, wiggle the doorknob, or cautiously look at the door as you lock it. Or maybe you avoid checking the door altogether and let your spouse check it. Catch new, small rituals before they grow into big ones. On the blank lines below, list any substitute rituals that you may be performing. Add them to your list of symptoms to be confronted in your Self-Directed Program.

_____

_____

_____

_____

Protective Distraction or Blocking

You may be distracting yourself or blocking the full impact of the exposure so you won't feel the anxiety. This is self-defeating. You need to feel the anxiety rise, then fall, in order for exposure and ritual prevention to work. List the ways that you may be distracting yourself or blocking anxiety during exposure and ritual prevention.

_____

_____

_____

_____

Avoidance

Be on the alert for all forms of avoidance. Do you avoid "contaminating" your hands—or do you keep one hand clean at all times? This is avoidance. Treat avoidance as you do rituals—with exposure and ritual prevention. List situations you avoid, rather than attacking them with exposure and ritual prevention. For example, do you refuse to use glue or paste so you won't "contaminate" your hands? Or do you not leave the house so you won't have to be faced with locking the door?

_____

_____

_____

Minimizing the Importance of Rituals

- "That's not really a ritual."

- "I can stop it whenever I want."

- "I just don't think I need to stop doing it."

A ritual is a ritual. Once you have attacked your major OCD rituals, go after your smaller ones. You may feel satisfied with only partial improvement of your OCD. You may have gotten rid of the major problems, and now you feel ready to stop working the program. Don't do it! This will increase the likelihood that you will relapse. If you were able to break free from major symptoms, you can break free from the minor ones, too.

You Need the Right Medication to Progress Further

Those people who are not taking anti-OCD medication should seriously consider it. If you already are on medications, you may need to change the medicine. Discuss with your physician the possibility of a change in type, dosage, or possibly augmenting your present medication regimen. For information on finding a qualified physician to prescribe the medicine, refer to chapter 17.

Many people with OCD have fears about taking medication. Their fear may be due to overall discouragement, a previous negative experience with side effects, a particular physician, or just plain old fear of the "what ifs . . . ":

- "What if the medicine doesn't work?" (If one doesn't work, another probably will.)

- "What if I have to take it the rest of my life?" (Not a bad trade-off for a lifetime of relief.)

- "What if I get addicted to it?" (OCD medicines are not addictive.)

- "What if I take medicine and don't get to the root cause?" (Your brain chemistry imbalance is the root cause!)

Don't give up! Take a chance and try again! Use the knowledge you've gained from this book to locate professional help that can help you find the right medication for you. It's worth it!

Family Problems

Flare-ups of family conflict, distress, and divisiveness can seriously interfere with your ability to maintain your progress. Ironically, family members may quite unconsciously sabotage your progress. Remember, when the person with OCD gets better, the family that once organized itself around the OCD symptoms has to reorganize itself. For example, you and your family members may find yourselves with time left over every day that was once spent participating in OCD rituals. What now? Family members may feel unneeded and actually resent you now that you are breaking free from OCD.

Together you must develop stronger relationships that are not dependent on OCD symptoms. Review chapter 16 to help you and your family deal more effectively with the OCD. If problems persist, you may want to consider seeking family therapy from a qualified mental health professional who is familiar with OCD. Chapter 17 can help you make decisions involved in getting professional help.

Lack of Social Support

Often, the discouragement and isolation of having OCD significantly interferes with making progress with your Self-Directed Program. This is why attending an OCD support group can be so important. When you are sharing openly with others the daily struggles and dilemmas of the disorder, a support group's acceptance and understanding can make a huge difference in your recovery from OCD. Chapter 17 provides suggestions for how to locate an OCD support group. If there isn't one in your area, consider starting one yourself. Guidelines for starting a support group can be obtained from the Anxiety Disorders Association of America (see the Resources section at the back of the book).

Lack of Motivation

Breaking free from OCD is hard work and it takes time. You may sometimes find your motivation weakening. Here's a nice tip: on the blank lines below write several reminders about how your life would be different without OCD. Be very specific. Then, write these reminders on small pieces of paper and tape them onto the surfaces in various places in your home, such as the refrigerator door or the bathroom mirror. When your enthusiasm wanes and you're tempted to give up, read what you've written. It will provide a quick boost to stay on track.

_____

_____

_____

_____

_____

Here is another tip. Compose a short, five- to ten-minute self-motivational narrative and record it on a cassette tape. Below are guidelines for composing your own self-motivation tape. Fill in the blanks using your particular symptoms and situation. Then, read it as one complete narrative, using lots of expression to make it believable. You may want to ask your spouse, parent, or therapist to record it for you in one of their voices to make it more believable. Or, you may want to record it in your own voice. The choice is yours.

"Hello _____ this is _____ speaking. I've (you have) had OCD for _____ years (months). My (your) problem is _____ (washing, checking, repeating, ordering, intrusive thoughts, etc.). This problem has prevented me (you) from living life freely. It has affected my (your) life in the following ways: _____ _____ (list several ways that OCD has negatively impacted your life in the areas of family and work, goals, hopes, and dreams). While neither I (you) nor anyone else is responsible for the fact that I (you) have OCD, I am (you are) responsible for taking every possible step to overcome it. I (you) have reached a point in my (your) life where I am (you are) unwilling to tolerate OCD symptoms anymore. I am (you are) committed to achieving a life with OCD as but a small, insignificant inconvenience.

To achieve this, I (you) must change my attitude from one of hopelessness and defeat to one of hope and possibility. I am (you are) no longer willing to hide in shame, in a dark corner with my (your) OCD. I am (you are) a whole person. I (you) have many great qualities. I am (you are) (list at least five positive qualities/strengths in yourself).

_____

_____

_____

_____

_____

I am (you are) not just my (your) OCD symptoms!

Despite feeling alone with this disease much of the time, I (you) now realize I am (you are) not alone. There are literally thousands who understand what I am (you are) going through. I can (you can) reach out to these people for help and understanding. And for those who do not understand, I (you) must give up my (your) anger, cynicism, and negativity. I (you) must learn patience. With proper information and education, many others will some day see the light and understand what OCD is, one person at a time. I (you) must give up my (your) insistence that the world change just for me (you). I (you) can promote change when I (you) begin to change myself (yourself), my (your) attitude, and my (your) OCD.

To live life free of OCD, I (you) must strive to change my (your) attitude from mistrust to trust. Though I've (you've) been disappointed and discouraged before, I (you) must wipe the slate clean. I (you) may need to put my (your) faith in a doctor, expert, group, person, or program that will help me (you) to confront and face the things I (you) fear, and guide me (you) toward the light of recovery. Though it's extremely scary, I'm (you are) ready and willing to do whatever it takes. I'm (you are) committed wholeheartedly to this.

I am (you are) committed to following through with medication—to take it religiously and only according to the directions of my (your) physician. I'm (you are) now ready to live a clean life, free of medication abuse that will only negatively affect the delicate balance of my (your) brain chemistry.

I'm (you are) willing to confront my (your) fears daily using the principles of cognitive-behavior therapy. I am (you are) working to recognize the differences between my logical brain and my OCD. I (you) realize that the irrational messages from my OCD brain are false and the compulsions and rituals only a waste of time. The obsessive thoughts are mere "ghosts and goblins," a "bad grade-B movie"—they may look real for a moment, but they are not.

If I (you) let the OCD trick me (you) into reacting to the images and messages as if they were real, the OCD wins and it gains more and more control over me (you). I (you) win when I (you) resist the magnetic pull of the compulsive urge. And although there is great discomfort in not giving in to it, if I (you) wait, and hang on through the discomfort, the urge will eventually diminish on its own. I am (you are) now willing to fight the battle of my (your) life to be victorious against this monster! I (you) hate this OCD so much, and my (your) commitment to recovery is so very strong, that I'm (you are) willing to put everything on the line and withstand the urge to perform a ritual. I am (you are) daily gaining the strength and courage to begin to take charge of my (your) OCD."

Complicating Illnesses

Depression, other anxiety disorders, attention deficit disorder (ADD), Tourette's syndrome, body dysmorphic disorder (BDD), trichotillomania, eating disorders, and substance abuse are just a few of the disorders that can complicate breaking free from OCD. See chapter 15 for a discussion of this issue. In obtaining an accurate medical diagnosis from a qualified mental health professional (the first important step before starting the Self-Directed Program), it can be determined what other conditions may be present that can complicate the process of recovery from OCD. Once these conditions are identified, a program of help/treatment can be better tailored to your specific problems.

Alcohol or Drug Addiction

These addictions greatly complicate OCD treatment. The chances are good that you are self-medicating to relieve your anxiety symptoms caused by the OCD. However, in addition to causing drug interactions, unwanted side effects, and toxic reactions, illegal drugs and alcohol can neutralize a prescribed medication's therapeutic effects. Due to the health risks of mixing illegal drugs or alcohol with anti-obsessive-compulsive agents, the obvious first step is detoxification and treatment from mental health professionals who specialize in "dual-diagnosis" psychiatric disorders.

Relapse: It Will Happen!

Expect relapse—especially upon making progress! OCD naturally waxes and wanes—expect it to happen throughout your life. The sooner you face the issue of relapse and learn some tools to cope with it, the better. The following suggestions can help you manage and survive symptom relapse:

1. After several weeks or months, you may feel you have it made. You may even think that you are cured! Don't be fooled! OCD is sneaky and persistent. It will give you a "sucker punch" when you least suspect it. In fact, we believe that progress without relapse is not true progress! Successfully managing relapses is a skill that will help you throughout your life with OCD.

2. Relapse is not a sign of failure. It's an opportunity to further refine the skills you've learned in the Self-Directed Program. Be honest with yourself. When you slip up and perform a ritual, admit it and make plans for how you can resist the compulsion in the future. Get back on track and don't get down on yourself—people with OCD are so very self-critical! If possible, immediately re-expose yourself to the feared situation again, and move on.

3. Pay attention to small symptoms before they grow into big ones. As you break free from your major rituals, you may find yourself doing smaller, less intrusive rituals. These may seem like harmless behaviors, but they aren't. They reinforce your belief that you need your rituals to ward off harm. Some examples of smaller rituals are touching the wall as you pass through doorways or checking the stove before you go to bed, even though you may not have used the stove at all that day. These may be new rituals or they may be old ones you overlooked when the major rituals overshadowed them. List below any "little" OCD symptoms you may still need to conquer:

_____

_____

_____

4. Look for a common theme. You may find that you have an underlying fear that connects the various obsessions and compulsions in your life. Cherry's major problem was checking, but she also had problems with hand washing, hit 'n run fears, and fears that she had said or done the wrong thing. The underlying fear was that she would do something or say something that would harm another. Exposure was aimed at this central obsession that was behind her many various compulsions. On the blank lines below, list any common themes that may underlie your OCD symptoms.

_____

_____

_____

5. Don't compare yourself with others—with or without OCD. Your OCD is uniquely your own; therefore, your recovery will be uniquely your own!

6. It is a very common, normal experience of people who make significant progress with their OCD to go through a phase of feeling depressed about the time that was lost to OCD. There may be a period of deep sadness and regret about what your life might have looked like had you recovered sooner. Forgive yourself and others for mistakes of the past! Remember that without all of those blind alleys, you would never have gotten to the point you are at today. They were an inevitable part of your recovery. Use the painful past to further safeguard and solidify the recovery you have achieved now.

7. The goal of this book is progress with your OCD, *not* a perfect cure. Be realistic in your expectations for recovery from OCD. Recovery is a life long process with many ups and downs.

8. Sometimes it will be just plain hard. When you are working hard at maintaining your previous gains, you may become discouraged and frustrated, as if you've accomplished nothing at all! It is at these times that you must not lose sight of the real progress you've made. Even at difficult times, give yourself a pat on the back for how far you've come!

9. Appreciate your small victories against OCD. Daily minor improvements eventually add up to larger gains.

10. Expect new symptoms to crop up—catch them early. You will also begin to notice symptoms you hadn't noticed before.

11. Step up your Self-Directed Program for a few weeks before stopping, reducing, or changing your medications. Be even stricter than usual as you resist rituals. It will make the transition much easier.

Make CBT a Part of Your General Lifestyle

Make the Self-Directed Program, and cognitive-behavior therapy, a major part of your lifestyle. Find ways to fit exposure and ritual prevention into your everyday life. Resist checking the door every time you leave the house, for example. A healthy lifestyle will help you stick with your program.

Fill the Empty Time

You may find yourself with huge chunks of time that were once filled with rituals. This time needs to be filled with productive activity or the OCD symptoms will sneak back into your life. List below several activities in which you would like to participate. Make sure they are activities you enjoy doing in a relaxed, nonobsessive way. If they are not, you may find yourself avoiding them. These activities may include hobbies, volunteer work, paid employment, drawing, journal writing—the possibilities are endless. Make plans to fill the time you once dedicated to OCD.

_____

_____

_____

Eat Right

A healthy, well-balanced diet will help you get the most out of the Self-Directed Program. Your body is made up of many substances, including nutrients, neurotransmitters, hormones, and enzymes, that must work together for your brain to function properly. There is no magic formula to make your brain function at its best except this: eat a healthy, well-balanced diet.

There are, however, a few dietary changes that can help you to control particular symptoms. Avoiding alcohol will not only help reduce anxiety, but will also have a positive effect on depression, because alcohol is a central nervous system depressant. At times, many people with OCD feel anxious or overstimulated. Many of the medications used to treat OCD can have overstimulation and anxiety as side effects. Staying away from foods with caffeine, such as coffee, many sodas, and chocolate, can help.

One of the most important dietary changes you can make is to avoid refined carbohydrates, such as candy and pastries. Stay away from anything with sugar in it. Replace refined sugar with fruits and complex carbohydrates, such as whole grain breads and pasta. This will help to even out your moods and counteract two common side effects of anti-OCD medication: weight gain and carbohydrate craving.

If you are one of those who experiences these side effects, knowing that they may occur and anticipating them will help you to control the weight gain.

Get Adequate Exercise

Don't go overboard. You probably don't need heavy-duty exercise to get positive results. Check with your doctor before beginning an exercise plan. Regular exercise has many benefits. It helps with weight loss by burning calories, increasing metabolism, and decreasing appetite. Exercise can reduce muscle tension, enhance concentration and memory, improve sleep, and reduce depression, anxiety, and stress. Not to mention that as you begin to look better, you will feel better about yourself, your confidence and self-esteem will improve, and your OCD will decrease.

Reduce Stress

Some particularly stressful times include periods of change and transition such as moving, illness, birth, and death. Even the in-laws visiting from out of town can provoke considerable stress. Since your OCD tends to act up more during stressful times, the Self-Directed Program will be much more difficult to accomplish then. Expect this and give yourself a break during these times. Be extra-tolerant of yourself when life gets in the way of your program and just do your best.

Make plans for reducing the stress of everyday life and find new ways to cope with stress. Take time to relax by listening to music, talking with a friend, or participating in a hobby. Excessive fatigue tends to make OCD symptoms worse.

Getting adequate sleep and rest is vitally important. See your doctor if your OCD medication interferes with your sleep. There are many books to help you learn relaxation exercises, reduce stress, improve your diet, and develop a personal fitness program. Find one that fits your lifestyle and learn from it.

On the blank lines below, write your plans for stress reduction, relaxation, diet, exercise, and general lifestyle changes:

_____

_____

_____

_____

_____

CHAPTER 14

It Happens to Children Too

If you're trying to achieve, there will be roadblocks. I've had them; everybody has had them. But obstacles don't have to stop you. If you run into a wall, don't turn around and give up. Figure out how to climb it, go through it, or work around it.

—Michael Jordan

Research studies have shown that one-third to one-half of OCD cases identified in adults began during childhood. The disorder may develop in childhood, adolescence, or young adulthood (March and Mulle 1998). About 1 percent of children, that is, some 200,000 American children and teenagers, have OCD (Yaryura-Tobias and Neziroglu 1997b). In childhood OCD, a family history of OCD is more frequent than in adult onset OCD, leading us to believe that genetic factors may play more of a role in childhood OCD (Geller 1998).

Months or years may pass before parents become aware that their child has a problem because children often hide their obsessions and compulsive behaviors. They try to suppress symptoms until they are alone, or at least until they get home from school. Children have a very strong need to feel accepted by others, to fit into their peer group. The strange behaviors and senseless compulsions are embarrassing to children, so they hide them.

It is best to treat OCD early. The longer it goes untreated, the more generalized the symptoms become. They invade more and more of the child's life and make OCD more difficult to treat (Yaryura-Tobias and Neziroglu 1997b).

With treatment, OCD may or may not follow the child into adulthood. Some children may have minimal symptoms as adults, or no symptoms at all. Others go into remission; their symptoms disappear, but return during adulthood. OCD often changes over time. Symptoms experienced as an adult may be different from those experienced as a child. Why do symptoms sometimes disappear with treatment and then reappear later in life? No one knows for sure, but hormones and stress may cause changes in biological makeup, and thus affect the expression of OCD symptoms (Yaryura-Tobias and Neziroglu 1997b).

Children and Rituals: Could It Be OCD?

At some point during the course of the disorder, adults with OCD recognize that their obsessions and compulsions are excessive or unreasonable. This requirement for diagnosis does not apply to children. They may lack adequate cognitive awareness to make this judgment (March and Mulle 1998). When they are anxious and obsessing, even adults with OCD may not realize they are being unreasonable.

Most children go through developmental stages characterized by compulsive behaviors and rituals that are quite normal. These behaviors are common between the ages of two and eight, and seem to be a response to children's needs to control their environment and master childhood fears and anxieties.

Compulsive behavior and rituals are most evident at bedtime. Children's words and actions become more repetitive. They may undress and dress several times, touch objects in a certain way, fix bed linens, or say good night repeatedly (Pedrick 1999). The child may, for example, require that the parent pull down the shades a certain way, kiss the child, and utter a specially worded "goodnight." If the routine is disturbed, a temper tantrum might result. If a single detail is forgotten or not done properly, the parent may be asked to do it over.

Dr. Henrietta Leonard, who studied the relationship between children's developmental rituals, superstitions, and OCD, wrote that between the ages of four and eight the developmental rituals are usually most intense (Leonard 1989). Boys express their belief that girls have "cooties," a form of imagined contamination where boys may vehemently avoid being touched by girls. By age seven, collecting things (hoarding in OCD) becomes common. Sports cards, comic books, toy figures, jewelry, and dolls are among the most popular collectibles. Between the ages of seven and eleven children's play becomes highly ritualized and rule-bound. Breaking the rules of a game is likely to be met with cries of "No fair!" In adolescence, rituals may subside but obsessive preoccupation with an activity or a music or sports idol is common.

Superstitions are ritual-like behaviors often seen in normal children. These are forms of "magical thinking" in which children believe in the power of their thoughts or actions to control events in the world. "Lucky" numbers and rhymes, such as "step on a crack, break your Momma's back," help to bring about a sense of control and mastery.

These normal childhood rituals advance development, enhance socialization, and help children deal with separation anxiety. Young children's rituals help them develop new abilities and define their environment. As they mature and develop into adulthood, most of these ritualistic behaviors disappear on their own. In contrast, the rituals of the child with OCD persist well into adulthood. These rituals are painful, disabling, and result in feelings of shame and isolation. Attempts to stop doing the rituals result in extreme anxiety.

Parents of a child with OCD are frequently frightened, confused, and frustrated by their child's persistence and preoccupation with cleanliness, orderliness, or checking rituals. Often, parents react at the extremes of either intimidation or passive enabling. If parents overreact and attempt to interrupt the behaviors, the child may become hostile and extremely anxious. If parents give in to the rituals, the child never learns to confront his or her fears. Out of frustration, many parents give in to the child and may even reluctantly assist in the rituals, for example, doing repeated loads of the child's laundry because he insists his clothes are "contaminated."

Wanda's Story

Art is usually a favorite subject of third graders. But not for Wanda. Sticky glue and paste, wet paint, powdery chalk, smelly clay. It was a nightmare. Her only escape was the bathroom.

She breathed a sigh of relief, jumped up, and flew to the door each time her teacher let her go. She would hurry to the bathroom down the hall. Fifty steps. She counted them and knew exactly how many; fifty steps every time.

Then the ritual would begin. It was always the same routine. After turning on the hot water, she'd spread her fingers out and rinse them. Then she pumped soap into the middle of her left hand. She felt relief as she washed each finger over and over. Twenty times for each finger. After washing, Wanda would get a paper towel and carefully turn off the water, making sure she didn't touch the faucet with her hands. If she did, she washed again. More and more often, she had to wash several times.

Bathroom breaks became more frequent, not just during art class, but all day. Unwanted thoughts seemed to pop into Wanda's head without warning. At first, washing her hands helped for a few hours, maybe for the whole day. But the thoughts came more and more often. And hand washing relieved her anxiety for only a few minutes.

Mrs. Chester, Wanda's teacher, became concerned about Wanda's frequent trips to the bathroom and her red chapped hands. Daydreaming was a problem too. The other children were starting to snicker when Wanda didn't seem to hear directions or failed to answer a question when she was called upon. Wanda's mother was worried about her behavior. She had tried several lotions to treat Wanda's red chapped hands. None of them helped.

"If you'd just stop washing your hands so much, they would heal," she told Wanda. "Just stop!" Wanda's mother didn't realize that Wanda couldn't "just stop." She had never heard of OCD and assumed the constant hand washing was a habit Wanda could stop with determination and willpower. Or maybe she would grow out of it. Kids go through stages. When Mrs. Chester recommended a psychiatric evaluation, she took Wanda to their pediatrician immediately. He referred her to a psychiatrist who diagnosed OCD.

Tom's Story

Once an A student, Tom was now getting C's and D's with an occasional F. He knew the material, but he rarely handed in his homework. When he did, it was late. He failed tests because he couldn't finish them. There just wasn't enough time. Was he lazy? Rebellious? No: he had OCD.

Tom feared making mistakes. He checked his homework papers repeatedly until they were past due. Then he figured there was no use turning the homework in. Tests were nightmares. He answered two questions, then checked his work, two more questions, and he checked it again. And his letters had to be just right: neat, orderly printing with none of the letters or numbers touching each other. His papers were filled with eraser marks, sometimes to the point of wearing holes in the paper.

Tom didn't check just papers. His bedtime checking often took a whole hour. First he had to check the door, then the stoves, appliances, windows, closets, and under the beds. His parents told him he didn't have to check these things, but he persisted. When they argued with him about it, he started over. So they learned to leave him alone while he checked. Like Wanda's parents, they thought he would outgrow it.

Tom's parents tried to talk him out of his checking rituals. What would happen if he didn't check? His answers were vague. Someone could be hurt. He wouldn't be able to sleep. Most often the answer was "I don't know, I just have to check."

His mother took Tom to the doctor, who referred them to a psychiatrist. After a thorough examination, the psychiatrist explained that Tom had a neurobiological disorder called obsessive-compulsive disorder. As the psychiatrist explained what OCD is, Tom's mother began to cry. "Doctor, I gave Tom OCD! He learned it from me. I don't check, but I worry about things and I arrange everything in a certain order. Everything in all the drawers and cupboards has a specific place."

The psychiatrist explained that she had not given Tom OCD. Obsessive-compulsive disorder is not learned. It is a neurobiological disorder. Sometimes several people in a family have OCD because it seems to have a genetic basis. After the diagnosis was completed, Tom and his mother both began to work on cognitive-behavior therapy together.

Cleaning, Checking, Counting, and Children

Obsessions that focus on contamination are the most commonly reported obsessions in children (Piacentini and Grawe 1997). Fears of contamination by dirt and germs lead to avoidance of the suspected contaminates and to excessive washing. Children may wash themselves in a self-prescribed manner, more frequently, or for excessive lengths of time.

An obsession with contamination sometimes produces the opposite effect. In these cases, fear of contamination of body parts, personal objects, or both leads to a reluctance or outright refusal to touch those parts or items. Watch for untied shoes, unbrushed teeth, sloppy clothing, and uncombed, dirty hair, especially in a child previously known to be neat and well-groomed.

Checking compulsions are also common in children and adolescents with OCD. These compulsions are often precipitated by fear of harm to self or others, or the child may be troubled by extreme doubt. Checking such things as doors, light switches, windows, electrical outlets, and appliances may take up hours of time every day. The child also may spend hours on a school assignment that should take only an hour, or feel compelled to check and recheck answers on assignments, to the point that the checking interferes with the completion of homework.

Some children with OCD have obsessions with numbers. They may have "safe" and "unsafe" numbers, repeat actions a certain number of times, or repeatedly count to a given number. Children may also repeat actions, such as walking through a doorway, until it "feels right" or in a self-prescribed manner. Look for repetitious questioning, reading sentences over and over, and numerous eraser marks on papers from erasing and rewriting words or numbers.

Symmetry rituals may manifest by tying and retying shoes or constantly rearranging objects until they are even. Items must be arranged in such a way that they appear symmetrical to the child (Pedrick 1997). Many children with OCD have difficulty wearing certain clothes. Hypersensitivities to touch, taste, smell, and sound are also common.

Fear of harming others or self, excessive moralization, and religiosity are often seen in children with OCD. Children and teenagers with OCD frequently have a tendency toward perfectionism and rigidity or stubbornness. They are likely to have above-normal intelligence, a more adultlike moral code, more anger and guilt, a more active fantasy life, and to be disruptive.

The following list indicates signs of OCD in children. Keep in mind when reading this list that, by definition, OCD symptoms must be time-consuming, cause marked distress, or significantly interfere with one's life. These are simply signals that there may be a problem. If you notice such signs, discuss them with your child in a nonthreatening way. If OCD is suspected, consult a psychiatrist who specializes in treating OCD.

Signs of Obsessive-Compulsive Disorder in Children

- Being overly concerned with dirt and germs

- Frequent hand washing or grooming, often in a ritualistic manner; red, chapped hands from excessive washing

- Long and frequent trips to the bathroom

- Avoidance of playgrounds and messy art projects, especially stickiness

- Untied shoelaces, because they may be "contaminated"

- Avoidance of touching certain "unclean" things

- Excessive concern with bodily wastes or secretions

- Insistence on having things in a certain order

- Having to count or repeat things a certain number of times; having "safe" or "bad" numbers

- Repeating rituals, such as going in and out of doors a certain way, getting in and out of chairs a certain way, or touching certain things a fixed number of times. This behavior may be disguised as forgetfulness or boredom

- Excessive checking of such things as doors, lights, locks, windows, and homework

- Taking excessive time to perform tasks. You may find a lot of eraser marks on school work

- Going over and over letters and numbers with pencil or pen

- Excessive fear of harm to self or others, especially to parents

- Fear of doing wrong or having done wrong

- Excessive hoarding or collecting

- Staying home from school to complete assignments, checking work over and over

- Withdrawal from usual activities and friends

- Excessive anxiety and irritability if usual routines are interrupted

- Daydreaming (the child may be obsessing)

- Inattentiveness, inability to concentrate or focus (often mistaken for ADD)

- Getting easily, even violently, upset over minor, trivial issues

- Repetitive behaviors including aimlessly walking back and forth in the halls

- Unexplained absences from school

- Persistent lateness to school and for appointments

- Excessive, repetitive need for reassurance for not having done, thought, or said something objectionable

- Asking frequent questions, when the answer has already been given

- Rereading and rewriting, repetitively erasing

(Adapted and expanded from "Ministering to Students with Obsessive-Compulsive Disorder," by Cherlene Pedrick, R.N., in *Teachers in Focus*, February 1999.)

Help for Children with OCD

Adults usually seek treatment because OCD is interfering with their lives. Children don't always recognize that they have a problem. They are often brought to the doctor when they exhibit unacceptable behavior and difficulty in school. Young people and their parents need to know there is hope and help for children with OCD.

As with adults, the combined use of medication and cognitive-behavior therapy (CBT) is widely recognized as the best treatment for childhood OCD (March and Mulle 1998). Discuss your options with your child's medical team. You may want to try CBT alone first, or combine CBT with medication. In severe cases, you will probably want to start medication before beginning CBT. Together, CBT and medication are powerful tools in the struggle against OCD.

Now, let's summarize medication treatment for children. However, a detailed discussion of medication treatment of obsessive-compulsive disorder is beyond the scope of this book. Remember, this is only a review.

Medication

As with adults, five medications make up the first line of defense in medication therapy for children with OCD: Anafranil, Prozac, Zoloft, Paxil, and Luvox. It takes up to twelve weeks at the proper dose to determine whether a medication is going to work. If one medication doesn't work, there is a good chance that another will. It is necessary for the child to make an attempt at resisting OCD symptoms while the medication is being tried. This is where cognitive-behavior therapy can be very helpful, by training the child in the techniques of confronting obsessive worries and resisting compulsions.

If adequate symptom relief is not achieved, other medications can be added to one of the selective serotonin reuptake inhibitors (SSRIs) listed above. Medications sometimes added to SSRIs are buspirone, clonazepam, and neuroleptics. Anafranil may also be combined with one of the SSRIs.

Behavioral side effects, including irritability, impulsiveness, and hypomania, are sometimes a problem in taking anti-OCD medications. If these side effects occur, the medication dosage can be adjusted, or another medication may be tried. Adjusting dosages in kids is tricky as one medication is withdrawn and another is introduced. A period of adjustment, if required, sometimes results in erratic changes in the child's behavior.

Many children treated with anti-OCD medications have problems with bedtime and sleep. It is important to determine if this is due to the medication or related to OCD symptoms. Obsessions and compulsions are often worse at bedtime. Intrusive thoughts may make it difficult for the child to get to sleep. Increasing the medication and focusing cognitive-behavior therapy on these issues can help. On the other hand, anti-OCD medication can interfere with sleep. Moving the dose to earlier in the day or decreasing the amount of the dose may help. Occasionally, the doctor will add another medication temporarily to aid sleep.

Children metabolize medications quickly so it is especially important to give the prescribed medications at regular intervals. This helps to maintain even blood levels and reduces the possibility of withdrawal.

Adolescence is a turbulent time for anyone, and teens with OCD are no different. Rebelliousness, acting out behavior, and lack of compliance can interfere with the treatment of OCD. Acting out behavior, agitation, and hyperactivity can be exacerbated by medications used to treat OCD. Cognitive-behavior therapy may make it possible to reduce side effects by decreasing medication dosages.

Cognitive-Behavior Therapy

Children can benefit from the Self-Directed Program with a few modifications and additions that are discussed in this chapter. The first step toward recovery is recognizing that the struggle with OCD is a team effort. Parents, siblings, other family members, therapists, doctors, and school personnel all play important roles. Working through the Self-Directed Program should be a team effort.

We strongly advise a thorough psychiatric examination by a psychiatrist who specializes in OCD treatment before beginning the Self-Directed Program with children. A specialist can be found through the listings of the Obsessive-Compulsive Foundation (203-878-5669). It is advisable to use this program with a therapist, but parents may assist their children using only the program. It is extremely important for parents to enthusiastically participate in the program. Enthusiasm is contagious. It will help their children to develop a stronger desire to get better.

The next step is educating the child and parents about OCD. This encourages cooperation with examination and treatment. Going to the doctor is scary for children, especially if they suspect they are crazy or that they have a serious illness that can't be helped. Learning the truth—that there's hope and help—greatly reduces their anxiety.

It is important at the outset to clearly and plainly label the OCD as the problem, *not* the child. Defining OCD as a medical problem involving brain function rightfully relieves the child and the family of guilt. This will enable the parents to direct energy where it belongs—toward the treatment of OCD.

Explain OCD and cognitive-behavior therapy to children in words they can understand. Depict OCD as a brain chemistry problem with terms such as "computer glitch," "squeaky brain circuit," or "brain hiccup." For example, compare behavior therapy to a car alarm. Remember the first time you heard a car alarm? You were probably concerned that someone's car was being stolen. After checking out a few cars when their alarms went off, you undoubtedly realized they were usually false alarms. You began to ignore them. Now when you hear a car alarm, you note it, then go on with what you were doing. With exposure and ritual prevention, we note the obsessions and try to ignore the anxiety. With practice, we realize they are false alarms. When we ignore the anxiety and prevent the compulsions, the anxiety gradually subsides.

Keys to Helping Children Break Free from OCD

- Emphasize that your child is *not* the OCD. The horrible thoughts and persistent worries are not who the child really is. It is only OCD.

- Explain OCD in understandable ways. Compare obsessions to hiccups, for example. They attack without warning and aren't easily controlled.

- Try to understand exactly what obsessions and compulsions your child is experiencing. Often children and teens are horrified by their obsessive thoughts and compulsive behaviors, thinking they are evil. They try to keep them a secret, even from their parents and therapists.

- Help your child distinguish between obsessions and compulsions because each is treated differently: exposure is used for obsessions and ritual prevention for compulsions. Trying to prevent obsessions is counterproductive.

- Give OCD a name. Mr. Worry, Mrs. Clean, Washy, Mr. Gooey, Checkers, and The Count are a few suggestions, or Fred, Sam, Pete, Molly, or Jane. This helps to "externalize" OCD. Have fun with your child as together you come up with a name for OCD. Using the name when talking about OCD reinforces the idea that OCD is the problem, *not* the child. It becomes an enemy rather than a bad habit. Teens may find this too childish and may prefer to call OCD by its medical term. That's okay because it still helps to externalize the disorder.

- Make the exposure work fun and challenging. Mom, Dad, and the child should be on a team, working together to battle the opponent—OCD. Teachers, counselors, doctors, and therapists are also important members of the team.

- Use a reward system to encourage your child to persist with the hard work of fighting OCD. A sticker chart works well. At the end of each week, give prizes according to the number of stickers earned. Rewards can also be computer, TV, and telephone time, and outings with family or friends. Computer-printed certificates can be used for rewarding achievement of special milestones in the Self-Directed Program. Rewards help the child remember that OCD is the enemy and bolster pride for winning over the disorder.

- Children handle OCD much better when they understand it is not their fault, and that they are not alone. This is where a support group for kids with OCD can be extremely beneficial. Contact the OCD Foundation for information about parent/child support groups in your area.

- Note that following the Self-Directed Program may simply be too overwhelming for many children and their parents. In this case, professional treatment is in order.

Pediatric Autoimmune Neuropsychiatric Disorder Associated with Streptococci (P.A.N.D.A.S.)

Childhood onset OCD has been linked to group A beta hemolytic streptococci (GABHS), the bacteria that causes strep throat. It is thought that the body forms antineuronal antibodies against the bacteria. These antibodies then interact with basal ganglia neural tissue in the brain. It is believed that this leads to OCD symptoms or intensifies existing symptoms. In other words, the body forms antibodies that not only combat the streptococci, they also attack brain tissue.

Children whose OCD is the result of this relatively rare autoimmune reaction of the body show significant improvement or even the elimination of OCD symptoms when the streptococcus infection is treated with antibiotics (March and Mulle 1998).

It is important to get prompt treatment for strep infections. A sudden onset or worsening of OCD symptoms accompanied by an upper respiratory distress warrants a trip to the doctor to check for signs of strep infection.

OCD and Related Disorders

Children and teenagers with OCD often have one or more other disorders. Tourette's syndrome, tic disorders, ADHD, learning disorders, disruptive disorders, depression, and other anxiety disorders are the most frequently seen disorders in children and teens with OCD. Depression tends to begin after OCD has been established. It is possible that the depression forms in response to the OCD (Piacentini and Grame 1997; March and Mulle 1998).

When children have one or more other disorders, it is important to coordinate cognitive-behavior therapy for OCD with the treatments for the other disorders. Doctors, therapists, teachers, counselors, and parents need to work as a team with the child to gain the upper hand over OCD and its related disorders.

Tourette's Syndrome

Tourette's syndrome (TS) is an inherited, neurological disorder that affects about 200,000 people in the United States (Koplewicz 1996). It is characterized by repeated and involuntary body movements and vocalizations. These are called tics. Symptoms begin before the age of twenty-one and last at least one year. Boys are three to five times more likely to have TS. It occurs in only one out of every 2,000 children, but as many as 15 percent of children have transient tics (Koplewicz 1996). These are tics that come and go. In a minority of cases, the vocalizations can include socially inappropriate words and phrases. This is called coprolalia. These vocal outbursts are neither intentional nor purposeful.

Involuntary movements can include eye blinking, repeated throat clearing or sniffing, arm thrusting, kicking movements, shoulder shrugging, and jumping. It is common for children and adults with TS to also have symptoms of obsessive-compulsive disorder (McDougle and Goodman 1997).

Tourette's Syndrome Checklist

Tics can be described as sudden urges to make virtually any movement or sound. These can include:

- eye blinking
- squinting
- lip smacking
- neck jerking
- shoulder shrugging
- arm flailing
- nail biting
- foot stomping
- barking
- coughing
- hissing
- humming
- stuttering
- sudden changes of voice tone, tempo, or volume
- short often meaningless phrases
- swearing

Many children with TS or tic disorders also have another neuropsychiatric disorder, such as ADHD or OCD. When a child has both TS and OCD, it is important to distinguish between tics and OCD symptoms because the treatments differ. It is often difficult to tell if a symptom is a tic or an OCD ritual. The major difference is that a tic is preceded by a sensory feeling, while an OCD compulsion is preceded by a thought.

Attention Deficit/Hyperactivity Disorder (ADD and ADHD)

Attention deficit hyperactivity disorder is the most common neuropsychiatric disorder in children. Affecting 3 percent to 5 percent of children, it occurs four to nine times more often in boys (Koplewicz 1996). Attention deficit disorder and attention deficit hyperactivity disorder are characterized by inattention and impulsivity: that is, difficulty keeping attention focused on one thing and being susceptible to a broad range of distractions. When attention deficit disorder (ADD) is accompanied by hyperactivity (excessive uncontrollable fidgetiness and inability to sit still to the point of interference with home and school), the term attention deficit hyperactivity disorder (ADHD) is used.

For ADHD or ADD to be diagnosed, the symptoms must be:

- present before the age of seven

- chronic (greater than six months duration)

- present at home and at school

- causing significant problems for the child

- present more often than not

Other disorders can cause inattention, impulsivity, and hyperactivity. These include anxiety disorders, depression, and P.A.N.D.A.S.

These should be considered when symptoms begin after the age of seven (Swedo and Leonard 1998). Most neuropsychiatric disorders can cause problems with attention and concentration similar to ADD symptoms. Children with OCD often appear inattentive and distracted when they are focusing on obsessive thoughts. Although some children with OCD also have ADD and ADHD, OCD symptoms are frequently confused with ADD and ADHD. Children with OCD who appear preoccupied with obsessive thoughts and are performing compulsive rituals are often misdiagnosed with ADD and ADHD.

Stevie's Story

Until he reached fourth grade, Stevie was a good student. But in fourth grade he became more and more inattentive and seemed to be daydreaming much of the time. When he wasn't daydreaming, he was out of his seat. "Sit down, Stevie!" became his teacher's constant refrain. Homework was rarely turned in because it was usually lost or forgotten. He failed tests because he never finished them.

At first glance, it might seem obvious that Stevie had ADHD. But careful evaluation would show that he had OCD. What are the clues to this diagnosis?

- Stevie's symptoms didn't start until he was nine years old.

- Further evaluation revealed that when Stevie was "daydreaming," he was actually focusing on obsessive thoughts.

- Stevie often left his seat in class, but there was a purpose to his movements. His obsessive thoughts involved fear of harm coming to his mother. He felt temporary relief by touching the door, wall, or window. What looked like aimless wandering was his disguise for touching rituals.

- Tests were not finished and homework was lost because of constant checking. Nightly, he spent hours doing homework, checking and rechecking his answers. Frustrated, he usually threw his homework out rather than turn in an imperfect paper.

By now, you undoubtedly realize the importance of proper diagnosis for children with neuropsychiatric disorders. Research has revealed which medications and therapies work best for each disorder. The first step is getting the right diagnosis. Then, family support is important for anyone struggling with OCD, but especially for children. Chapter 16 will help you further as your family works as a team to fight OCD.

Family Help for Children with OCD

Family involvement is important to anyone striving to break free from OCD. For children, family involvement is crucial. The family needs to work as a team in the fight against OCD. There are some specific areas where parents can assist their children as they struggle with OCD. The rest of this chapter discusses those areas and offers practical, concrete suggestions for the parents of children with OCD to help them help their children.

Acceptance and Fairness

Obsessive-compulsive disorder is not fair! It is not fair for the child with OCD, and it is not fair for the child's siblings. The brothers and sisters of a child with OCD may feel that he or she "gets away" with misbehavior because of the disorder. They're probably right. Again, education will help the entire family understand OCD behavior. Giving OCD a name helps. Instead of blaming the child, brothers and sisters can blame OCD.

Help family members understand the difference between fairness and equality. We're all different. We all have different abilities, needs, and problems. The child with OCD just happens to have OCD as a problem. All children need to be treated according to their individual needs. This may not be equal, but it is fair.

Use examples from everyday life to illustrate this difference between equal and fair. Tommy may be in Boy Scouts. Would you buy a Boy Scout uniform for Sally too? Of course not, but if she is involved in soccer, you would buy her a soccer uniform. If Sally wears glasses, would you make Tommy wear glasses to make Sally feel better? Would you tell Sally she can't wear glasses because Tommy doesn't have glasses? Of course not, that wouldn't be fair. Point out that everyone is different. We don't treat everyone the same. Instead, we take each person's needs into account.

Now, list examples of the different interests and needs of each of your children: _____

_____

_____

_____

Do you treat them differently? Is that fair?_____

_____

_____

List examples of the different interests and needs of your children's friends. _____

_____

_____

Do your children play different games with different friends? Is that fair?_____

_____

_____

Structure and Discipline

Structure is very important in any family. Children feel more secure when they know they can depend on a daily routine. Obsessive-compulsive symptoms tend to become more severe when routines are broken by life changes. Vacations are fun, but they can bring with them a whole new set of obsessive thoughts and compulsive behaviors. A child with OCD does best in a structured environment, and such an environment will benefit the rest of the family also.

Set clear rules and expectations. Post them on the refrigerator. State the rules in a positive way. "You will do your homework before watching TV," instead of "No TV until your homework is done." "You may watch TV two hours today," instead of "No more than two hours of TV."

List some of your major family rules: _____

_____

_____

Schedule activities. They don't have to be the same activities every day, but let your child know what the schedule will be for each day. Try to have dinner, homework, and bedtime at the same time most days. What if things get off schedule? Help your child accept the changes. People with OCD tend to dislike change, but this is a part of life. We need to accept that.

What is your family schedule?

Breakfast: _____

Lunch: _____

Dinner: _____

Homework: _____

Bedtime: _____

Other activities: _____

_____

Stress exacerbates OCD, especially in the beginning of treatment. Try to maintain a non-stressful environment. A structured environment, positive attitude, and unconditional acceptance will greatly reduce stress in the home.

Sometimes children find it less frightening to be punished than to fight OCD. Misbehavior might be part of a compulsion or it could be avoidance behavior. Of course, misbehavior may or may not have anything to do with OCD. What about discipline for disobedience that has nothing to do with OCD? Use your stickers! Set up a sticker chart for all the children. Reward positive behavior with a sticker. These behaviors may be different for each child, depending on age, temperament, and personality. Get the children involved in setting goals and choosing behaviors to be rewarded. At the end of each week, give small rewards for the stickers. Accompany stickers and rewards with praise. Even when children don't earn a reward, give praise for trying.

Gather the family together. What behaviors do you want to reward? _____

_____

_____

List some things that could be used as rewards: _____

_____

_____

Children with OCD may need reminders when their behavior is out of control. Prearrange a signal to be used when behavior is inappropriate. Cherry's husband does this. When they are around other people and he knows she is engaging in compulsive behavior, he gives her a little nudge. Don't expect perfection. If they have a goal, people with OCD want to achieve that goal right now and to perfection. Help your child understand that perfection is not necessary.

Children with OCD misbehave in the same ways that children without OCD misbehave. They need discipline for misbehavior that they can control. As medication and cognitive-behavior therapy begin to help, the parents' expectations should be increased. Cherry admits she used her OCD as an excuse for inappropriate behavior for some time. "People will just have to understand—I have OCD." That was her excuse. Your child's therapist can help you decide which negative behaviors should be disciplined, and which should not.

Time-out is a great discipline technique. Choose a place for time-out. The bedroom may not be the best place. One minute time-out per year of age is a good rule of thumb. Time-out for a four-year-old would be four minutes, for example. Be clear about what behaviors will earn a time-out. "But when I give my child a time-out, I'm in time-out too," you say? This is true! Plan activities you can do during the time-out. For example, this would be a good time for you to read a magazine.

Homework

Even with kids who do not have OCD, the home can turn into a battlefield at homework time. It can be extra frustrating for many of the children with OCD. There are, however, some things you can do to help your child with homework.

To get an idea of what your child is facing, try to do a page of his/her homework with the obsessions and compulsions your child is experiencing. For example, write very neatly, erasing when a "mistake" is made. Mistakes might be any letters that touch each other or letters that are not neat enough. When you get halfway through, throw it away and start over. Or do a page of homework while repeating a worry your child might have. Repeat it over and over, at least every thirty seconds.

Think about what it must be like for children who demand perfection from themselves. Not only must they get the homework done, but it must be perfect. They must get an A. Surely, you can see how it might be tempting to avoid homework or not do it at all.

Schedule homework time. The time just before or just after dinner is a good time for many families. Plan quiet activities before homework. It's often hard to focus on homework after playing hard outside. Try not to let your child get involved in another activity that cannot be finished before homework is done. Many people with OCD have difficulty leaving things before they are completed.

Have a homework time every night—even when there is no homework. If your child does not have school assignments, encourage the child to read a book, write a story, practice math, or do some other learning activities. Or distribute "Mom's Assignments" or "Dad's Assignments." Children soon learn that these will likely be rougher than the ones their teachers give. Try to have at least thirty minutes of homework time. Help your child break assignments into small tasks to make them seem less overwhelming. Breaks between tasks might help. Let kids get up and move around a bit—without getting involved in another activity.

Homework should be done in the same place whenever possible. Provide good lighting and keep plenty of supplies nearby. Stock the area with paper, pencils, pens, crayons, scissors, whatever is frequently needed for homework. This reduces the need to go searching for things. Allow your child to help choose a place to do his homework. If homework cannot be done in the same place every night, put the supplies in a box that can be moved from place to place.

Communicate with the teachers. Is your child turning in assignments? Keep a log of how much time your child spends on homework. If it is excessive, maybe the teacher will reduce the amount of homework until the OCD improves some.

Reward completion of homework—without complaints and tantrums—with praise. Incorporate homework rewards into your sticker chart. Homework completion gets a sticker good toward rewards. Homework without complaint gets another sticker.

Finally, we would like to make a recommendation that *is* challenging. Turn off the TV and get the entire family involved in homework time. Mom and Dad can use this time to read or work on bills and paperwork. Nothing is more encouraging than seeing Mom and Dad reading books. If you have preschoolers, use this time to read a book to them or work on numbers, letters, and shapes.

Our family's homework time: _____ to _____

What will family members do when they don't have homework? _____

_____

_____

School

A child's teacher and school counselor are important team members in the struggle with OCD, but school personnel may lack knowledge about the disorder. As a parent, you can help by providing information to your local schools.

The booklet *School Personnel: A Critical Link*, by Gail B. Adams, Ed.D. and Marcia Torchia, R.N., is an excellent resource for school personnel on identification, treatment, and management of OCD in children and adolescents. It can be obtained through the Obsessive-Compulsive Foundation (see the Resources section at the back of the book), and is a valuable resource for teachers.

Teaching the Tiger, by Marilyn P. Dornbush, Ph.D., and Sheryl K. Pruitt, M.Ed., is an excellent handbook for school personnel involved in teaching children and adolescents with OCD, attention deficit disorder, and Tourette's syndrome. (See the Resources section.) Many of the principles can be applied to family situations.

If you have a local Obsessive-Compulsive Foundation affiliate or support group, request that a representative provide an in-service presentation at your child's school. This will help school personnel better understand OCD and its management. If no one is available, the video, *The Touching Tree* (also available through the Obsessive-Compulsive Foundation), will improve understanding. It is about a boy with OCD whose teacher recognizes that he has a problem and assists him in getting help.

Communicate with your child's teachers through visits, phone calls, and notes. Inform them of new symptoms, medication changes, side effects of medications, progress of cognitive-behavior therapy, and behavior for which to praise your child.

Portions of this chapter were adapted from a continuing education course for nurses, *Obsessive-Compulsive Disorder*, by Cherlene Pedrick, RN. It was published in 1997 by the National Center of Continuing Education, Inc., and is used here with permission.

CHAPTER 15

OCD and Company

Even if you're on the right track, you'll get run over if you just sit there.

—Will Rogers

Other psychiatric disorders resemble OCD. Like OCD, they include symptoms such as intrusive thoughts or repetitive behaviors. We call these OCD-related or OC Spectrum disorders (OCSDs). Some disorders have symptoms that are so similar to OCD that diagnosis can be difficult. These include trichotillomania, monosymptomatic hypochondriasis, body dysmorphic disorder, and some eating disorders. Other disorders, such as depression, also are seen frequently in people with OCD. These are called co-morbid disorders because they coexist with OCD.

Treatment of OCSDs and co-morbid disorders is challenging. The mental health professional must plan a comprehensive treatment strategy for each disorder. Often, more than one mental health professional must be involved.

Trichotillomania

Trichotillomania (TTM) is characterized by chronic, repetitive pulling of bodily hair. The sites of hair pulling include the scalp, eyelashes, eyebrows, axillary (armpit), body, and pubic area. Hair pulling tends to occur in episodes, exacerbated by stress, or sometimes by relaxation (when reading a book or watching television, for example). All other causes of hair loss, including medical and dermatological problems, must be considered and ruled out before the diagnosis of TTM is confirmed. People with TTM experience an increasing sense of tension immediately before pulling out a hair or when attempting to resist hair pulling. When the hair is pulled, they experience immediate feelings of pleasure, gratification, and relief.

Once thought to be rare with a prevalence of only .05 percent to .6 percent, recent studies estimate a prevalence of 2 percent to 3 percent of the population (Keuthen, O'Sullivan and Jeffrey 1998). As with OCD, people with TTM are often highly secretive about their symptoms. They may hide their symptoms by pulling hair from those parts of the body that are not easily visible, or they wear wigs or hair styles that conceal the head areas where their hair has been pulled.

Children with trichotillomania demonstrate a male to female ratio of 1:1. By adulthood however, more women are diagnosed with TTM. The onset usually occurs in childhood or adolescence, although it can begin before the age of one or as late as middle age. There appears to be a subgroup of TTM with an onset before the age of five (Keuthen, O'Sullivan and Jeffrey 1998).

Trichotillomania is often co-morbid with other psychiatric disorders, including anxiety disorders, depression, eating disorders, attention deficit disorder (ADD), Tourette's syndrome, and body dysmorphic disorder. Interestingly, one study observed a significantly higher rate of hair pulling in patients with both Tourette's syndrome and OCD than in patients with either Tourette's or OCD alone (Keuthen, O'Sullivan and Jeffrey 1998).

Complications of TTM are alopecia (baldness), infection, and scarring at hair extraction sites, slowed or stopped hair growth, and changes of hair texture or color. Some people eat the hair they have pulled and are at risk for stomach pain, gastrointestinal obstruction, peritonitis, and, in rare cases, even death (Keuthen, O'Sullivan and Jeffrey 1998). The repetitive arm and hand movements involved in hair pulling can cause carpal tunnel syndrome and other neuromuscular problems (Keuthen, O'Sullivan and Jeffrey 1998).

What causes trichotillomania? No one knows for sure, but evidence is growing that brain function and structure may be involved. The abnormalities found in the brains of people with TTM overlap with those found in OCD and Tourette's syndrome. Dr. Susan Swedo and her colleagues have proposed that streptococcus infections may be involved in some cases of early onset hair pulling (Keuthen, O'Sullivan and Jeffrey 1998).

Trichotillomania can be effectively managed with medication and behavior therapy. The most widely studied and used behavioral technique is habit reversal training (HRT) (Azrin and Nunn 1973). It involves several components, including the following:

- **Awareness training.** Monitor for one week all urges to pull, actual occurrences of pulling, when and where they occur, emotions just prior to pulling, and feelings immediately after pulling.

- **Identifying response precursors.** What do you do with your arms and hands just before starting to pull? Do you touch or stroke your hair? Touch your face, eyelashes?

- **Response detection procedure.** Describe and experience the muscles you use when pulling, using the following exercise: Extend arm straight and hold for 10 seconds. Slightly tighten muscles in arm. Then, begin moving clenched arm slowly toward your head. At one-quarter of the way, *stop* and hold for 10 seconds. At halfway, stop and hold for 10 seconds. At three-quarters of the way, *stop* and hold for 10 seconds. When your hand is at the top of your head, *stop* and hold for 10 seconds (*do not touch your hair*). Repeat entire sequence until the urge to pull subsides.

- **Competing response training.** Choose an incompatible behavior, one that prevents hair pulling. It must be a physically inconspicuous activity, such as muscle tightening, hand grasping, clasping or clenching an object, your belt, or a Koosh ball, for example. Practice for three minutes, then release for one minute. Then repeat five more times.

- **Identifying habit-prone situations.** Talking on the phone, watching TV, driving the car, for example. These are situations that typically trigger pulling. Practice competing responses in situations most likely to trigger pulling.

- **Relaxation training.** Training in deep muscle relaxation, deep breathing exercises. Use these when urge to pull strikes, or when stress is high.

- **Positive attention (overcorrection).** If pulling should occur, practice positive hair care by extensive brushing or by repairing eye makeup. This is intended as a mildly aversive behavior. If done consistently, it makes hair pulling less satisfying.

- **Prevention training.** Practice a competing response when and where pulling is likely to occur.

Other Methods for Managing TTM

Hair collecting is a mildly aversive technique and requires that the sufferer collect all of the hair that has been pulled. Cognitive-behavior therapy has also been used to help counteract maladaptive thought patterns that precede hair pulling. Case studies on the use of hypnosis with TTM indicate that hypnotic techniques can benefit some hair pullers. (Please note that hypnosis has been proven of *little* value with classic OCD.) The focus of the hypnotic techniques is on enhancing habit awareness and reinforcing behavioral control of the hair pulling.

More research is being done on this disorder and there is much hope. A good source for the latest information is the Trichotillomania Learning Center. Their address and website URL is in the Resources section. Information on TTM is also available through the Obsessive-Compulsive Foundation.

Body Dysmorphic Disorder

People with body dysmorphic disorder (BDD) have a preoccupation with a minor bodily defect or imagined defect which they believe to be conspicuous to others. It causes clinically significant distress or impairment in functioning. The name is derived from the Greek word *dismorfia*: *dis* meaning abnormal or apart, and *morpho* meaning shape. Before 1987, BDD was referred to as dysmorphobia, so named by psychopathologist Enrique Morselli in 1891.

Most people with BDD are not "ugly" at all. Their physical appearance is likely to go unnoticed. They are usually shy, seldom make eye contact, and have low self-esteem. They often go to extremes to camouflage their imagined ugliness, wearing sunglasses, hats, or bulky clothing.

Several studies have found that almost 90 percent of BDD obsessions are face-related, followed by hair, skin, and eyes (Yaryura-Tobias and Neziroglu 1997b). But any body part can be the focus of concentration. Often, people with facial and skin dysmorphia pick and dig at their skin. Some have concerns involving body symmetry. Others have muscle dysmorphia, a type of BDD in which patients worry that their bodies are too small and puny. Usually just the opposite is true: typically, they are large and muscular. BDD by proxy is a form of the disorder in which a person obsesses about supposed flaws in another person's appearance.

People with BDD frequently lack insight or awareness of their problem. They frequently seek cosmetic surgery or dermatologic treatment for their perceived physical defects and are highly unlikely to seek help from a mental health professional until depression becomes a significant factor in their distress. There is often a high degree of overvalued ideation or even delusional thinking. In addition to the obsessional nature of BDD, one study found that 90 percent of patients with the disorder performed one or more repetitive and time-consuming behaviors (Phillips 1998). These are behaviors intended to examine, improve, or hide imagined defects, such as mirror checking, grooming, shaving, washing, skin picking, weight lifting, and comparing self with others. People with BDD either may seek reassurance from others or try to convince others of their defect.

Body dysmorphic disorder usually begins in adolescence, though it can start in childhood. There seems to be a slightly higher prevalence in males—one large study reported 51 percent were men. Obsessive-compulsive disorder is common in people with BDD, occurring in over 30 percent of patients. In one study, depression had a 60 percent rate of occurrence (Phillips 1998).

Although most patients with BDD are reluctant to take medication, serotonin reuptake inhibitors (SRIs) are the medications of choice to treat BDD. Successful medication therapy can result in a decrease in the time spent preoccupied with the imagined defect, less time occupied with associated compulsive behavior, less distress, and reduced depressive symptoms. Often, patients gain improved insight into their BDD problem. As with OCD, relapse is usually a problem when medication is stopped.

Preliminary studies suggest that cognitive-behavior therapy can be helpful for people with BDD. Exposure and response prevention combined with cognitive techniques were effective in 77 percent of BDD patients in one study (Phillips 1998). Often the challenge is getting someone to accept psychiatric treatment rather than dermatological, surgical, or other medical treatments. More research into BDD is needed. But there is hope. There are good treatments available for BDD.

Depression

As mentioned in chapter 2, depression often occurs with OCD. It is the most common co-morbid disorder. Many people with OCD suffer from some degree of depressive symptoms ranging from mild ("the blues") to severe, life-threatening depressive illness. This is characterized by strong, persistent feelings of sadness, hopelessness, helplessness, loss of interest in normal activities and pursuits, lack of energy, impaired sleep and appetite, and frequently suicidal feelings.

Controversy has existed for many years over whether depression is a separate disease, independent from OCD, or a secondary disease, caused by the OCD itself. In one study, 56.9 percent of patients with OCD were diagnosed with a major depressive episode first. Yaryura-Tobias and Neziroglu estimate that 90 percent of OCD patients have depression secondary to their OCD (1997b). Many of the same medications used to treat depression also work well with OCD. This leads us to believe that patients with obsessive-compulsive disorder and depression may share some of the same brain structure and neurochemical abnormalities. Undoubtedly, further research will reveal more about the connection between OCD and depression. Perhaps depression is a natural outgrowth of a devastating disease such as OCD. Indeed, it can be depressing to suffer from OCD!

The presence of severe clinical depression complicates the treatment of OCD. Severely depressed OCD patients cannot benefit fully from the Self-Directed Program due to the learning and memory deficit symptoms typical of clinical depression. The diagnosis of depression is best made by a licensed mental health professional who may use a variety of clinical tools to assess the likelihood and severity of depression. A self-administered questionnaire called the Zung Self-Rating Depression Scale (Zung 1965) follows. It can help you determine whether or not you should consult a mental health professional about depression in addition to OCD.

Zung Self-Rating Depression Scale*

Instructions: For every statement in the left column, circle the number of the response that describes how you presently feel.

1. I feel downhearted, blue, and sad   1) Never, 2) Sometimes, 3) Most of the time, 4) All the time

2. Morning is when I feel the best   1) Never, 2) Sometimes, 3) Most of the time, 4) All the time

3. I have crying spells or feel like crying   1) Never, 2) Sometimes, 3) Most of the time, 4) All the time

4. I have trouble sleeping through the night   1) Never, 2) Sometimes, 3) Most of the time, 4) All the time

5. I eat as much as I used to — 1) Never, 2) Sometimes, 3) Most of the time, 4) All the time

6. I enjoy looking at, talking to, and being with attractive women/men — 1) Never, 2) Sometimes, 3) Most of the time, 4) All the time

7. I notice that I am losing weight — 1) Never, 2) Sometimes, 3) Most of the time, 4) All the time

8. I have trouble with constipation — 1) Never, 2) Sometimes, 3) Most of the time, 4) All the time

9. My heart beats faster than usual — 1) Never, 2) Sometimes, 3) Most of the time, 4) All the time

10. I get tired for no reason — 1) Never, 2) Sometimes, 3) Most of the time, 4) All the time

11. My mind is as clear as it used to be — 1) Never, 2) Sometimes, 3) Most of the time, 4) All the time

12. I find it easy to do the things I used to do — 1) Never, 2) Sometimes, 3) Most of the time, 4) All the time

13. I am restless and can't keep still — 1) Never, 2) Sometimes, 3) Most of the time, 4) All the time

14. I feel hopeful about the future — 1) Never, 2) Sometimes, 3) Most of the time, 4) All the time

15. I am more irritable than usual — 1) Never, 2) Sometimes, 3) Most of the time, 4) All the time

16. I find it easy to make decisions — 1) Never, 2) Sometimes, 3) Most of the time, 4) All the time

17. I feel that I am useful and needed — 1) Never, 2) Sometimes, 3) Most of the time, 4) All the time

18. My life is pretty full — 1) Never, 2) Sometimes, 3) Most of the time, 4) All the time

19. I feel that others would be better off if I were dead — 1) Never, 2) Sometimes, 3) Most of the time, 4) All the time

20. I still enjoy the things I used to do — 1) Never, 2) Sometimes, 3) Most of the time, 4) All the time

Scoring:

For questions 1, 3, 4, 7, 8, 9, 10, 13, 15, and 19, give yourself: 1 for *Never*, 2 for *Sometimes*, 3 for *Most of the time*, and 4 for *All of the time*. For questions 2, 5, 6, 11, 12, 14, 16, 17, 18, 20 give yourself a: 4 for *Never*, 3 for *Sometimes*, 2 for *Most of the time*, and 1 for *All of the time*. Then, total your score. For your rating:

Rating = (Your Score)/80 x 100
Divide your score by 80, then multiply by 100. This number is your depression rating.

If your rating is:

Below 50 = within the normal range
50–59 = Presence of minimal to mild depression
60–79 = Presence of moderate to marked depression
70 and over = Presence of severe to extreme depression

Use this scale to determine where you might stand. If you find that you are moderately to severely depressed, take this score into your doctor immediately and discuss it with him or her. Effective treatment for depression is widely available. Lifting of depression can pave the way for you to break free from OCD.

* Printed with permission from the American Medical Association. Copyright 1965.

PART IV

CHAPTER 16

OCD Is a Family Affair

Alone we can do little; together we can do so much.

—Helen Keller

The family plays an important role in OCD treatment and recovery. Family stress and dysfunction, while not a direct cause of OCD, can powerfully affect the person with OCD and the severity of symptoms (March and Mulle 1998). Similarly, OCD in the family can contribute to disruption, discord, and serious misunderstanding (Yaryura-Tobias and Neziroglu 1997b).

What often gets lost is that *OCD, not the person suffering from it,* is the enemy. Fighting it and managing OCD, therefore, must be a team effort. This chapter will help family members to understand what it takes to support and encourage the person with OCD toward healing.

Support Starts with Each Family Member

Coping with OCD within the family unit is largely determined by each family member's capacity to deal with discomfort, frequent confusion, and conflicting emotions toward the disease and the person with OCD. Because OCD can be so taxing on the emotional resources of the family, at times members may become overwhelmed and resort to attitudes and behaviors that are destructive to the person with OCD, such as ridicule, neglect, or outright hostility.

Inadvertent reinforcement of the OCD symptoms is another common outcome of the tension that can arise within the family. By using the following strategies, however, the family can come together to promote recovery and optimize wellness in the person with OCD.

Get the Facts First

If a member of your family is exhibiting the signs and symptoms of OCD, you must first learn as much as you can about the disorder. Much anxiety about OCD is allayed by acquiring good, solid facts and information about the disorder. Talk frankly to trusted professionals and experts about your family's problem. Become an "expert" in the disorder that is affecting your family. There is more quality information about OCD available now than ever before. The

Appendix contains a short introduction to OCD and its treatment. This is a good starting point for family members. The first chapters of this workbook build on that basic information and will help you understand what the family member who is working his or her way through the Self-Directed Program is experiencing.

Quit the Blame Game

Shame, guilt, and self-blame among family members are impediments to effective management of OCD within the family. Note that for decades it was fashionable to blame the cause of OCD on inadequate child rearing practices, a chaotic family environment, and the like. If only human behavior was so simply explained!

The fact is there is not a shred of evidence that early family interactions directly cause OCD (March and Mulle 1998). As we explained in chapter 2, genetics and biology are the likely culprits when someone has OCD. A family affected by OCD should feel no more shame about it than they would if someone in the family had diabetes, heart disease, or any other chronic medical condition.

Get OCD Out of the Closet

Often, family members and caregivers feel a collective sense of shame about having OCD in the family. They fear others may regard them with scorn, as bad parents, brothers, sisters, or children. Don't allow the ignorance of others to dictate your feelings about having someone with OCD in your family. Talk openly about it with people who you believe are capable of understanding and support. Find an OCD support group in your community and start learning more about OCD.

Share the information you will find in the Appendix with your extended family members. It is clear and concise enough for those who just want to know the basics. There is an old phrase used in Alcoholics Anonymous that may apply here: "You are only as sick as your secrets!"

Manage Your Negative Feelings

Once you have achieved some understanding of OCD, the next step is to manage your negative feelings about the presence of OCD in the family. These include anger, resentment, and frustration.

1. **Let go of anger**. Work on accepting the facts of your family as they are, yet find the strength and wisdom to change what you can. Acceptance does not mean doing nothing. It means spending your energies finding effective solutions, not wasting energy being angry and resentful. These emotions only waste your valuable energy and time. Work on letting go of the anger and finding forgiveness for the sufferer and, most of all, yourself! You did nothing to cause it, or to "deserve" this. It just is.

2. **Control the feeling that others should understand also**. No one is obligated to feel as you feel or do as you do just because you want them to. Arm yourself with facts and solid information and bring these educational materials into your home. Share the information with interested family members in a gradual, nonthreatening way.

3. **Expect and accept resistance**. Because of the lack of understanding about mental illness, many family members have their own preconceived ideas about what causes OCD. Therefore, *expect and anticipate resistance to even the best, most qualified sources of information.* You can try, but don't expect to change entrenched attitudes. Resist viewing the most antagonistic and biased individuals as "wrong" and therefore "bad," but rather as "yet to be educated." Over time, patience and persistence can change even the most entrenched attitudes.

4. **Be a good listener**. Don't lecture. Siblings of a child with OCD often have deeper issues, such as unexpressed anger, guilt, or resentment that may require professional guidance. By talking about these feelings and learning more about OCD they are more likely to resist making hurtful remarks and criticizing.

How Family Members Can Help the Person in the Self-Directed Program

Once the person with OCD begins the Self-Directed Program, family members can play important roles in that person's progress and recovery. People with OCD often need a support person at home to assist them with the exposure tasks and homework assignments. However, before you take on the role of support person, learn what will be expected of you. This will be a long-term project, often requiring regularly scheduled time to help with home practice. Are you prepared for such a serious commitment?

Family members and friends who are not taking on the role of support person can also help the person with OCD. This next section is for anyone who cares for someone with OCD.

Communicate with the Health Care Team and with Each Other

Keep communication simple and clear. OCD symptoms wax and wane. Keep this in mind when the OCD seems worse than usual. Lower your expectations for the time being and encourage everyone in the family to express their feelings about how the OCD is affecting the family. Together, remember other times when the OCD seemed especially bad, but then things got better.

If the person with OCD is a child, you will want to establish close communication with the health care team. Adults with OCD are a different story. Ask the person with OCD how much he or she wants you to be involved. Ask other members of the family for their opinions, too. If the person with OCD gives consent, contact any therapists treating your loved one. Ask about what role you can play in the treatment process.

Don't Participate in OCD Rituals

One of the negative ways caregivers and family members deal with the disruption caused by OCD behaviors in the family is to participate in the OCD. Participation, also called "enabling," is the family's way of "keeping the peace" in the face of the sufferer's persistent demands for immediate relief from obsessive worries. Often, enabling is a last-ditch path of least resistance for dealing with compulsions that are out of control and extremely disruptive to the family. However, the unfortunate, disastrous result of enabling/participation in OCD rituals is that OCD symptoms are reinforced and strengthened with the family immersed within them.

Typical Ways Family Members Participate in OCD Behaviors

- Doing the laundry for the person with OCD, who treats unworn or briefly worn clothing as "contaminated" and therefore in need of constant and unnecessary laundering.

- Responding with "You don't have AIDS and you won't get sick" every time the person with OCD—who never engages in unsafe behaviors—repeatedly asks whether he or she might be sick with the virus.

- Reassuring the person with OCD—who takes hours checking door locks and appliances to ensure they are completely shut and "off"—that all items are secure or locked, or assisting with the checking rituals.

- Reassuring repeatedly that no pedestrian was harmed while riding in the car with the person with OCD who obsesses about the possibility of hitting someone while driving.

- Helping the person with hoarding obsessions who fears throwing away something "important" by examining each piece of trash before throwing it away.

- Changing your clothes in the garage before coming into the home to avoid causing anxiety to the person with OCD fearful of "contaminating" the house with outdoor "contaminants."

- Avoiding the purchase of chemicals, particular household products, or pesticides because the OCD sufferer believes these to be dangerous or "contaminated."

- Giving in to persistent, often exhausting, requests by the person with OCD for verbal reassurance that something is "right" or "okay" or "correct" or "not bad, harmful or dangerous." Until the "right" response is provided, the request may be repeated over and over.

- Trying to reason the OCD away. By offering endless reiterations of facts or theories about how AIDS is caught, for example, or how unreasonable the obsessive concern is, the family member only neutralizes the obsessive thought, and thereby encourages its persistence.

With the above-described behaviors in mind, take a close look at your family situation and your individual responses to the person with OCD and write on the blank lines below whatever participation behaviors you and/or family members have engaged in with the person with OCD:

1. _____

2. _____

3. _____

4. _____

5. _____

6. _____

7. _____

8. _____

9. _____

10. _____

How to Stop Enabling OCD

Should you suddenly just quit giving reassurance and participating in rituals? Probably not. Stopping your participation without first enlisting the cooperation of the person with OCD is likely to cause tremendous anxiety and disruption. The best plan of action is to collaborate on a plan *with* the person with OCD *before* beginning to disengage from rituals. Ideally, this is best accomplished at the time the sufferer is ready to begin the Self-Directed Program. The assistance of a counselor or therapist familiar with OCD can be especially useful here.

Guidelines for Disengagement

1. Anticipate that the person with OCD will see the anxiety go up for a while before it goes down. Heightened anxiety in the patient may be disruptive at first, but it's a sure sign of change. Stay cool.

2. Decrease your participation gradually, though not too gradually. For example, cut your participation in half to start, and decrease by one-half every week or two. Use the Weekly Plan for Disengagement form below to plan your strategy.

3. Plan on completely stopping all participation in compulsive rituals after an agreed-upon period of time. Make this nonnegotiable.

4. Discuss all disengagement plans openly with the person with OCD before implementing them. No surprises.

5. Expect a certain amount of resistance to your decreasing participation in rituals. Resistance may range from mild discomfort to anger, rage, even violence, though this is rare. Violent behavior should never be tolerated.

6. Explain your reasons for disengagement clearly and honestly to the sufferer. Remain calm, yet firm and straightforward. It is very important to respond in a consistent manner.

7. When demands to neutralize anxiety occur, family members should state in a calm, reasonable, and low-keyed manner any of the following:

   - "I must refuse to help you neutralize your anxiety because it is destructive to your health in the long run."

   - "Because I love you, I refuse to participate in harmful behavior."

- "While I might be helping you feel better in the short run, in the long run I'll only be harming you."
- "I know it's hard and may be upsetting to you, but it's best if I not do that ritual for you."
- "Dr. _____ has instructed me to not participate and he/she knows what he/she's talking about and we decided to trust the doctor's judgment."

8. If total nonresponse to requests for reassurance is unrealistic, agree with the sufferer that you will respond to requests *only once* per day. Use this agreement as a stepping-stone to eventual total prevention of all reassurance behaviors.

9. Prior to beginning the disengagement, fill out the OCD Enabler's Declaration of Independence. Make a copy, sign it, and place it in a prominent place within your home.

OCD Enabler's Declaration of Independence

Date _____

Dear _____

I'm offering this to you from a deep and profound sense of respect, love, and acceptance that you have an illness that has caused you to be very difficult to be with. As someone who has been involved in your OCD symptoms, I have come to realize that by participating in your OCD, I have not only hurt myself, I also have contributed to your OCD problem without meaning to do that. Some of the ways that I've been enabling you are these:

- *Assisting in or carrying out your compulsive behaviors in order to make you more "comfortable" and to shield you from discomfort*
- *Assisting in or carrying out your compulsive behaviors in order to keep "peace and quiet" in the family*
- *Assisting in or carrying out your compulsive behaviors because I was afraid you would*

  _____

- *Lying to myself and others both about your condition and the pain your OCD symptoms have caused*
- *Making my life into an unhealthy extension of your illness. In trying to help you and relieve your pain, I have gotten further and further from the person I really am, and I have unintentionally reinforced your illness and my entrenchment in it*

I hereby place you on notice that from this moment on, I will lovingly and respectfully refuse to assist in any of your compulsive rituals. I will lovingly decline to satisfy your compulsive requests for reassurance. This means that I love you more than I can describe. It means that my belief in you and your capacity for health and wellness is so great, so overwhelming, that I will hold to this with the greatest resolve.

I believe in you!

Signed

Date

How to Deal with Obsessive Reassurance Seeking

Obsessive reassurance seeking is a particularly distressing and annoying symptom of OCD with which family members become entangled. It usually occurs in the following sequence:

1. **Obsessive worry intrudes**. The person with OCD experiences an obsessive thought that could be about almost any frightening or uncomfortable idea or notion such as:

   - "Maybe I'll get AIDS and die a slow death."
   - "What if my parents leave me, get divorced, or die?"
   - "What if the pantry is not clean and I become contaminated?"
   - "Maybe there are bugs under the counter and they'll get on my food!"

2. **A jolt of anxiety**. At the moment the thought strikes, severe discomfort occurs. Under extreme anxiety, people with OCD have an extremely limited capacity to "self-soothe" or resolve the discomfort of the thought through productive, logical self-talk or self-reflection.

3. **Urge for tension relief**. Instead of self-soothing, they experience an uncontrollable urge to obtain immediate relief from outside themselves in the form of a question posed specifically to receive verbal reassurance from a trusted source of comfort or authority figure.

4. **Getting the "fix."** A family member, sensing this severe anxiety, offers the verbal reassurance intended to calm the person down such as: "No, you won't get AIDS," or "Mommy will be right back," or "Don't worry, it's clean." However, the response often must be repeated, over and over again, until the anxiety of the thought is neutralized, and the person with OCD feels "better."

5. **Over and over again**. Then the cycle starts over. Over time the annoying pattern becomes ingrained, and becomes a learned habit that is difficult to break.

Use Humor to Disengage from Obsessive Reassurance Seeking

Although no laughing matter, demands for reassurance about an obsessive thought are often best met with a humorous remark to lighten the tension. Avoid an angry and critical tone. Some examples follow:

If the person with OCD asks: Did I check the door locks enough times?

Answer: *I think Ft. Knox could use your talents* or *We'll just donate everything we own to the Lonely Home-Invaders Society.*

If the person with OCD asks: Am I a good person? Did I harm anyone (anything)?

Answer: *You left a trail of death in your wake. You and Jack the Ripper should compare notes.*

If the person with OCD asks: Are you coming back?

Answer: *No, I'm going to Hollywood to make it big.*

If the person with OCD asks: Will I get sick from AIDS?

Answer: *We might as well make funeral arrangements now.*

If the person with OCD asks: Did I hurt your feelings?

Answer: *Yes, and I'll just never recover from it.*

Your Plan to Disengage from Participating in the OCD

Now that you understand better how participation in the OCD is harmful, even destructive, describe your personal plan to stop participating in and enabling OCD in the family.

The rituals my family members and I have been participating in or enabling are: _____

_____

_____

We've been neutralizing the anxiety of the person with OCD in the following ways: _____

_____

The feelings that have kept me involved as an enabler to the OCD are: _____

_____

_____

Weekly Plan For Disengagement

	Rituals I Will Disengage From	How Much Will I Reduce Involvement? (Be specific)	Did the Sufferer Collaborate? Y or N
Week 1			
Week 2			
Week 3			
Week 4			

Additional Guidelines for Dealing with OCD in the Family

- **Encourage compliance with medication and cognitive-behavior therapies**.

Due to side effects, the person with OCD may need reminders to take his/her medication. If necessary, place medications in a weekly reminder box to avoid missed or extra doses. Encourage the sufferer to follow the physician's directions. Sometime this means to "hang in there" with the medication even when side effects are bothersome and symptom relief hasn't yet begun. Patience with the medication is a must!

Encouragement will also be needed as the person with OCD works through the Self-Directed Program. Familiarize yourself with the program so you can be an effective cheerleader. It is hard work and often discouraging, but patience and persistence will be rewarded by a better quality life for the whole family.

- **Be supportive and encouraging**.

Setting expectations too high sets people up for failure. However, not progressing fast enough can be discouraging. Help your family member set reasonable goals. Recognize and encourage even small signs of success. Avoid comparisons with others who have OCD or with family members without the disorder. The person with OCD probably already has a low self-image.

OCD is demoralizing. People with OCD are often ashamed of their behavior. They know it is irrational. Often shame about the behavior results in shame about the self. The thought, "OCD makes me do weird things," turns into "I am weird." People need to know they are not "weird" or "crazy" because of their OCD behavior. They are not their OCD. Separating their wonderful selves with their many positive attributes from the OCD is important. Offer praise for positive behavior. Reward even small steps in the Self-Directed Program with praise.

- **Reduce stress.**

Reducing stress is especially important during early treatment. Keep the family routine as normal as possible. Stress exacerbates OCD symptoms. Even happy, satisfying events such as vacations can cause an increase of symptoms.

- **Become familiar with signs of relapse.**

Chapter 10 may help you and your family member with OCD to recognize the signs of worsening OCD symptoms. It will also help maintain the gains made in the Self-Directed Program.

- **Take care of *yourself*.**

Taking good care of yourself is perhaps the most important guideline. OCD tends to take over one's entire life, then proceeds to dominate family life. Don't let OCD rule your home. Take time out to get away by yourself. Care for your needs and the needs of other family members. Join a support group for family members of people struggling with OCD. Such a group will help you discover how others are dealing with OCD in their families and also help you find the strength, courage, and wisdom to intervene effectively.

- **Turn off the TV!**

Television, originally intended to entertain and inform, has become a breeding ground for fear and worry in people with OCD. Tabloid TV news programs and so-called human interest programs attract and keep viewers watching by presenting stories purposely intended to instill some degree of fear of harm or potential danger in the world.

People with OCD tend to absorb fear the way a sponge absorbs water. They tend to overestimate risk and misperceive the presence and likelihood of danger and harm, and in many cases find it difficult to objectively appraise the true risk-potential depicted in a well-intended, provocative TV news segment. Thus, they are particularly susceptible to overreaction to provocative news stories, especially if the story is presented in such a manner as to appear highly credible and authoritative.

For example, they find particularly disturbing stories about a hidden, unsuspected danger of disease affecting children, or unforeseen dangers and pitfalls inherent in previously unsuspected, innocuous activities of day-to-day life. Such stories can trigger fresh, new obsessions or exacerbate existing obsessive worries. Consider doing what you can to reduce the amount of TV watched in the family, or be much more selective in the choice of programming your family views.

- **Commit to change.**

Sometimes it helps to put commitments in writing. If you haven't already done so, review the OCD Enabler's Declaration of Independence with your family member who struggles with OCD. Discuss it and make any changes you like. We left space at the end to write anything else you would like to say. Then sign it. Commit to change the way you respond to OCD, and help your family member break free from OCD.

Assisting the Family Member Who Won't Acknowledge Having OCD and Refuses Help

In some cases, family members or friends may recognize signs of OCD years before the person with OCD acknowledges and accepts it. In spite of serious impairment, the person may deny the illness and refuse to seek help, thus causing a great deal of pain and hardship to the entire family. Feelings of depression, hopelessness, and helplessness may prevail among family members who are at a loss as to how to help the sufferer in denial.

When all efforts to convince the person in denial to get help have failed, confront the sufferer using the following guidelines:

1. Since there is strength in numbers, it is helpful to confront the person with OCD as a unified group.

2. Obtain the help of a trained family therapist or a counselor familiar with OCD who can assist in facilitating communication between family members and the sufferer.

3. Firmly, yet compassionately, explain specifically how the OCD behavior is affecting the family. Explain how the situation is intolerable and stress the family's commitment to helping. Acknowledge that the person is in pain, yet may lack the support, knowledge, or tools to face the disorder. Emphasize that it is the OCD behavior that is intolerable and not the sufferer.

4. If the person persists in denial, state that denial of the illness is a sure symptom of the illness. Offer to help and explain that doing nothing is not an acceptable option. Each family member must state what each is willing to do to help change the present situation. Give a time frame for obtaining help and state clear contingencies if the plan is not fol-

lowed within the specified time frame, such as moving the person to a group home, hospital, or other custodial living situation.

5. Be firm, yet flexible and realistic. If change appears unlikely, what is most important is to take whatever measures are necessary to ensure that the sufferer lives independently, with dignity and has ample opportunities to improve his/her standing in life.

CHAPTER 17

Where to Get Help?

Talk doesn't cook rice.

—Chinese proverb

From the beginning of this workbook we have recommended that you consult a mental health professional before starting the Self-Directed Program. This can be a very helpful step that can contribute significantly to your progress in recovering from OCD. Many of you have put off discussing your OCD problem with a mental health professional or have been seeing a professional for other problems. You may be ready to tackle the issue of your OCD with a professional, but don't know where to start. This chapter addresses your questions and concerns.

Professional Help for OCD

The best professional to help you with your OCD is someone who knows a good deal about OCD and how it is treated. Usually, this will be a psychiatrist or psychologist. Psychiatrists are medical doctors who specialize in treating disorders of the brain and mind. Their primary role is to prescribe medications for OCD. They are usually not trained to do cognitive-behavior therapy (CBT), but they are well aware of it. On the other hand, psychologists, therapists, and counselors who treat OCD cannot prescribe medication, but they are usually trained in CBT. It is rare that one doctor does both. So the likelihood is that many of you will need to see two separate professionals—one for the medication and one for the CBT.

Whether you begin treatment with medications or cognitive-behavior therapy does not matter. As we have stressed throughout this workbook, the optimum treatment is the combined use of medications and CBT. Both play important roles in recovery. The person with OCD who chooses one and ignores or avoids the other is receiving only partial treatment and therefore only partial results.

Remember, too, that different people respond differently to medications and CBT. In other words, there are some recovering persons with OCD who consider medication the key factor in their recovery, and CBT a less important factor. And there are others who, with equal fervor, will state that CBT is the key ingredient in their recovery. Many also contend that both treatment modes are equally important. Everyone responds differently to different treatments. The one that is right for you can only be determined by your efforts to obtain combined treatment.

If is very important that the psychiatrist and therapist you consult are experienced in treating OCD. Although any licensed physician can administer medication for OCD, consulting a psychiatrist who understands treatment of the disorder is by far the best choice. The Obsessive-Compulsive Foundation (see Resources section) maintains a listing of psychiatrists and therapists who claim to have additional knowledge and experience in the treatment of OCD. Because the Obsessive-Compulsive Foundation does not specifically research the credentials and qualifications of every doctor and therapist on their referral list (this would be an overwhelming and expensive process), consumers must still maintain caution. This would be only the first, though very useful, step toward identifying a qualified professional in your area.

The Obsessive-Compulsive Information Center (Dean Foundation), the Obsessive-Compulsive Foundation, the Anxiety Disorders Association of America (ADAA), and the Association for Advancement of Behavior Therapy also maintain listings of therapists who have indicated special interest in treating obsessive-compulsive disorder. Addresses for these groups are in the Resources section.

If an experienced therapist is not available locally, you may choose to travel to one of a number of centers where OCD is treated. Contact the Obsessive-Compulsive Foundation for a current list of inpatient and outpatient programs. You could stay in a motel or with friends and attend an outpatient clinic for evaluation and intensive therapy. Subsequent sessions may be possible by telephone. Inpatient treatment may be necessary if there is substantial risk of self-harm or danger as a result of your OCD symptoms.

Because treatment can be expensive in terms of time and finances, select your therapist carefully. Use the Counselor Selection Interview Form that appears later in this chapter as a guide to evaluate the therapist. Consider asking for the opinions of other professionals who may know of the therapist in question. Get feedback from former patients who have been helped by the professional you are considering. Beware, however, of the tendency to obsess about making the "perfect" decision. This can delay getting the vital help you need. Go with your gut feelings about what is best—*do it and stick to it!*

Questions to Ask Prospective Therapists

1. What techniques do you generally use to treat OCD?
   "Cognitive-behavior therapy" or "behavior therapy" are good answers. Cognitive-behavior therapy means that cognitive change principles (targeting changing beliefs and attitudes) are used with the behavioral change principles (targeting compulsive behaviors and rituals). Go a step further and ask therapists what kind of behavior therapy they use. If exposure and response prevention or exposure and ritual prevention (both terms are used) is not mentioned, you may want to look for a different therapist. After reading through this book you should have a pretty good understanding of what exposure and ritual prevention is. If you do not, review chapters 3–6.

2. Are you licensed by the state?

3. What are your credentials?
   A master's degree in a mental health discipline is the minimal acceptable training. Do not be overly impressed by credentials, however. A talented, skilled master's level therapist with significant experience with OCD can be many times more helpful than an M.D. or Ph.D. with lots of education but little real knowledge of OCD. Look for membership in the OC Founda-

tion, the Anxiety Disorders Association of America (ADAA), or the Association for the Advancement of Behavior Therapy (AABT).

4. Do you have OCD or know anyone personally who has it?
An excellent question, if a little brazen. Though few qualified mental health professionals are likely to have OCD, a number do have personal experience with family members or others who have the disorder. This may be a sign that the doctor understands OCD well.

5. Where did you learn about OCD treatment?
Training is important, as is experience. A single weekend professional workshop on OCD is insufficient. Look for a background that includes intensive training in cognitive-behavioral therapy for anxiety disorders and ongoing case supervision. Psychiatrists should have evidence of having received continuing education specifically about the pharmacology of OCD treatment.

6. How many OCD patients have you actually treated *for OCD*?
There is no magic number, but it is important that the therapist has experience treating OCD patients *for OCD*. Many nonspecialists help people with OCD with all kinds of general life-stress issues. Although this contributes somewhat to their knowledge of OCD, it is not sufficient background and experience to treat OCD patients *for OCD*.

7. Did your OCD patients get better?
Always expect a "yes" response, but look for the therapist who emphasizes the *combined* use of medications and cognitive-behavioral therapy.

8. How many of your current patients have OCD?
The more that OCD and anxiety disorders are a focus of the therapist's practice, the better. However, be aware that only in the case of an OCD or anxiety disorders *specialist* is the therapist likely to have more than just a few, if any, patients currently being seen specifically for OCD.

9. Would you be willing to leave your office to do behavior therapy if needed?
Flexibility is the key here. If exposure work requires a home visit or a series of visits, is the therapist willing to do what is needed?

10. During behavior therapy, are you available between sessions if I get "stuck" or need support while doing exposures?
Again, flexibility is the key. The therapist must understand fully the enormous stress that exposure work may entail and must be willing to be available between sessions for brief telephone support and monitoring

11. Do you support the use of appropriate medication for OCD?
Be wary of any therapist who holds an overly strong, biased view against the use of medication—or holds the view that medication is the cure-all for OCD.

12. How "cured" will I be by the end of treatment?
Walk out if the therapist offers you a "cure" for OCD, or boasts a laundry list of "cured" patients. Most qualified, competent therapists will not promise a cure, but instead will offer hope for significant symptom relief and assistance with learning to live a more satisfying life, despite the OCD.

Other Considerations

13. Do you get along with the therapist?
It is vital you feel comfortable talking and opening up to your therapist. You must **trust this** person and be willing to do whatever he or she says is necessary to make progress.

14. If not experienced with OCD, does the therapist indicate a willingness to learn more about it?
Therapists experienced in the treatment of OCD are not available in many areas. One who is willing to learn and help you work through the Self-Directed Program is next best.

Counselor Selection Interview Form

Name: _____

Cost of appointments: _____

Estimated number of visits expected: _____

Credentials, education, experience, training: _____

_____

_____

Number of OCD patients, current and past: _____

Willingness to leave office to do behavior therapy: _____

Psychiatrist to whom patients are usually referred if medication appears to be indicated: ___

_____

Who takes calls when therapist is not available (e. g., when the therapist is out of town or on a vacation): _____

Overall impression: _____

_____

_____

_____

_____

Support Groups

If there is a support group in your area, a good one can help you reach your goal of breaking free from OCD. It can be an enormous relief to realize your symptoms are not unique. Support groups also can be helpful for the families of people with OCD, especially parents of children and adolescents. Support groups can play an important role in education about OCD. A list of OCD support groups meeting throughout the country and internationally is available through the Obsessive-Compulsive Foundation (see Resources section).

Obsessive Compulsive Anonymous (OCA) is a support group founded in 1988 by Roy C. Obsessive Compulsive Anonymous utilizes principles similar to other twelve-step programs such as Alcoholics Anonymous, Narcotics Anonymous, Gamblers Anonymous, and Alanon. The program is described in the book by Roy C., *Obsessive Compulsive Anonymous—Recovering from Obsessive Compulsive Disorder*. A list of groups is available on their website or by phone (see Resources section).

GOAL (Giving Obsessive-Compulsives Another Lifestyle) is a support group format begun by a Philadelphia OCD support group. Their emphasis is on choosing behavioral goals to work on between meetings. Dr. Jonathan Grayson, Ph.D., one of GOAL's founders, advises having a professional person who is experienced with OCD assist the group. This person answers questions, helps keep the meetings on track, and gives individual assistance when needed.

Local support groups may use one of these formats or they may use another one that has proven to work for them. A list of OCD support groups in your area is available through the Obsessive-Compulsive Foundation.

Help in Cyberspace

Support for people with OCD and their families is available on the Internet. Several discussion groups exist for people with OCD and their families. The largest of these groups, the OCD-L, is a moderated discussion group (called a "mail list") with over 400 subscribers. To subscribe, send an e-mail to OCD-L@VM.MARIST.EDU. Put "subscribe" followed by your name in the subject area. E-mail messages with the ongoing discussion go out to everyone on the discussion list, so everyone gets several e-mail messages a day. OCD-L is expertly moderated by Chris Vertullo of Marist College. She insures that the discussion stays relevant and appropriate to the topic of OCD. (Cherry believes this discussion group has been responsible for 80 percent of her ongoing recovery. She met people who have problems similar to hers who offered support, concern, and friendship.)

Another discussion group for people with OCD is the Usenet newsgroup at alt.support.ocd. Usenet is a worldwide distributed discussion system sponsored over the Internet by UUNet, a worldwide Internet service provider. It consists of a set of "newsgroups" with names that are classified by subject. There are over 40,000 newsgroup discussion groups covering every conceivable topic. Both popular web browsers, Netscape Navigator and Internet Explorer, support Usenet newsgroup access. Find your newsgroup screen and type in alt.support.ocd. Unlike the OCD-L, alt.support.ocd is an unmoderated discussion group, which means there is no one in charge to monitor content. As a result, alt.support.ocd tends to be a bit more raw in its content and veers off topic more frequently. Both discussion groups include commentary from various mental health professionals who donate their time to field questions and contribute their knowledge and support.

Online chat is an excellent way to meet others with OCD. It enables you to converse in "real time" with others over the Internet using your computer's keyboard to send and receive text.

Excellent chat areas related to OCD exist on the Internet. The Obsessive-Compulsive Spectrum Disorders Association (OCSDA) sponsors a free monthly online Marathon Support Weekend (MSW). These are moderated online chats on various topics related to OCD. Experts in the field of OCD and anxiety treatment are featured. They field questions and promote lively discussions of the many issues important to people with OCD and their families. Visit OCSDA's website at http://www.ocdhelp.org for details on accessing the MSWs.

Another way to access chat rooms about OCD is through Internet Relay Chat (IRC). Separate "chat" software is required, such as "mIRC32" (you can download it from many shareware websites such as CNet at www.download.com or Tucows at www.tucows.com). Using standard chat software, log on to an IRC server at port 6667. Type /NICK <name> to register. Type /JOIN ##OCD to find listserv members. Then type /NAMES ##OCD to get a list of current users. Best times vary. Try from 12 noon to 2 P.M. EST and from 8 to 10 P.M. EST.

The following proprietary subscriber online services also feature OCD Chat services:

- Prodigy On-line Bulletin Board Service for OCD can be found by: (jump) medical support bb; choose topic "anx/dep/ocd"; look in subject area for subjects beginning with "OCD."

- America Online has an OCD Chat every Wednesday at 9 P.M. EST. It can be found by keyword: PEN. America Online also has an OCD message board in the mental health section.

There are many websites dedicated to providing information about OCD. Many of them have an "Ask the Expert" page, message boards, chat rooms, and resources for finding help dealing with OCD. We have listed some of our favorite websites in the Resources section.

As we end this *OCD Workbook*, it is our hope that you are well on your way to breaking free from obsessive-compulsive disorder. The Resources section is filled with more help and hope. Besides lists of websites and support groups, we have listed many printed resources and organizations that are working to help people break free from OCD.

Appendix

A Brief Introduction to Obsessive-Compulsive Disorder for Family and Friends

Obsessive-compulsive disorder is characterized by obsessions and/or compulsions that are time-consuming, distressing, and interfere with normal routines, relationships with others, and/or daily functioning. *Obsessions* are persistent impulses, ideas, images, or thoughts that intrude into a person's thinking and cause excessive worry and anxiety. *Compulsions* are mental acts or repetitive behaviors performed in response to obsessions to relieve or prevent worry and/or anxiety. They often have the intention of magically preventing or avoiding a dreaded event such as death, illness, or some other perceived misfortune.

A diagnosis of OCD is made on the basis of a psychiatric examination, a history of the patient's symptoms and complaints, and the degree to which the symptoms interfere with daily functioning. Based on the nature, length, and frequency of the symptoms presented, the doctor will differentiate OCD from other medical diseases with similar symptoms.

Studies have shown that 80–99 percent of all people experience unwanted thoughts. But most people can hold unpleasant thoughts in their minds without too much discomfort, or they can easily dismiss the thoughts entirely. Their thoughts are shorter in duration, less intense, and less frequent than the intrusive thoughts of those who suffer from OCD. The obsessive thoughts of OCD, on the other hand, usually have a specific onset, produce significant discomfort, and result in a powerful, overwhelming urge to neutralize or lessen them.

People with OCD frequently suffer from depression. Approximately one-third have depression at the time they seek treatment. About two-thirds of people with OCD have had at least one episode of major depression in their lifetime. Many others suffer from lesser forms of depression. It's very important to watch for warning signs of depression.

What causes OCD? No one knows the exact answer to that question yet, but researchers are piecing together the puzzle. There is growing evidence that it tends to run in families and is caused by subtle variations in brain structure and circuitry. The most widely held theory is that the cause is related to abnormal levels of one of the brain's vital neurotransmitters, serotonin. Brain imaging studies have demonstrated abnormalities in several parts of the brains of people with OCD. These include the thalamus, caudate nucleus, orbital cortex, and cingulate gyrus.

How is OCD treated? Medication and cognitive-behavior therapy are the most effective treatments for OCD. They can be used alone, but applied together they can be powerful weapons in the struggle with OCD. The medications most effective for treating OCD belong to the family of drugs known as serotonin reuptake inhibitors (SRIs). They include fluvoxamine (Luvox), fluoxetine (Prozac), sertraline (Zoloft), paroxetine (Paxil), citalopram (Celexa), and clomipramine (Anafranil). They help to correct the chemical imbalances and relieve OCD symptoms. Some people will have to try more than one of these medications to find the one that works best for them. Others will need to take a combination of medications.

Cognitive-behavior therapy helps by providing the person with OCD the necessary tools to manage their obsessions and compulsions. Initially, it can appear quite challenging, even scary—but obtaining relief from OCD symptoms makes it all worthwhile. When used together, medication and cognitive-behavior therapy complement each other. Medication alters the level of serotonin, while cognitive-behavior therapy helps to modify behavior by teaching the person with OCD the skills to resist compulsions and obsessions. Medication can reduce the anxiety level, thus making it easier to implement cognitive-behavior therapy principles.

Exposure and ritual prevention **(ERP)**—also called exposure and *response* prevention—is the principal behavioral technique for treating OCD. This involves prolonged exposure to the real-life anxiety and ritual-evoking stimuli. For example, the person with OCD may be asked to actually touch or directly contact some feared object, such as an empty garbage pail or other "contaminated" object, without relieving his or her anxiety by hand washing. Through repeated practice, the person realizes that the feared disastrous consequences do not and will not occur, and the severe anxiety initially associated with that situation decreases. This is the process of *habituation*. Exposure is best done in stages, taking baby steps toward the ultimate goal of complete habituation to the feared object or situation.

The purpose of ritual prevention is to decrease the frequency of rituals. The person with OCD is instructed to face feared stimuli, experience the urge to do rituals, and then *simultaneously* to block ritual behaviors such as hand washing or excessive checking. At first the person may be instructed to delay performing a ritual, and gradually work toward totally resisting the compulsion.

The OCD Workbook leads people through the Self-Directed Program to break free from OCD. The primary tool is exposure and ritual prevention. The program also uses cognitive therapy principles. This involves changing distorted thinking and beliefs. Cognitive therapy encourages the person to identify inaccurate thoughts and attitudes, and to replace them with healthier, more accurate ones.

How can you help? Be an encourager. Read the first few chapters of *The OCD Workbook* to get a better understanding of OCD. Chapter 16, "OCD Is a Family Affair," will help you to provide needed support, acceptance, and encouragement as your loved one struggles to break free from OCD.

Yale-Brown Obsessive-Compulsive Scale (YBOCS)

Questions 1 to 5 are about your obsessive thoughts.

Obsessions are unwanted ideas, images, or impulses that intrude on thinking against your wishes and efforts to resist them. They usually involve themes of harm, risk, and danger. Common obsessions are excessive fears of contamination; recurring doubts about danger; extreme concern with order, symmetry, or exactness; fear of losing important things.

Please answer each question by writing the appropriate number in the box next to it.

1. Time Occupied by Obsessive Thoughts

Q. How much of your time was occupied by obsessive thoughts?

0 = None - If you checked this answer, also check 0 for questions 2, 3, 4 and 5 and proceed to question 6.

1 = Less than 1 hour per day, or occasional occurrence.

2 = 1 to 3 hours per day, or frequent occurrence.

3 = More than 3 hours and up to 8 hours per day, or very frequent occurrence.

4 = More than 8 hours per day, or nearly constant occurrence.

2. Interference Due to Obsessive Thoughts

Q. How much do your obsessive thoughts interfere with your work, school, social, or other important role functioning? Is there anything that you don't do because of them?

0 = None

1 = Slight interference with social or other activities, but overall performance not impaired.

2 = Definitive interference with social or occupational performance, but still manageable.

3 = Causes substantial impairment in social or occupational performance.

4 = Incapacitating.

3. Distress Associated with Obsessive Thoughts

Q. How much distress do your obsessive thoughts cause you?

0 = None

1 = Not too disturbing.

2 = Disturbing, but still manageable.

3 = Very disturbing.

4 = Near constant and disabling distress.

4. Resistance Against Obsessions

Q. How much of an effort do you make to resist the obsessive thoughts? How often do you try to disregard or turn your attention away from those thoughts as they enter your mind?

0 = Try to resist all the time.

1 = Try to resist most of the time.

2 = Make some effort to resist.

3 = Yield to all obsessions without attempting to control them, but with some reluctance.

4 = Completely and willingly yield to all obsessions.

5. Degree of Control Over Obsessive Thoughts

> **Q.** How much control do you have over your obsessive thoughts? How successful are you in stopping or diverting your obsessive thinking?

0 = Complete control

1 = Usually able to stop or divert obsessions with some effort and concentration.

2 = Sometimes able to stop or divert obsessions.

3 = Rarely successful in stopping obsessions or dismissing obsessions, can only divert attention with great difficulty.

4 = Obsessions are completely involuntary, rarely able to even momentarily alter obsessive thinking.

The next several questions are about your compulsive behaviors.

Compulsions are urges that people have to do something to lessen feelings of anxiety or other discomfort. Often they do repetitive, purposeful, intentional behaviors called rituals. The behavior itself may seem appropriate but it becomes a ritual when done to excess. Washing, checking, repeating, straightening, hoarding, and many other behaviors can be rituals. Some rituals are mental. For example, thinking or saying things over and over under your breath.

6. Time Spent Performing Compulsive Behaviors

> **Q.** How much time do you spend performing compulsive behaviors? How much longer than most people does it take to complete routine activities because of your rituals? How frequently do you do rituals?

0 = None.

1 = Less than 1 hour per day, or occasional performance of compulsive behaviors.

2 = 1 to 3 hours per day, or frequent performance of compulsive behaviors.

3 = More than 3 hours and up to 8 hours per day, or very frequent performance of compulsive behaviors.

4 = More than 8 hours per day, or near-constant performance of compulsive behaviors (too numerous to count).

7. Interference Due to Compulsive Behaviors

> **Q.** How much do your compulsive behaviors interfere with your work, school, social, or functioning? Is there anything you don't do because of your compulsions?

0 = None.

1 = Slight interference with social or other activities, but overall performance not impaired.

2 = Definite interference with social or occupational performance, but still manageable.

3 = Causes substantial impairment in social or occupational performance.

4 = Incapacitating.

8. Distress Associated with Compulsive Behavior

> **Q.** How would you feel if prevented from performing your compulsion(s)? How anxious would you become?

0 = Not at all anxious.

1 = Only slightly anxious if compulsions prevented.

2 = Anxiety would mount but remain manageable if compulsions prevented.

3 = Prominent and very disturbing increase in anxiety if compulsions interrupted.

4 = Incapacitating anxiety from any intervention aimed at modifying activity.

9. Resistance Against Compulsions

Q. How much of an effort do you make to resist the compulsions?

0 = Always try to resist.

1 = Try to resist most of the time.

2 = Make some effort to resist.

3 = Yield to almost all compulsions without attempting to control them, but with some reluctance.

4 = Completely and willingly yield to all compulsions.

10. Degree of Control Over Compulsive Behavior

Q. How strong is the drive to perform the compulsive behavior? How much control do you have over the compulsions?

0 = Complete control.

1 = Pressure to perform the behavior but usually able to exercise voluntary control over it.

2 = Strong pressure to perform behavior, can control it only with difficulty.

3 = Very strong drive to perform behavior, must be carried to completion, can only delay with difficulty.

4 = Drive to perform behavior experienced as completely involuntary and overpowering, rarely able to even momentarily delay activity.

TOTAL

Note: Based upon the author's experience, scores on the YBOCS can be interpreted as follows:

0–14: non-significant to mild OCD

15–23: mild to moderate OCD

23–29: moderate to severe OCD

30–40: severe to disabling OCD

This adaptation of the Y-BOCS is printed with the permission of Wayne Goodman at the University of Florida, College of Medicine, Gainesville, Florida 32610. The original version was published by: Goodman W.K., Price, L.H., Rasmussen, S.A., et al. "Yale-Brown Obsessive Compulsive Scale I: Development, Use and Reliability." *Arch Gen Psychiatry* 1989. 46:1006–1011.

Resources

Self-Help Books

Adams, Gail B., and Marcia Torcia. *School Personnel: A Critical Link in the Identification, Treatment, and Management of OCD in Children and Adolescents.* P. O. Box 70, Milford, CT: Obsessive-Compulsive Foundation.

Baer, Lee. 1992. *Getting Control: Overcoming Your Obsessions and Compulsions.* New York: Plume.

C., Roy. 1990. *Obsessive Compulsive Anonymous, Recovering from Obsessive Compulsive Disorder.* New Hyde Park, NY: Obsessive Compulsive Anonymous, Inc.

C., Roy. 1993. *Obsessive Compulsive Disorder, A Survival Guide for Family and Friends.* New Hyde Park, NY: Obsessive Compulsive Anonymous, Inc.

Ciarrocchi, Joseph W. 1995. *The Doubting Disease: Help for Scrupulosity and Religious Compulsions.* Mahwah, NJ: Paulist Press

de Silva, Padmal, and Stanley Rachman. 1998. *Obsessive-Compulsive Disorder: the Facts, Second Edition.* New York: Oxford University Press.

Dumont, Raeann. 1996. *The Sky Is Falling: Understanding and Coping with Phobias, Panic, and Obsessive-Compulsive Disorders.* New York: W. W. Norton.

Foa, Edna B., and Reid Wilson. 1991. *Stop Obsessing! How to Overcome Your Obsessions and Compulsions.* New York: Bantam Books.

Gravitz, Herbert L. 1998. *Obsessive Compulsive Disorder: New Help for the Family.* Santa Barbara, CA: Healing Visions Press.

Greist, John H. 1995. *Obsessive Compulsive Disorder: A Guide.* Madison, WI: Dean Foundation for Health, Research and Education.

Greist, John H. 1993. *Obsessive-Compulsive Disorder in Children and Adolescents: A Guide.* Madison, WI: Dean Foundation for Health, Research and Education.

Johnston, Hugh F., and J. Jay Fruehling. *OCD and Parenting.* Madison, WI: Child Psychopharmacology Information Center, University of Wisconsin (Department of Psychiatry).

Neziroglu, Fugen, and Jose A. Yaryura-Tobias. 1995. *Over and Over Again: Understanding Obsessive-Compulsive Disorder.* New York: Lexington Books.

Osborn, Ian. 1998. *Tormenting Thoughts and Secret Rituals: The Hidden Epidemic of Obsessive-Compulsive Disorder.* New York: Pantheon Books.

Rapoport, Judith L. 1989. *The Boy Who Couldn't Stop Washing: The Experience and Treatment of Obsessive-Compulsive Disorder.* New York: E. P. Dutton.

Santa, Thomas. 1999. *Understanding Scrupulosity: Helpful Answers for Those Who Experience Nagging Questions and Doubts.* Liguori, MO: Liguori Publications.

Steketee, Gail, and Kerin White. 1990. *When Once Is Not Enough: Help for Obsessive Compulsives.* Oakland, CA: New Harbinger Publications, Inc.

Schwartz, Jeffrey, with Beverly Beyette. 1996. *Brain Lock: Free Yourself from Obsessive-Compulsive Behavior.* New York: Regan Books.

VanNoppen, Barbara L, Michele Tortora Pato, and Steven Rasmussen. 1997. *Learning to Live with OCD: Obsessive Compulsive Disorder, Fourth Edition.* Milford CT: Obsessive Compulsive Foundation.

Professional Books

Hollander, Eric, and Dan J. Stein, eds. 1997. *Obsessive-Compulsive Disorders: Diagnosis, Etiology, Treatment.* New York: Marcel Dekker.

Jenke, Michael A., Lee Baer, and William E. Minichiello, eds. 1998. *Obsessive-Compulsive Disorders: Practical Management, Third Edition.* St. Louis, MO: Mosby, Inc.

March, John S., and Karen Mulle. 1998. *OCD in Children and Adolescents: A Cognitive-Behavioral Treatment Manual.* New York: The Guilford Press.

Steketee, Gail S. *Treatment of Obsessive Compulsive Disorder.* 1993. New York: The Guilford Press.

Yaryura-Tobias, Jose A., and Fugen Neziroglu. 1997. *Biobehavioral Treatment of Obsessive-Compulsive Spectrum Disorders.* New York: W. W. Norton.

Yaryura-Tobias, Jose A., and Fugen Neziroglu. 1997. *Obsessive-Compulsive Disorder Spectrum, Pathogenesis, Diagnosis, and Treatment.* Washington, DC: American Psychiatric Press, Inc.

Mental Health Books

Depression and Anxiety Disorders

Burns, David D. 1990. *The Feeling Good Handbook.* New York: Plume.

Copeland, Mary Ellen. 1992. *The Depression Workbook, A Guide to Living with Depression and Manic Depression.* Oakland, CA: New Harbinger Publications, Inc.

Copeland, Mary Ellen. 1994. *Living with Depression and Manic Depression.* Oakland, CA: New Harbinger Publications, Inc.

Copeland, Mary Ellen. 1998. *The Worry Control Workbook.* Oakland, CA: New Harbinger Publications, Inc.

Childhood OCD and Related Disorders

Dornbush, Marilyn, and Sheryl Pruitt. 1993. *Teaching the Tiger: A Handbook for Individuals Involved in the Education of Students with Attention Deficit Disorders, Tourette's Syndrome or Obsessive-Compulsive Disorder.* P. O. Box 188, Duarte, CA: Hope Press.

Koplewicz, Harold S. 1996. *It's Nobody's Fault: New Hope and Help for Difficult Children.* New York: Times Books.

Rapoport, J. L. 1989. *Obsessive-Compulsive Disorder in Children and Adolescents.* Washington, DC: American Psychiatric Press.

Swedo, Susan, and Henrietta Leonard. 1998. *Is It "Just a Phase": How to Tell Common Childhood Phases from More Serious Problems.* New York: Golden Books.

Body Dysmorphic Disorder

Phillips, Katharine A. 1996. *The Broken Mirror: Understanding and Treating Body Dysmorphic Disorder.* New York: Oxford University Press.

Mental Health

Ratey, John J., and Catherine Johnson. 1997. *Shadow Syndromes: Recognizing and Coping with the Hidden Psychological Disorders That Can Influence Your Behavior and Silently Determine the Course of Your Life.* New York: Pantheon Books.

Swedo, Susan, and Henrietta Leonard. 1996. *It's Not All in Your Head. Now Women Can Discover the Real Causes of Their Most Commonly Misdiagnosed Health Problems.* San Francisco: HarperSanFrancisco.

Mental Health Organizations

American Foundation for Suicide Prevention, 120 Wall Street, 22nd Floor, New York, NY 10005. 212-363-3500. Internet: http://www.afsp.org

Anorexia Nervosa and Related Eating Disorders, Inc., P.O. Box 5102, Eugene, OR 97405. 541-344-1144. Internet: http://www.anred.com

Anxiety Disorders Association of America (ADAA), Dept. A. 6000 Executive Blvd., Suite 513, Rockville, MD 20852. 301-231-9350. (Or 11900 Parklawn drive, Suite 100?). Email: AnxDis@aol.com Internet: http://www.adaa.org

Association for the Advancement of Behavior Therapy, 305 Seventh Ave., New York, NY 10001-6008. 212-647-1890. Internet: http://server.psyc.vt.edu/aabt/

Children and Adults with Attention Deficit Disorders (C.H.A.D.D.), 499 Northwest 70th Avenue, Suite 308, Plantation, FL 33317. 305-587-3700. Internet: http://www.chadd.org

Kidscope, Obsessive-Compulsive Foundation, PO Box 70, Milford, CT 06460-0070. (children=s newsletter)

National Alliance for the Mentally Ill, 200 N. Glebe Rd., Suite 1015, Arlington, VA 22203-3754. 800-950-NAMI (800-950-6264).

National Anxiety Foundation, 3135 Custer Drive, Lexington, KY 40517-4001. 606-272-7166. Internet: http://lexington-on-line.com/naf.ocd.2.html

National Association of Anorexia Nervosa and Associated Disorders, Box 7, Highland Park, IL 60035. 847-831-3438. Internet: http://www.healthtouch.com

National Attention Deficit Disorder Association, P.O. Box 972, Mentor, OH 44061. 800-487-2282 or 216-350-9595. Internet: http://www.add.org

National Depressive and Manic-Depressive Association, 730 North Franklin, #501, Chicago, IL 60610. 800-82N-DMDA.

National Foundation for Depressive Illness, P.O. Box 2257, New York, NY 10116. 800-248-4344.

National Institute of Mental Health, 9000 Rockville Pike, Building 10. Room 30-41, Bethesda, MD 20892. 301-496-3421. Information services: Panic and other anxiety disorders: 800-647-2642. Depression: 800-421-4211

National Mental Health Association, 1201 Prince St., Alexandria, VA 22314-2971. 703-684-7722

National Mental Health Consumers= Self-Help Clearinghouse, 1211 Chestnut St., Philadelphia, PA 19107. 800-553-4539.

Obsessive Compulsive Anonymous, Inc. (OCA) P.O. Box 215, New Hyde Park, New York 11040. 516-741-4909. Internet: http://members.aol.com/west24th/index.html

Obsessive-Compulsive Foundation, Inc. (OCF) P.O. Box 70, Milford, CT 06460-0070. 203-878-5669. Email: info@ocfoundation.org. Internet: http://www.ocfoundation.org

Obsessive Compulsive Information Center, Madison Institute of Medicine, 617 Mineral Point Rd., Suite 300, Madison, WI 53717. Internet: http://www.healthtechsys.com/mim.html

Our Courage Defines Us (OCDU), PO Box 9123, Niskayuna, NY 12309-0123 (newsletter)

Scrupulous Anonymous, Liguori, MO 63057 (newsletter) http://www.liguori.org/apostolc/cssr/newsltr.htm

Tourette Syndrome Association, Inc. 42-40 Bell Boulevard, Bayside, New York 11361-2820. 718-224-2999. Email: tourette@ix netcom.com

Trichotillomania Learning Center, 1215 Mission Street, Santa Cruz, CA 95050. 408-457-1004. Email: trichster@aol.com Internet: http://www.trich.org/

Mental Health Websites

Awareness Foundation for OCD and Related Disorders—http://members.aol.com/afocd/afocd.htm

Center for Psychiatric Rehabiliation at Boston University—http://www.bu.edu/sarpsych/jobschool

Cherry's Website—http://members.aol.com/Cherlene

Dr. Bob's Psychopharmacology Tips—http://uhs.bsd.uchicago.edu/dr-bob/tips/tips.html

Doubt and Other Disorders—http://www.geocities.com/HotSprings/6209/index.html

Fairlite OCD Server—http://fairlite.com/ocd/

Internet Mental Health Infosource—http://www.mhsource.com

Mental Health—http://www.mentalhealth.com/fr20.html

National Anxiety Foundation—http://lexington-on-line.com/naf.html

Obsessive-Compulsive Anonymous—http://members.aol.com/west24th/index.html

Obsessive-Compulsive Disorder Resource Center—http://www.ocdresource.com/

Obsessive-Compulsive Foundation—http://www.ocfoundation.org

Obsessive Compulsive Information Center—http://www.healthtechsys.com/mim.html

OCD-L Email List—listserv@vm.marist.edu

OCD Online—http://www.ocdonline.com

OCD Resource Center of South Florida—http://www.ocdhope.com

OC & Spectrum Disorders—http://www.ocdhelp.org

Psych Central - Dr. John Grohol's Mental Health Page—http://www.psychcentral.com

Scrupulous Anonymous—http://www.liguori.org/apostolc/cssr/newsltr.htm

Shrink-Rap Press (two Australian psychiatrists that publish children's books on anxiety disorders and ADHD)—http://www.shrinkrap.com.au

Trichotillomania Learning Center—http://www.trich.org/

References

Alsobrook, II, John P., and David L. Pauls. 1998. Genetics of obsessive-compulsive disorder. In *Obsessive-Compulsive Disorders: Practical Management, Third Edition,*edited by M. Jenike, L. Baer, and W. Minichiello. St. Louis, MO: Mosby, Inc.

American Psychiatric Association. 1994. *Diagnostic and Statistical Manual of Mental Disorders*, Fourth Edition (*DSM-IV-R*). 1400 K St. N.W., Washington, DC: American Psychiatric Association.

Azrin, N., and R. G. Nunn. 1973. Habit reversal: A method of eliminating nervous habits and tics. *Behavioral Research and Therapy* 11:619-628.

Baer, L., and M. Jenike. 1998. Personality disorders in obsessive-compulsive disorder. In *Obsessive-Compulsive Disorders: Practical Management*, edited by M. Jenike, L. Baer, and W. Minichiello. St. Louis, MO: Mosby, Inc.

Beck, A. T., G. Emery, and R. L. Greenberg. 1985. *Anxiety Disorders and Phobias: A Cognitive Perspective.* New York: Basic Books.

Ciarrocchi, Joseph. 1995. *The Doubting Disease: Help for Scrupolosity and Religious Compulsions.* Mahwah, New Jersey: Paulist Press.

———. 1998. Religion, scrupolosity, and obsessive-compulsive disorder. In *Obsessive-Compulsive Disorders: Practical Management, Third Edition*, edited by M. Jenike, L. Baer, and W. Minichiello. St. Louis, MO: Mosby, Inc.

Damecour, C. L., and M. Charron. .1998. Hoarding: A symptom, not a syndrome. *Journal of Clinical Psychiatry* 59:5, May.

Ellis, A. 1962. *Reason and Emotion in Psychotherapy.* New York: Lyle Stuart.

Freeston, M. H., R. Rheaume, R. LaDoucheur. 1996. Correcting faulty appraisals of obsessional thoughts. *Behaviour Research and Therapy* 34(5):433-446.

Freeston, M. H., R. LaDoucheur, F. Gagnon, N. Thibodeau, R. Rheaume, H. Letarte, and A. Bujold. 1997. Cognitive-behavioral treatment of obsessive thoughts: A controlled study. *Journal of Consulting and Clinical Psychology* 65(3):405-413.

Freeston, M. H., and R. LaDoucheur. 1997. What do patients do with their obsessional thoughts? *Behavior Research and Therapy* 35(4):335-348.

Frost, R., and R. Gross. 1993. The hoarding of possessions. *Behavioral Research and Therapy* 31:367-381.

Frost, R., and R. Steketee. 1998. Hoarding: clinical aspects and treatment strategies. In *Obsessive-Compulsive Disorders: Practical Management, Third Edition.* edited by M. Jenike, L. Baer, and W. Minichiello. St. Louis, MO: Mosby, Inc.

Geller, Daniel A. 1998. Juvenile obsessive-compulsive disorder. In *Obsessive-Compulsive Disorders: Practical Management, Third Edition*, edited by M. Jenike, L. Baer, and W. Minichiello. St. Louis, MO: Mosby, Inc.

Greenberg, D. 1984. Are religious compulsions religious or compulsive? *American Journal of Psychotherapy* 38:524-532.

Greenberg, D. 1987. Compulsive hoarding. *American Journal of Psychotherapy.* XLI:409-416.

Greist, J. H., and J. W. Jefferson. 1995. *Obsessive-Compulsive Disorder Casebook.* Washington, DC: American Psychiatric Press, Inc.

Hecht, A. M., M. Fichter, and P. Postpischil. 1983. Obsessive-compulsive neurosis and anorexia nervosa. *International Journal of Eating Disorders* 2:69-77.

Jenike, Michael, Hans C. Breiter, Lee Baer, David N. Kennedy, Cary R. Savage, Michael J. Olivares, et al. 1996. Cerebral structural abnormalities in patients with obsessive-compulsive disorder: A quantitative morphometric magnetic resonance imaging study. *Archives of General Psychiatry* 53:625-632.

Jenike, Michael. 1996. *Obsessive-Compulsive Foundation: Special Report, Drug Treatment of OCD in Adults.* Milford, CT: Obsessive-Compulsive Foundation.

———. 1998. Theories of etiology. In *Obsessive-Compulsive Disorders: Practical Management, Third Edition,* edited by M. Jenike, L. Baer, and W. Minichiello. St. Louis, MO: Mosby, Inc.

Keuthen, Nancy, Richard L. O' Sullivan, and Donald E. Jeffrey. 1998. Trichotillomania: Clinical concepts and treatment approaches. In *Obsessive-Compulsive Disorders: Practical Management, Third Edition,* edited by M. Jenike, L. Baer, and W. Minichiello. St. Louis, MO: Mosby, Inc.

Koplewicz, Harold S. 1996. *It's Nobody's Fault.* New York: Times Books.

Leonard, Henrietta. 1989. Childhood rituals and superstitions: Developmental and cultural perspectives. In *Obsessive-Compulsive Disorder in Children and Adolescents,* edited by J. L. Rappoport. Washington, DC: American Psychiatric Press.

March, John, and Karen Mulle. 1998. *OCD in Children and Adolescents: A Cognitive-Behavioral Treatment Manual.* New York: The Guilford Press.

McDougle, Christopher J., and Wayne K. Goodman. 1997. Combination pharmacological treatment strategies. In *Obsessive-Compulsive Disorders: Diagnosis; Etiology; Treatment,* edited by Eric Hollander and Dan J. Stein. New York: Marcel Dekker, Inc.

Niehous, Dana J. H., and Dan J. Stein. 1997. Obsessive-compulsive disorder: Diagnosis and assessment. In *Obsessive-Compulsive Disorders: Diagnosis; Etiology; Treatment,* edited by Eric Hollander and Dan J. Stein. New York: Marcel Dekker, Inc.

O'Sullivan, G., H. Noshirvani, and I. Marks. 1991. Six-year follow-up after exposure and clomipramine therapy of obsessive-compulsive disorder. *Journal of Clinical Psychiatry* 52:4.

Pedrick, Cherlene. 1997. *Obsessive-Compulsive Disorder.* P. O. Box 1407, Roseville, CA: National Center of Continuing Education, Inc.

———. 1999. Ministering to students with obsessive-compulsive disorder. *Teachers in Focus,* February.

Phillips, Katherine A. 1998. Body dysmorphic disorder: Clinical aspects and treatment strategies. In *Obsessive-Compulsive Disorders: Practical Management, Third Edition,* edited by M. Jenike, L. Baer, and W. Minichiello. St. Louis, MO: Mosby, Inc.

Piacentini, John, and Flemming Grawe. 1997. Childhood OCD. In *Obsessive-Compulsive Disorders: Diagnosis; Etiology; Treatment,* edited by Eric Hollander and Dan J. Stein. New York: Marcel Dekker, Inc.

Salkovskis, P. M. 1985. Obsessive-compulsive problems: A cognitive-behavioral analysis. *Behavior Research and Therapy* 23:571–583.

Salzman, L. 1973. *The Obsessive Personality: Origins, Dynamics and Therapy.* New York: Jason Aronson.

Schwartz, Jeffery M., with B. Beyette. 1996. *Brain Lock: Free Yourself from Obsessive-Compulsive Disorder.* New York: HarperCollins.

Seuss, L., and M. S. Halpern. 1989. Obsessive-compulsive disorder: The religious perspective. In *Obsessive-Compulsive Disorder in Children and Adolescents,* edited by Judith L. Rappoport. Washington, DC: American Psychiatric Press.

Steketee, Gail S. 1993. *Treatment of Obsessive-Compulsive Disorder.* New York: The Guilford Press.

Steketee, Gail S., Randy O. Frost, Jose Rhaume, and Sabine Wilhelm. 1998. Cognitive theory and treatment of obsessive-compulsive disorder. In *Obsessive-Compulsive Disorders: Practical Management, Third Edition*, edited by M. Jenike, L. Baer, and W. Minichiello. St. Louis, MO: Mosby, Inc.

Swedo, Susan Anderson, and Henrietta Leonard. 1998. *Is It "Just a Phase"? How to Tell Common Childhood Phases from More Serious Promlems*. New York: Golden Books.

Wegner, D. M. 1989. *White Bears and Other Unwanted Thoughts*. New York: Viking Penguin.

Yaryura-Tobias, Jose A., and Fugen A. Neziroglu. 1997a. *Biobehavioral Treatment of Obsessive-Compulsive Spectrum Disorders*. New York: W. W. Norton & Company.

———. 1997b. *Obsessive-Compulsive Disorder Spectrum: Pathogenisis, Diagnosis, and Treatment*. Washington DC: American Psychiatric Press.

Zung, W. W. K. 1965. A self-rating depression scale. *Archives of General Psychiatry* 12:63-70.

More New Harbinger Titles

HEALING FEAR
New Approaches to Overcoming Anxiety

Therapist Edmund Bourne shares the hard-won wisdom and the healing techniques that helped him overcome his own struggle with anxiety.

Item HFR Paperback, $16.95

THE ANXIETY & PHOBIA WORKBOOK

This comprehensive guide is the boook therapists most often recommend to clients struggling with anxiety disorders.

Item PHO3 $19.95

WHEN PERFECT ISN'T GOOD ENOUGH

Exercises help you challenge unrealistic expectations and work on the specific situations in your life where perfectionism is a problem.

Item PERF $14.95

AN END TO PANIC

A state-of-the-art treatment program helps you take charge of fear-fueling thoughts, cope with phobic situations, and begin to live life in the here and now.

Item END2 $19.95

BETTER BOUNDARIES
Owning and Treasuring Your Life

If you feel like you have trouble saying no to others, this book can help you establish more effective boundaries.

Item BB $15.95

THE DAILY RELAXER

Distills the best of the best to bring together the most effective and popular techniques for learning how to relax.

Item DALY Paperback, $12.95

THOUGHTS & FEELINGS
Taking Control of Your Moods and Your Life

Now in its second edition, the most complete and useful guide to cognitive-behavioral techniques ever written is better than ever.

Item TF2 Paperback, $18.95

Call **toll-free 1-800-748-6273** to order. Have your Visa or Mastercard number ready. Or send a check for the titles you want to New Harbinger Publications, 5674 Shattuck Avenue, Oakland, CA 94609. Include $3.80 for the first book and 75¢ for each additional book to cover shipping and handling. (California residents please include appropriate sales tax.) Allow four to six weeks for delivery.

Prices subject to change without notice.

Some Other
New Harbinger Titles

Your Surviving Spirit, Item 3570 $18.95

Coping with Anxiety, Item 3201 $10.95

The Agoraphobia Workbook, Item 3236 $19.95

Loving the Self-Absorbed, Item 3546 $14.95

Transforming Anger, Item 352X $10.95

Don't Let Your Emotions Run Your Life, Item 3090 $17.95

Why Can't I Ever Be Good Enough, Item 3147 $13.95

Your Depression Map, Item 3007 $19.95

Successful Problem Solving, Item 3023 $17.95

Working with the Self-Absorbed, Item 2922 $14.95

The Procrastination Workbook, Item 2957 $17.95

Coping with Uncertainty, Item 2965 $11.95

The BDD Workbook, Item 2930 $18.95

You, Your Relationship, and Your ADD, Item 299X $17.95

The Stop Walking on Eggshells Workbook, Item 2760 $18.95

Conquer Your Critical Inner Voice, Item 2876 $15.95

The PTSD Workbook, Item 2825 $17.95

Hypnotize Yourself Out of Pain Now!, Item 2809 $14.95

The Depression Workbook, 2nd edition, Item 268X $19.95

Beating the Senior Blues, Item 2728 $17.95

Shared Confinement, Item 2663 $15.95

Handbook of Clinical Psychopharmacology for Therpists, 3rd edition, Item 2698 $55.95

Getting Your Life Back Together When You Have Schizophrenia, Item 2736 $14.95

Do-It-Yourself Eye Movement Technique for Emotional Healing, Item 2566 $13.95

Stop the Anger Now, Item 2574 $17.95

The Self-Esteem Workbook, Item 2523 $18.95

The Habit Change Workbook, Item 2639 $19.95

The Memory Workbook, Item 2582 $18.95

Call **toll free, 1-800-748-6273,** or log on to our online bookstore at **www.newharbinger.com** to order. Have your Visa or Mastercard number ready. Or send a check for the titles you want to New Harbinger Publications, Inc., 5674 Shattuck Ave., Oakland, CA 94609. Include $4.50 for the first book and 75¢ for each additional book, to cover shipping and handling. (California residents please include appropriate sales tax.) Allow two to five weeks for delivery.

Prices subject to change without notice.